Hospitality Activities Management

HOSPITALITY ACTIVITIES MANAGEMENT

Monica Sharma

CENTRUM PRESS
NEW DELHI-110002 (INDIA)

CENTRUM PRESS
H.O.: 4360/4, Ansari Road, Daryaganj,
New Delhi-110002 (India)
Tel: 23278000, 23261597, 23255577, 23286875

B.O.: No. 1015, Ist Main Road, BSK IIIrd Stage,
IIIrd Phase, IIIrd Block, Bengaluru-560085 (INDIA)
Tel: 080-41723429

Email: centrumpress@gmail.com
Visit us at: www.centrumpress.com

Hospitality Activities Management

First Edition, 2013

ISBN 978-93-81460-27-6

PRINTED IN INDIA

Printed at Balaji Offset, Delhi.

Contents

Preface

The tourism sector has experienced rapid growth and gained in importance for the economies of many developing countries and even for several developed countries. Active travel refers to an approach to travel and transport that focuses on physical activity (walking and cycling) as opposed to motorised and carbon-dependent means. Given that in the UK over 50% of car journeys are under 5 km, there exists considerable scope to replace motor car journeys with more active forms of travel. Doing so would have the multiple benefits of increasing levels of physical fitness and reducing rates of obesity, whilst reducing the consumption of fossil fuels and consequent Carbon emissions. Global climate change due to fossil fuel usage, and the continued increase in obesity are amongst the most serious health and environmental problems the world is currently facing.

In response to this, a recent movement has emerged led by Public Health and environmental campaigners to advocate for stronger policies and practices that promote active travel, and make cycling and walking safer and more attractive. The intention being that these modes could in many instances replace car usage for everyday journeys to school, shops, public services etc. To facilitate this would require local planning and highway authorities to invest in ensuring safe routes are available to these destinations (danger from other road traffic is frequently cited as the primary reason for not cycling.) In many areas the current focus of development for cycle provision is on isolated leisure trails, resulting in highly fragmented cycle routes and pavements/ sidewalks, which do not link effectively to everyday destinations. Archaeological tourism can include all products associated with public archaeological promotion, including visits to archaeological sites, museums, interpretation centres, reenactments of historical occurrences, and the rediscovery of indigenous products, festivals, or theatre. Archaeological tourism walks a fine line between promoting archaeological sites and an area's cultural heritage and causing more damage to them, or to risk becoming invasive tourism. As such sites are often run by tourist boards that place ticket fees and souvenir revenues as a priority, the question remains whether a site is worth opening to the public or remaining closed and keeping the site out of harm's way. Adventure travel is a type of tourism, involving exploration or travel to remote, exotic and possibly hostile areas. Adventure tourism is rapidly growing in popularity, as tourists seek different kinds of vacations. According to the U.S. based Adventure Travel Trade Association, adventure travel may be any tourist activity, including two of the following three components: a physical activity, a cultural exchange or interaction and engagement with nature.

The primary aim of writing this book on this subject is to present the subject matter in a concise and an intelligible form, keeping in view the needs of the average student.

—Author

1

Management and Planning of Nature based Tourism

Introduction

Nature based tourism is one of Australia and the world's fastest growing tourism markets, as residents and visitors go to natural and cultural areas and sites to experience beautiful landscapes, flora and fauna and our European and Indigenous culture. In the ACT, even without significant promotion, visitation to natural areas and cultural sites is steadily growing.

Nature based tourism is tourism focussing on visitation to natural or near natural area, including recreation, visits to European and Indigenous cultural sites and simple sightseeing. As a nature based tourism destination the ACT is unique within Australia and possibly the world. Compared to a national average of 8% for land designated as parks and reserves, 53% of the ACT is made up of either national park or nature reserves with a further 10% of the Territory composed of plantation forests. Given this wealth, the ACT's natural areas represent significant recreation and tourism resources. Indeed, experiences of unspoiled natural environments, unique landscapes and wildlife, as well as significant Indigenous and European heritage and cultural resources, offer considerable potential to contribute to the Territory's tourism promotion and positioning.

Canberra's high quality urban environment also provides an opportunity for the ACT to develop an image as a diverse and healthy leisure destination. The Bush Capital's open spaces, parks, walking and cycling trails as well as close proximity to substantial and significant nature parks and reserves provide a wide range of opportunities for Canberrans and visitors to relax, recuperate and revitalise.

This Strategy sets out the ACT Government's directions and priorities for the further development of nature based tourism in the territory. The Strategy has been developed as one component of the ACT Tourism Master Plan. Ongoing community involvement in both experiencing our wonderful assets and in working with the Government in refining and developing the Strategy is actively sought.

Why an ACT Nature Based Tourism Strategy?

Nature based tourism can deliver a range of environmental, social and economic benefits to the ACT community, including:

- increased community and visitor environmental awareness and understanding;
- promotion of environmental and cultural values;
- generation revenue for the conservation and management of natural and cultural heritage;
- greater community and visitor enjoyment of natural and cultural sites and facilities; and
- employment opportunities, utilising local knowledge and facilities.

In addition, nature based tourists tend to be high yield tourists, spending more, and staying longer in a destination than general tourists. Importantly, as tourism, and in particular nature based tourism, is essentially about the environment in which we live, work and play the ACT's natural assets also represent significant community resources and recreational opportunities. Many of those visiting the Territory's natural and cultural sites and attractions are and will continue to be Canberra residents and their visiting friends and relatives.

What is Nature Based Tourism?

Nature based tourism can be defined as visitation to natural or near natural areas. This includes ecotourism, adventure tourism, rural tourism, visits to European or Indigenous cultural and heritage sites, and simple sightseeing and recreation. Ecotourism is a niche component of nature based tourism, with a focus on education and interpretation of the natural and cultural environment.

The ACT has a wide range of significant nature based tourism assets and resources, including Namadgi National Park, Tidbinbilla Nature Reserve, Canberra Nature Park, Murrumbidgee River Corridor and Googong Foreshores. Other assets include:

- the Australian National Botanic Gardens;
- the National Aquariums and Australian Wildlife Sanctuary;
- Canberra's city parks and lakes, managed by the ACT Government and the National Capital Authority;
- European and Indigenous cultural heritage sites and objects; and
- plantation pine and native forests managed by ACT Forests.

Who are the Nature Based Tourists?

We are all nature based tourists. Most of us enjoy getting out into the natural environment, and most of us seek a range of experiences, from wilderness trekking and bush walking through to less demanding activities such as scenic driving and casual visits to nature reserves and parks. Bureau of Tourism Research (BTR) data notes that:

- the appeal of nature based tourism experiences are similar across most age and life cycle groups;
- educative and interpretive experiences are of similar appeal amongst both sexes and across age and life cycle groups (although people with children are more likely to see learning about nature as important than those without children);
- nature based and ecotourists tend to be more educated than non-ecotourists and often have higher incomes; and
- as experiences become more physically demanding, more expensive or specialised the nature based tourism market quickly narrows.

Thus there is no single nature based tourism market, rather a range of markets and market segments that flow into one another as the tourists seek a range of experiences. These experiences range from what can be described as 'hard' nature based such as wilderness trekking and bush walking through to less demanding or 'soft' nature based activities such as scenic driving, and casual visits to nature reserves and parks. Many visitors to natural and cultural heritage sites are Canberra residents - families and friends wishing to simply experience nature and culture.

Plantation Forests

Approximately 10% of the Territory is plantation pine and other forests managed by ACT Forests. About 1.1 m residents and visitors come to the forests each year. These areas are managed as multiple purpose forests, being both commercial forest and available for a wide range of recreational activities. Of the 26,900 hectares managed by ACT Forests, about 16,000 hectares is pine plantation. The remainder comprises nature reserves, native vegetation corridors, water bodies and streams and over 1200km of forest roadway. The range of activities available in these areas is much wider than in the national parks and nature reserve areas, and includes car rallies, paint ball, sled dog trials, horse riding, cycling, orienteering and off-lead areas for dogs. ACT Forests offer a range of activities including bush walks, fishing and camping. The forests also contain a diversity of European and Aboriginal heritage sites, as well as several arboreta and the largest cork oak plantation in the southern hemisphere. The less restricted use of the forests also reduces any pressure to use the more sensitive natural areas for more intensive activity, for example the FAI Rally of Canberra, a major car rally, is also held in ACT Forests areas.

In contrast to the other states and territories, the ACT's bush parks and forests are relatively close to our urban areas, enabling easy access for both residents and visitors to experience the ACT's natural and cultural heritage.

The Environment Green Evaluation Programme

Balatonfüred managed environment protection as an important mission even before the political –economical changes of '89. But the real progress started only in the nineties. The Self-government created its own Local Order of Environment amongst the first towns in the country, introduced selective waste collection subsided financially by EU after a successful PHARE submission, joined local forces of NGOs interested in environmental issues.. As a continuation of this progress the Self-government participated in a large international environmental project led by the Union of Baltic Cities along with Siófok and Lake Balaton Development Coordination Agency.

The goal of the project is to create and introduce an up to date, environment conscious managing system in the participating cities for a sustainable urban environment. Dr. Bóka István. the mayor of Balatonfüred signed the co-financing statement on 26th March 2004. The Kick-off meeting was held in Riga on 13th -14th June, 2005. where the most important steps and the frameworks of co-operation of the three years long project were discussed. Only after this meeting, on 21st July, 2005. the Partnership and Grant Agreement was signed by UBC and Balatonfüred.. Yet in Riga on the starting plenary conference the frameworks and the forms of co-operation and the schedule of work were determined.

First of all the preparation of a Baseline Review and then a Strategic Program were decided. After having collected the available necessary local documents and refreshing data Balatonfüred has compiled its Baseline Review. As a part of this work, the SWOT analysis gives a proper starting point for the Strategic Program of the town, as it formulates step by step the strengths to be exploited consciously better in the future, weaknesses we have to eliminate as far as possible, or to reduce their negative effects and the possibilities we are to make the best and the threats which are to avoid.. This Strategic Program was compiled following the structure of the BR. In the process of creation of SP the still existing documents (City Developing Concept, Urban Organization Plan, for Public Health, etc) and the newest developing ideas were highly taken into consideration Evaluation of the present situation (SWOT analysis) Environmental elements

The natural environment of town Balatonfüred belongs to the most beautiful and most precious sites in the country. This beauty has not only aesthetic but a high economic value, as it considerably contributes to the tourist attractiveness of the town itself. Thus protecting and improving the natural environment is a basic interest of the community.

The Koloska valley, the Tamás hill and the Malom valley are the most precious outskirt areas of Balatonfüred. These sites along with the other outings are threatened mostly by two main dangers. The first is building up and fencing (illegally or evading the law) and the illegal waste deposits. Building up and fencing endangers mostly Tamás hill and the other higher areas where the beautiful panorama induces such needs and intentions. Illegal waste deposits have been occurring in decades long on certain places well accessible by cars and lorries, mainly by the roadsides leading out of town.

The Strategic Program is to preserve the natural environment by the following measures: On the non built green areas of Tamás hill total ban of construction is to introduce except those improvement involved in the Strategic Program. It is to acquire the ownership the areas around Jókai lookout tower and the paths leading to the summit. More frequently emptied and more numerous waste containers are to be placed on the most often visited illegal deposits by the roads leading out of the town- The control of these area must be realized by joining forces of official and voluntary environmentalists.

Besides preservation of the natural environment it is to make efforts to a careful and cautious exploitation of these values, as the improving ecotourism, and with raising incomes increase the city welfare. The Strategic Program supports the following improvements: Ecological recreation of the streambed of Malom valley brook and establishment a fee fishing pond above the Dobogóhid section of the brook. Previously or simultaneously The recultivation of the neighbouring dumpsite is to be completed.

A cable lift is to establish on the slopes of Tamás hill. Its incomes are to ensure the costs of a permanent warding of the natural environment. It is a further benefit, that heart patients and disabled people can enjoy the beauty of the panorama. On the still existing forest paths of the northern slopes a system of jogging tracks is to establish. This can also be used as cross country sky courses in winter. Summer bobsleigh course is also supported by the Strategic Program. The excursion centre in the Koloska valley needs a better and easier access and a higher level of services and more comfort. The Strategic Program supports such improvements. Besides this a cautious riverbed recreation on the lower sections of the brook is allowed. On the upper sections it is only the installation of small wooden barrages to retain water what is supported by the SP. The middle section of the brook is to remain in its natural condition.. The renovation of the Füredi Kiserd (Small Forest Park) is supported but the old and precious wood stock must be preserved. The Balaton shoreline is to be protected.

Further concrete walls and stoning is allowed only sections where the Shoreline Rehabilitation Plan indicates boat jetties or yacht harbours. Reeds and natural shoreline are to be protected even at that sites. A mobile, floating aquarium and ecological showplace is to be built and placed between Tagore Promenade and the Annabella beach Efforts are to be made for the most detailed mapping of underground mineral carbonic water bases. Further research drillings must be carried out in order to substantiate an improving medicinal spa culture. Constructed environment The three historical centre of the town, Fured Old Village, the Resort Quarter and Aracs historical village core is to preserved and developed according to the traditions.

At a different extent these three areas became city centres by the commerce, catering and services focused here. Further improvement is possible and desirable mostly by the private investments attracted here, but for the preserving renovation of public places financed by municipal and granted funds is also necessary.. The "Mainstreet program" aims at the development of the main street of the Old Village besides preserving the picturesque values, strengthen the functions of town centre. The improvement of the historical village centre of Aracs has already commenced. It must be completed by reconstructing the municipality owned buildings into a centre of education, culture and services.

The partly finished renovation of the Resort Quarter is to be extended with the reconstruction of Gyogyter (Medicinal square), and east and westward continuation of the Tagore Promenade. In the eastern section of the littoral zone between the two main beaches on the plot of the Anglers' Association a municipal water sport centre is to be established. This places will afford possibilities for fishing rowing and sailing first of all for the local people. The former Huray –market (once the village football ground in the old times) building up is allowed only with establishments for only cultural and /or entertaining activities.

On the public plots behind it recreational or educational establishments are to be built. Building areas for economical activities which are not desirable in residential districts will be provided primarily by the northern side of Aszof road, towards the dumpsite and on itself the dumpsite after its restoration. The building of the west bypass road is the most important traffic task. Renovation of pavements and urban streets must be continued. The number and the length of bike roads are to be increased. This improvement is desirable primarily in the case of bike roads joining to the Balaton Bike road and leading north out town, thus the background settlements, the stations of wine routes, and the values of nature can get an easy access. The total renovation of the rainfall system is vitally necessary. Humane factor First rank task is to increase the number of birth.

It can be realized by increasing the certainty of existence (creating new places of employment, flat building programs) education and by the financial support for young mothers and newborns We have to protect our fundamentally good education system of the unfavourable effects, spreading from outside. Further co-operation of our primary schools is desirable. In health aspect the conditions of the environmental elements are generally suitable. Occasional air pollution from traffic will be reduced by building bypass roads, and the sporadic water and soil pollution will also diminished by perfecting the sewage system.

The main mortal risk factors are to be reduced by proper and effective health education and by the extension of screening tests. At present only the State and the local Self-government play essential role in social care. It is desirable to establish and support civil organizations with a vocation to such aims and goals. The crime status is rather suitable in the city.

The main figures in crime reports are ceasing year by year. The Self Government, NGOs and enterprises support effectively the work of the Police and other crime pursuing organizations through the Foundation for Property Defence.. To counter against drugs and other addictions prevention is the number one tool, and secondly a more effective crime pursual work and a rising social support is to be achieved. The seasonal (autumn, winter) unemployment is a very characteristic and impending factor on city development.

Thus the main goal is to increase the numbers of permanent work places. City function and management The Mayor's Office, which is responsible for city function and management carries out its task profoundly suitable. Its co-operation with the elected city management, the Self-government is also proper. Within the Office the co-operation between the departments must be strengthen.

Regular heads of departments meetings-are to be held, where they report on the achievements and where the tasks for the next period will be shared out. Reinforcement of environmental affairs with minimum one new staff member is absolutely necessary. In the case of public space wards the situation is similar. Employment of an additional staff member is justified as well as the widening of their authority and competence. The clarks' ability of communication in a foreign language are to be improved. Employment of a new civil servant ought to be conditioned by a communicative skill in a foreign language. It is the PROBIO zRT which performs definitely the communal duties of the town in a suitable and a improving way. This company is responsible for collecting, transport and deposit of communal waste on a dumpsite operated by itself. The dumpsite is to be operated until the start up of the regional waste management system including the new dumpsite. Then the old dumpsite must be recultivated and environment friendly activities are to be settled here.

We have to stimulate and increase the selective waste collecting and the in situ composting on the detached estates with a garden. The self-government has to review the whole city function especially the energy supply of the town. It is vitally important to compile an energy concept and an energy action plan. The Self-government and the Mayor's Office are to be committed to be the vanguard promoting the utilization of alternative energy resources. Therefore an action plan must be worked out for the installation of public buildings with solar collectors. The Self-government is to encourage the establishment of small local di- and trigeneration power stations for new public establishments and bigger private buildings.

For the realization of this program a conscious and well prepared project strategy is to be compiled. This is the way to acquire the majority of the necessary financial funds. A local program is to be worked out for the renovation of public and private buildings introducing more efficient heat isolation technologies. Economy The economy of the city is mostly based on summer tourism. This must be changed in two ways. First the tourist period must be widened, and secondly other economical activities must be settled in the town. The extension of tourist season has already begun. The Balaton Congress and Leisure time Centre has built and organises diverse programs, the year round functioning Aqua park opened for the public.

Three four star hotels affording high level services all the year are going to be finished and opened at the end of this year. The still existing older hotels are to be renovated thus joining to the season elongating program. The sport tourism is also improving thanks to the new possibilities by the opening of BCLC and by building new yacht harbours. Former institute offers place for sport events all the year, sailing life is restricted to the period from the late spring until early autumn. Establishment of an ice stadium would give an additional push to the development of sport tourism.

As this establishment needs much energy it is to be built and operate by the most modern and effective energy utilization. The cultural tourism also has got a huge possibility by the opening of BCLC. A new theatre performing all the year around would significantly animate the cultural life in the town.

The traditional wine tourism is the only economical activity what is based on agriculture and has significant role in the town. Its quantitative improvement is hardly possible. Further development seems to be possible in the still existing estates, achievements of a better access to the wine route stations and improving better services. Fishing tourism is to be also improved. The Balatonfüredi Horgasz Egyesulet has to get a possibility to build a new jetty and fishing clubhouse, which can afford a proper level of services for guest anglers. The careful improvement of natural environment mentioned under will also contribute to the prolongation of the tourist season. For the sake of creating new jobs. it is also vital to attract other economical activities in the city. First of all economical, logistic and financial centres are to be settled as they won't spoil the tourist appeal of the town. Different kinds of environment friendly artisan manufactures are also welcome Certain faculties of high school education according to character of the region (environmental, nature protection, hydrobiology or tourism and economy, possibly faculty of law) would animate the local economy and the whole spirit of the town.

The growth in alternative forms of tourism has occurred simultaneously with an increased recognition of the need to implement the concept of sustainable development. Eco-tourism has been widely assumed to be inherently sustainable, although few attempts have been made to verify this assumption. Eco-tourism incorporates environmental and cultural conservation objectives, and emphasizes economic benefits to local communities.

Hence, eco-tourism would appear to be, and is increasingly presented as, a tool for sustainable development. However, it also has the potential to be more environmentally damaging than mass tourism since it typically occurs in fragile environments and opens up previously undiscovered destinations to the mass market.

By the late 1980s, a shift in the tourism industry's marketing strategy occurred alongside the emergence of the global environmental movement. In the decade of "green consumerism", critical consumers were soon leading the demand for "environmentally sound" holidays. Tour operators and travel companies began to promote themselves and their products as "environmentally friendly", and a number of companies published ethical and environmental codes of conduct and guidelines for travellers as well as guidelines for self-regulation. Tour companies also started to promote eco-tourism holidays to all corners of the world, to coincide with the inclusion of the environment on the mainstream political agenda. At the same time the tourist hunting industry has expanded dramatically.

Literature Survey

Sustainable Development

In the 1987 Brundtland Report of the World Commission on Environment and Development, sustainable development is defined as the " development that meets the needs of the present without compromising the ability of future generations to meet their own needs" (World Commission on Environment and Development, 1987:43). To meet the needs of the present, the new development has to provide ground on which the basic necessities of all humans and the opportunities for a better life can be satisfied.

Sustainable development is being discussed for the last two decades, mostly among academicians. The core elements of these discussions are:

- The idea that the needs of present and future generations must be considered;
- The need to ensure that renewable and non-renewable resources are conserved, not exhausted;
- The requirement that access to and use of natural resources must take fair account of the needs of all people;
- A recognition that issue of environment and sustainable development must be treated in an integrated manner.

Sustainable Tourism Development

The tourism and recreation industry is at a crossroads in its development. Now as one of the world's largest industries, it is increasingly confronted with arguments about its sustainability and compatibility with environmental protection and community development. Consideration of tourism, the environment, and concepts of sustainability should consider four key challenges: (1) a better understanding of how tourists value and use natural environments; (2) enhancement of the communities dependent on tourism as an industry; (3) identification of the social and environmental impact of tourism; and (4) implementation of systems to manage these impacts. The tourism and recreation industry is confronted with serious and difficult choices about its future. The decisions made now will for decades affect the lifestyles and economic opportunity of residents in tourism destination areas. Many of these decisions are irreversible because once communities lose the character that makes them distinctive and attractive to nonresidents, they have lost their ability to vie for tourist-based income in an increasingly global and competitive market place.

Owen (1993) characterizes sustainable tourism development as:

- Tourism should be one part of a balanced economy.
- The use of tourism environments must allow for long-term preservation and for use of those environments.
- Tourism should respect the character of an area.
- Tourism must provide long-term economic benefits.
- Tourism should be sensitive to the needs of the host population.

Butler suggests the following working definition of sustainable development in the context of tourism: "tourism which is developed and maintained in an area (community, environment) in such a manner and at such a scale that it remains viable over an indefinite period and does not degrade or alter the environment (human and physical) in which it exists to such a degree that it prohibits the successful development and well being of other activities and processes".

The growth in alternative forms of tourism has occurred simultaneously with increased recognition of the need to implement the concept of sustainable development. As with "eco-tourism", "sustainable development" is another environmental catch phrase with no single definition. On the face of it, no other economic activity would appear to lend itself to sustainable development better than tourism. Alternative forms of tourism that incorporate environmental and cultural conservation objectives with an emphasis on economic benefits to local communities would appear to be a panacea for sustainable development. Because damage to the environment threatens the resource base on which alternative forms of tourism depend, it would be logical to expect all involved in tourism to ensure the protection of these resources. All forms of tourism consume resources such as land and energy.

However, when practiced against the standards of its definition, the small scale and dispersed nature of eco-tourism, combined with connotations of sound environmental management, means that it has the potential to consume far less basic resources than other forms of tourism or other developments.

A recent article in the UK Youth Hostel Association's magazine, Triangle, takes up this theme: "Spending your holiday in one of the latest artificial all-weather tropical pleasure domes or in intensely developed but properly managed holiday resorts like Benidorm and Torremolinos can be more environmentally friendly than indulging in trips to remote or fragile areas where tourism is more likely to be environmentally and culturally damaging and puts little or nothing back into managing and protecting the environment" (YHA, 1996).

Quoted in the same article, the popular conservationist David Bellamy comments "Eco-tourism is already a dirty word. Hill walking, jungle trekking and all the rest are just as potentially harmful as conventional resort holidays, if not more so. Most of the tourism industry is simply sponging off clean water, fresh air, the natural and cultural environment and is putting nothing back in. But there are praiseworthy exceptions, which not only do not damage the environment, but also actually help to restore it. This is real eco-tourism." (YHA, 1996).

In addition to the potential damage caused locally to tourist destinations, the air transport of tourists to remote areas of the globe seriously undermines the concept of sustainability of the industry as a whole. For example, air travel contributes 2-3 percent of global emissions of fossil fuel derived carbon dioxide, the principal greenhouse gas, as well as nitrogen oxides, which contribute to low-level ozone formation. Paradoxically, nitrogen oxides released at high altitudes also contribute to the thinning of the protective ozone layer over the earth.

Not all of the impacts of tourism are necessarily negative. If development and change are bound to occur in a particular site from some activity or other, tourism may be a far less damaging alternative than many other more polluting industries. The Overseas Development Association (ODA) Manual of Environment Appraisal (1996) provides a checklist to help develop management strategies to minimize negative impacts and maximize positive benefits. Therefore, alternative or other forms of tourism are not necessarily a panacea for sustainable development, unless well planned and well regulated.

In most countries, there usually is no coordination between programs that promote and market tourism and those that manage environment and culture. On the other hand, agencies dealing with the promotion of tourism are not involved with the evaluation of its effects or with advance planning and management of the adverse impacts of tourism through avoidance, mitigation, and compensation strategies.

Eco-tourism

The term "eco-tourism" is often assumed largely to alternative tourism that involves international travel by people from rich developed countries to developing countries, as a means of providing much needed foreign exchange for hard-pressed national economies, and earnings for poor rural people. The notion of these interrelated conservation and economic benefits has led to much confusion surrounding the variety of terms currently in use that appear to have similar meanings and aims. These include "alternative tourism", "sustainable tourism", "soft tourism", "special interest tourism", "green tourism", and "eco-tourism". Some of these terms frequently appear to be used interchangeably, while others may be defined in a variety of ways.

In reality, eco-tourism has become widely adopted as a generic term to describe tourism that has, as its primary purpose, an interaction with nature, and that incorporates a desire to minimize negative impacts. Implicit in the term is the assumption that local communities should benefit from tourism and will help to conserve nature in the process. In this study, the term "Eco-tourism" will be used to generalize all the other terms, and if a specific section of eco-tourism like wildlife tourism or alternative tourism is explained, then those terms will be used specifically. The terms "eco-tourists" and "eco-tours" will be used in this study to summarize the group of tourists and the tours created for them in the name of eco-tourism. As with the term "eco-tourism", there is similar confusion regarding the term "alternative tourism" that is often used as a generic term encompassing a range of variations such as eco-tourism and green tourism, all of which purport to offer a more benign alternative to conventional mass tourism. Indeed, eco-tourism has been described as "one of the most widely used and abused phrases of the last decade", which it is argued can mean anything to anyone.

A few definitions of "Eco-tourism":

"An enlightening nature travel experience that contributes to the conservation of the ecosystem while respecting the integrity of host communities".

"Responsible travel to natural areas, which conserves the environment and improves the welfare of local people".

"Purposeful travel that creates an understanding of cultural and natural history, while safeguarding the integrity of the ecosystem and producing economic benefits that encourage conservation".

Eco-tourism can contribute enormously to the management of protected areas. Benefits include foreign exchange revenues, employment opportunities, improving awareness of conservation objectives and stimulation of economic activity. While protected areas are major destinations for eco-tourists, private enterprise is playing an increasing role in the eco-tourism sector. In addition, eco-tourism is a major vehicle for realizing tangible benefits of conservation for local communities with wildlife populations occurring on their land. However, the benefits accruing to local communities from tourism have so far been overstated. The type and magnitude of the environmental impacts associated with eco-tourism vary with the type of tourist activity pursued. Some impacts are obvious and easily identifiable, while others are indirect and difficult to quantify.

Strategies to manage the impacts arising from eco-tourism may also be direct or indirect. Direct strategies include limiting the total numbers of visitors to an area; dispersing visitors; zoning; using fixed viewing points; and setting guidelines for minimum viewing distances. Indirect strategies are those that aim to modify the behaviour of tourists. One of the most important ways of achieving this is to educate visitors about the potential disturbance they can cause and to provide advice on how to reduce it. Eco-tourism has the potential to be more damaging than mass tourism since they often occur in fragile or unique environments. Small-scale operations in environmentally sensitive locations may eventually turn into much larger and more destructive operations. Eco-tourism may simply represent the early stages of the conventional tourist destination life cycle. The life cycle concept essentially revolves around the premise that, unless intervention occurs, tourist destination areas and resources inevitably will become over-used and, consequently, will decline. The six stages of the cycle are as follows:

- Exploration (few tourists, poor access and facilities, environment unchanged);
- Involvement (local initiatives, some promotion, increasing numbers);
- Development (many tourists, locals lose control, deterioration of environment);
- Consolidation (tourist numbers exceed local residents, all major chains represented);
- Stagnation (numbers peak, destination falls out of fashion, environmental and social problems);
- Decline or Rejuvenation (or intermediaries).

This cycle has a number of obvious implications for sustainability, based on the consideration of factors such as carrying capacity, local participation, ownership, social and environmental impacts.

Mass tourists may have less impact than eco-tourists, because they tend to limit themselves to well known, easily accessible areas and insulate themselves from the local people. In some instances, the zoning of mass tourism (or enclave tourism) is adopted as a deliberate policy by a host country. For example, tourists in the Maldives are confined to self-contained, purpose built resorts on isolated, often formerly uninhabited islands, in order to avoid a culture clash between bikini-clad tourists and the conservative, Islamic islanders. Bhutan limits the annual foreign tourist entrance to their country to 3,000 pax only.

Eco-tourism proved to be a very lucrative sector of the industry, and commercial considerations of marketing the latest "undiscovered" paradise quickly overshadowed any concerns for environmental or cultural degradation. Indeed, the marketing of eco-tourism may well have accelerated social degradation, because more and more previously unknown destinations were discovered and subsequently opened up to mass tourism.

Turkey & Sustainable Tourism Development

Without giving due regard to the underlying principles of eco-tourism, tour operators and even governmental agencies seem to be securing the short-term economic benefits to sell regions or products.

As a developing country, Turkey's choice of pursuing a tourism development strategy is to create opportunities for economic improvement, since it suffers from deficit in the balance of payments. Tourism is also a tool for decreasing unemployment, because it is a labour-intensive industry. Turkey is trying to secure the short-term inflow of the foreign currency by increasing its bed capacity and trying to attract more tourists.

Although the industry is centralized as being governed by the ministry, there are not any records available of any act for sustainable tourism development. Some accommodation units and travel agencies to a certain extent, as a tool for revenue generation, only use sustainable tourism. Accommodation units try to decrease the operational costs like usage of sun energy. Some demand less usage of towels. Clearly, the aim of these acts is not to maintain sustainable tourism, but to minimize their costs. Indeed, the travel agencies' main concern is to maximize the total number of tourists to increase their profit. Therefore, the carrying capacity is totally ignored.

Like many other developing country governments, Turkish governments have helped the fast development of tourism without taking into account the factors of local culture and environment. All governmental acts have been related to monetary gains, since Turkey have been used to economic crises during the last decade. Even IMF has expected certain tourism income figures in order to give credits.

Research Methodology

The purpose of the research was to explore the perceptions of and the possible commitments of Turkish travel agencies engaged in eco-tourism to sustainable tourism development. An exploratory study were undertaken since not much was known about the situation at hand, and there were not any information available on how similar problems or research issues have been solved in the past. In other terms, there were not any previously defined theoretical framework and any hypothesis to test, so this research was to develop related subjects and their groupings by content analysis.

In order to address the quality of information obtained about nature tour operators, substantial attention will be given to survey design and administration. The aim of the research was to examine how travel agencies perceive the impacts of their development and to evaluate their level of response to environmental concerns. In order to satisfy these aims, the objective was to obtain rich data. This pointed towards using a qualitative method involving relatively few people. According to Oppenheim (1992) 'the longer, the more difficult and the more open-ended the questions schedule is, the more we should prefer to use interviews.' In the light of this, a decision was made to undertake face-to-face, in-depth interviews.

In order to reach desired information, directors or senior personnel of ten TURSAB member agencies who are engaged in eco-tourism as the unit of analysis were interviewed. Having obtained the booklet of TURSAB listing the agencies as the population frame, the initial intention was to undertake systematic random sampling; however, this method of sampling proved unsatisfactory due to the high number of companies unwilling to participate and the fact that only around one-third of the population were in Istanbul, making the rest impossible to reach regarding the time limits. The choice of researcher was, therefore, very much decided on by the respondents' willingness to participate, i.e. the first ten agencies in Istanbul to agree. Given the seniority of all the interviewees, this was effectively 'elite interviewing': the individuals are influential and in a position to report on their organizations policies and future plan. Furthermore, 'elites respond well to... intelligent, provocative, open-ended questions'. Among the total population of 362, 135 were located in Istanbul and the rest 227 were located especially where eco-tourism activities took place. A limitation should be noted that the number of agencies rapidly change and figures of 2000 may not be the exact values of today, yet helped us for a fair idea of the population, since links on TURSAB website of the updated lists of agencies did not work during research process.

The research was a cross-sectional study with respect to time horizon, because data were gathered by the interview once, for a period of days.

In-depth, face-to-face interviews with managers of travel agencies engaged in eco-tourism have been used as the data collection method. Other data sources were used during the literature survey such as publications, manuals, archives, journals and related books.

For qualitative data analysis, systematic coding by content analysis was used to analyze the transcripts of the interviews. In this method, the researcher analyzed interview answers and prepared a list of subjects. The researcher and one independent sorter categorized these subjects independently. After a discussion between the researcher and the independent sorter, who was a manager of one of the visited travel agencies, a common categorization was agreed upon. For reliability testing, two independent graduate students who have studied research methodology also categorized the subjects.

According to the reliability test, the results of the content analysis came out to be significant.

Findings & Discussions

Types of Tours

According to the segmentation like mass tourism and eco-tourism, travel agencies engaged in eco-tourism also sell tours for the mass market. When the respondents were asked to compare the two types of tours with respect to sustainability, there was a clear dichotomy between the two segments. At the first glance, special tours and eco-tours might be considered more sustainable;

their volumes are lower, they are more likely to use local accommodation, local guides and services, and attract more environmentally aware clients. However, a differentiated tour for the mass market may attract eco-tourists as well. On the other hand, some specialist markets are evolving into mass markets, because of the increase in volume and the rapidly changing markets. This shows the danger of using broad statements, as eco-tours are more sustainable.

Types of Activities

According to the frequency order derived from the answers of the respondents, the following activities are marketed by the travel agencies: Walking/rambling, alternative water sports, trekking, golf, adventure, cycling, hunting, safari, photographing, mountaineering, rafting, horseback riding, fishing, alternative winter sports, bird watching. Many of the agencies sell more than one type of tours.

Why to Sell Alternative Forms of Tourism?

Travel agencies sell alternative forms of tourism in order to earn more money. Other reasons are to reach the young generation, to increase the variety of products and to enter a new market. Travel agency executives feel that their companies should be considered like markets or small shops in evaluation of any effects of operations, but they forget the fact that they do not sell products of another company like a market, but they produce the eco-tours themselves and sell them. Since those tours selling the nature are their products, they are responsible for the positive or negative effects of their products. These effects may be to the environment, to the local culture or to other aspects related to sustainable tourism. Travel agencies do not seem to accept the fact that some of the activities they make are acting against sustainable tourism by opening new areas to tourism without considering carrying capacity, using the nature as a marketing concept and allowing uncontrolled contact with local culture and tourists.

Sustainable Tourism

Sustainable development is a new subject of concern that many of us are not familiar with. Sustainable tourism development is also new, but it is being discussed in meetings of many international organizations. The first and obviously the main finding was that most of the interviewed senior personnel or managers of travel agencies in Turkey that are engaged in eco-tourism do not even know what sustainability is all about.

Interesting answers on the definition of sustainability, which were totally unrelated to it, reminded the researcher the fact that many of the employees and managers in the tourism industry are uneducated or did not have their education on tourism. This was proved by the respondents' education levels, which were mostly high-school graduates. The most interesting answer for the researcher was: 'Sustainable tourism,... should be related to renovations of the hotels, planes... it should not be related with travel agencies, we sustain tourism'. No matter the answer is funny or dramatic, but it seemed to be the reality for general knowledge of travel agency executives in Turkey related to sustainability. So, the respondents did not take into consideration the important aspects of sustainability like local culture or environment, since they did not know the term.

Who is More Responsible for Realization of Sustainable Tourism?

Economically, travel agencies feel that any attempt to take steps on sustainable tourism will put them at a commercial disadvantage because of increasing costs. They agree on helping the realization of sustainable tourism only if the tourists accept to pay more. Therefore, they feel that governments are more responsible for imposing restrictions, limiting growth and controlling volumes and so helping sustainable tourism. The result of this study showed that, travel agencies are willing to comply with regulations if governments impose them to the whole sector. Another point that Turkish travel agencies engaged in eco-tourism mentioned is their operations are too small with respect to the whole market to make any influence.

Conclusion & Implications

This study has examined the social, environmental and cultural impacts of alternative tourism activities with regard to the travel agencies in Turkey engaged in eco-tourism. First conclusion is that it has become harder to segment the market into mass tourism and eco-tourism, since the two segments are becoming more integrated into each other and there are products, which cannot be put under a certain category. Second conclusion is that, although these travel agencies sell eco-tours and earn money, they believe that government has the major responsibility to ensure sustainable development. The third general conclusion is the fact that most of the travel agency executives has learned the definition of sustainability after the general explanation of the researcher.

It is easy to make an assumption like because travel agencies are small enterprises; their responsible behaviour may have a very small effect on sustainable tourism. Yet, specialist tours take tourists deeper into nature and sensitive local culture, and import the necessary skills instead using local work force.

Environmental policies and sustainable acts have become nothing more than a marketing ploy and a vehicle or eluding regulation. Environmental departments and affiliations with glossy campaigns have arguably become a PR exercise designed to meet the growing awareness in some markets to appear environmentally sound and to attract higher spending tourists. For sustainable tourism to be a marketable concept, tourists themselves have got to really buy on it.

To conclude, the researcher wants to point out that sustainability is mostly considered as an utopia and will probably never be achieved.

2

Appropriate Planning for Coastal Tourism

Coastal Tourism and Recreation and the U.S. Economy

Growth in International Travel and Tourism

Travel and tourism is the world's largest industry. As reported by the World Tourism Organization, travel and tourism involved more than 528 million people internationally and generated $322 billion in receipts in 1994. In 1995, travel and tourism generated an estimated $3.4 trillion in gross output¾ creating employment for 211.7 million people, producing 10.9 percent of world gross domestic product, investing $693.9 billion in new facilities and equipment, and contributing more than $637 billion to global tax revenues.

The mammoth global tourism industry is a "massive consumer of energy and resources", and is expected to continue to grow significantly in the future. In 1995, the World Tourism Organization forecasted international arrivals worldwide to reach 661 million by the year 2000, up from 528 million in 1994, with arrivals predicted to reach 937 million by 2010. By 2005, it is estimated that the industry will have expanded globally, generating employment for 305 million people, producing 11.4 percent of world gross domestic product, investing $1,613 billion in new facilities and equipment, and contributing more than $1,369 billion in tax revenue. This growth in world tourism is related to three main factors: increased personal incomes and leisure time, improvements in transportation systems, and greater public awareness of other areas of the world due to improved communications. Foreign tourism has been a very important factor for the U.S. economy. In 1994, 45.5 million international visitors came to the United States, according to the Department of Commerce, and spent $60 billion dollars. The U.S. travel and tourism industry, with 6 million jobs, represents the second-largest employer in the United States after health care.

In 1986, the United States was the world's leading tourism destination. However, since that time, the U.S. leadership position in world tourism has been eroding; in 1996, France became the world's leading tourism destination. In 1995, the Commerce Department projected a 2.5 million dip in the number of international visitors to the United States and a dip in tourism revenues of 2.7 percent. Continuing economic difficulties in Europe and the strengthening of the U.S. dollar could account for some of this decline.

Balance of Payments Contributions of International Travel and Tourism

In 1994, the Wall Street Journal estimated that the United States receives over 45 percent of the developed world's travel and tourism revenues and 60 percent of its profits. While the United States runs a substantial merchandise trade deficit, it has a trade surplus in the service sector, with travel and tourism accounting for the largest and most rapidly growing part of this surplus.

According to Business Week, "foreign visitors spend about $80 billion a year in the United States, producing a $26 billion U.S. trade surplus in travel and tourism". Likewise, this publication reports 1.4 million U.S. jobs are supported by foreign tourism¾ ten times the number of jobs in the U.S. steel industry.

Foreign tourism to the United States in 1995 was expected to generate a trade surplus of $26 billion compared to a surplus of $17 billion in 1992 and a deficit of $7 billion in 1986. U.S. employment due to international tourism has been projected to grow by as much as 18 percent annually during the 1995-2000 period, doubling the number of tourism-related jobs every four years. The Department of Commerce has estimated that foreign tourist spending in the United States will rise to $132 billion dollars in the year 2000.

Tax Revenue Contributions of International Travel and Tourism

It has been estimated that travel and tourism produces tax revenues for all levels of government of about $58 billion annually. Of this total, foreign tourism is responsible for tax revenues of about $7.5 billion, about $4 billion of which goes to the federal government. Houston has observed that federal expenditures for beach re-nourishment have averaged only $34 million a year between 1950 and 1993 (in 1993 dollars), noting that the federal government receives tax revenues from foreign tourism that are 180 times its expenditure on the nation's beaches.

Promotion of International Tourism to the United States

The United States lags far behind other nations on spending on tourism promotion. Ronald Allen, chairman of Delta Air Lines, Inc., notes "...The Republic of Ireland, with a population of less than 4 million people, spends $45 million in public funds annually to promote tourism. This country, with 260 million people, spends less than $17 million in federal money" Wildavsky, 1995, p. 2280). Spain, with its attractive beaches and climate, spends 10 times more than the United States in advertising to attract international tourists. The United States ranks 31st in the world in international tourist market advertising.

Indeed, there has been a debate at the national level in the United States on whether a greater national presence concerning tourism promotion is needed, with industry advocates arguing for a greater role to eliminate "creeping neglect by public policy makers". Opposition to this has been expressed by economists and others who argue that private companies, not taxpayers, should bear the costs of promotional activities that benefit the U.S. tourism industry.

Coastal and Marine Tourism in the United States

The precise magnitude of foreign and domestic tourism in U.S. coastal and marine areas is not clear, since no separate statistics are kept for foreign or domestic tourists to these areas. Figures on foreign tourism receipts are generally based on surveys of departing travellers, generating data which are "imperfect and cannot be compared over time with precision". Data on tourism in coastal areas cannot easily be disaggregated from national-level statistics, but impressionistic evidence as well as a number of recent works on the subject suggest continued growth of tourism in coastal and marine areas in the United States and worldwide. Detailed information on the economic impact of domestic tourism has been difficult to find, but growth in all forms of recreation in coastal areas in which both foreign and domestic tourists partake is readily apparent.

Such activities include beach going, recreational boating, cruises, marine mammal watching, recreational fishing, underwater recreation, bird watching, nature appreciation, and the like.

In terms of U.S. tourism, studies have shown that beaches are the leading tourist destination while national parks and historic sites are the second most popular destination. Consistent with these findings, approximately 180 million people visit the coast for recreational purposes, with 85 percent of tourist related revenues generated by coastal states.

In addition to growing numbers of visitors, the permanent population of U.S. coastal regions is also increasing at a faster rate than the population as a whole. The population of coastal counties has increased by approximately 25 percent since 1970. In California, for example, Wilson and Wheeler (1997) provide the following estimates for the annual contribution of various ocean industries to the California economy.

Their study shows that tourism (predominantly coastal) is the largest contributor at $9.9 billion, with the next largest contributor being ports at $6.0 billion. Offshore oil accounted for $860 million, and fisheries and mariculture combined contributed $550 million. Similarly, between June 1995 and May 1996, 2.5 million visitors to Monroe County, Florida (in the Florida Keys) spent about $1.2 billion. Recreation and tourism (all coastal) accounted for over 60 percent of output/sales, 45 percent of income, and over 46 percent of all employment.

Recently the Environmental Protection Agency (EPA) undertook a national study on the benefits of water quality improvement in terms of numbers of people involved and the economic value of the activities in which they participate (EPA, 1996). This study provides some valuable quantitative information on the importance of coastal tourism and recreation:

- Saltwater fishing generates expenditures of over $5 billion annually, a total economic output of $15 billion, total earnings (wages) of over $4 billion, and over 200,000 jobs.
- Over 77 million Americans participate in recreational boating (NMMA, 1996). The number of recreational boats in the United States almost doubled from 1970 to 1990 (16.2 million), and is expected to increase by a further four million by the year 2000 (EPA, 1996). In 1996, Americans spent approximately $17.7 billion on boats and directly related items (NMMA, 1996).
- Over 80 million Americans participate in outdoor (non-pool) swimming, with visitors to beaches and lakes increasing from 18 million in 1981 to 23 million in 1989. In seven states, beachgoers spent $74 billion with the most popular recreational activities being swimming, sunbathing, and walking in coastal areas (EPA, 1996).
- Birdwatching is estimated by the U.S. Fish and Wildlife Service to generate spending of about $18 billion per year by over 24 million "birders" and other wildlife watchers, a generous proportion of which occurs in coastal regions (EPA, 1996).

A number of the estuary programs that make up EPA's National Estuary Program have undertaken studies of the economic activity generated by the coastal and estuaries resources in their region. Some findings related to coastal tourism and recreation are given below (EPA, 1997): Corpus Christi, Texas. Nature tourism in Corpus Christi is the fastest growing component of a tourism sector that generates $23 billion annually. Recreational fishing provides aggregate net benefits to the area of $83 million, including $37 million per year in state and local taxes, with a regional economic impact of $546 million. Non-fishing coastal recreational activity adds another $23 million in state and local taxes, and $340 million in regional economic impact.

Long Island Sound, New York. The economic impact of water quality-dependent uses in Long Island Sound, including boating, commercial and sport fishing, and swimming, is estimated at more than $5 billion annually. Commercial and recreational fishing contributed more than $1.2 billion to the total, while beachgoing has a direct benefit of more than $800 million annually.

Indian River Lagoon, Florida. The Indian River Lagoon region is a popular resort and vacation destination which received over six million visitors in 1995 and provided economic benefits of approximately $730 million.

Santa Monica Bay, California. Tourism is the Los Angeles region's second largest industry with 392,000 full and part-time jobs contributing $3.6 billion annually to the region's payroll. With nearly four million tourists annually, and over 45 million beach visits per year, Santa Monica Bay contributes significantly to the regional economy.

San Francisco Bay, California. The economy of the 12 counties bordering this estuary exceeds $175 billion and supports more than four million jobs. Many of these jobs are dependent on the estuary's natural resources or are water-related. Revenues from maritime activities exceed $5.4 billion each year, and marinas annually generate some $167 million. Tourism, which generates over $4 billion annually, is likewise strongly tied to the aesthetic values of the estuary.

Policy Frameworks for Coastal Recreation and Tourism: an Assessment

Understanding Tourism

A perusal of the literature on tourism suggests that it is easy to make generalizations: on the positive side, to extol its huge economic development potential; on the negative side, to decry impacts on the environment, overuse of resources and energy, ignorance of local culture, and absence of local benefits. For analytical purposes, it is best, however, to consider tourism in neutral terms as an agent of development and change which may have both positive and negative effects, as the following quote suggests:

"As Butler (1990) points out, tourism, like other industries, is an agent of development and change and must be recognized as such. It is consumptive like any other industry and the level of consumption is determined by the scale and style of tourism development. At low levels and with careful design, tourism may be able to operate at a sustainable level. However, controlling the level and style of development over the long term presents challenges which, to this point, have not been successfully met. Because of its potentially high impact, tourism should be considered in the same manner as any other industry and should be subjected to the same environmental and social impact assessment processes during the planning stages".

Butler suggests the following working definition of sustainable development in the context of tourism: "tourism which is developed and maintained in an area (community, environment) in such a manner and at such a scale that it remains viable over an indefinite period and does not degrade or alter the environment (human and physical) in which it exists to such a degree that it prohibits the successful development and well being of other activities and processes".

Tourism has often been ignored by public sector agencies. Where it has been considered as a specific development feature, it has often been viewed as a "soft" option, which can be pursued relatively easily and which does not require much in terms of specific planning or resources. While this view has changed somewhat in recent years as the magnitude and importance of tourism has begun to be appreciated, ignorance about tourism and many of the processes associated with it is still widespread.

The lack of attention by public agencies to tourism is especially problematic in the case of marine and coastal tourism. In most countries, there usually is no coordination between programs that promote and market tourism and those that manage coastal and marine areas. Integrated coastal management often tends to be done within environmental or planning agencies. On the other hand, agencies dealing with the promotion of tourism are not involved with the evaluation of its effects or with advance planning and management of the adverse impacts of tourism through avoidance, mitigation, and compensation strategies. Hence, one of the greatest challenges facing coastal managers in the United States and elsewhere is how to integrate tourism development within the ambit of integrated coastal management, and thus increase the likelihood of long-term sustainability.

The Role of the Federal Government in Coastal Tourism Management

As an economic activity, tourism is difficult to influence and manage directly. Like most coastal development in market economies, tourism-related development is driven largely by the private sector and its assessment of economic opportunities. Miller and Auyong (1991) point out that tourism involves mainly three sets of actors: tourists, locals (those who reside in the region of tourism destinations but are unconnected to the tourism industry), and two categories of brokers (those in the private sector who are engaged in the business of tourism, and those in the public sector who in one way or another monitor, manage, or govern tourism). Tourism tends to be globally driven by market forces influenced by such factors as advertising (by public or private agents at the tourist destination), the perceptions of the travelling public about security, amenity values, etc., and, in the case of international tourists, by currency factors.

Notwithstanding these difficulties, there is much that the federal government, working with the states and localities, does to ensure that coastal tourism is conducted in a sustainable manner, thereby ensuring long term economic and environmental benefits for coastal communities and the nation. Sustainable development of coastal tourism is dependent on:

1. *good coastal management practices* (particularly regarding proper siting of tourism infrastructure and the provision of public access);
2. *clean water and air, and healthy coastal ecosystems;*
3. *maintaining a safe and secure recreational environment though the management of coastal hazards (such as erosion, storms, floods), and the provision of adequate levels of safety* for boaters, swimmers, and other water users;
4. *beach restoration efforts* that maintain the recreational and amenity values of beaches; and,

Sound Policies for Wildlife and Habitat Protection.

While there are separate federal programs dealing with each of these areas, some more successfully than others, in recent years there has been a growing realization among a number of federal agencies that these factors are interconnected and that all are needed to achieve healthy ecosystems and sustainable economies in coastal communities. To cite just one example, the Sustain Healthy Coasts 5-year Implementation Plan, developed by NOAA's Office of Ocean and Coastal Resource Management, defines the following objective: "Foster well-planned and revitalized coastal communities that are compatible with the natural environment, minimize the risk from natural hazards, and provide access to coastal resources for the public's use and enjoyment."

In the sections that follow, existing efforts by federal agencies the categories outlined above are reviewed and assessed. The small but growing sector of ecotourism, and the need to manage this activity carefully to avoid adverse impacts on protected species and sensitive habitats, is also discussed.

Coastal Management and Planning

The United States has the oldest national coastal management and planning program in the world, initiated under the Coastal Zone Management Act of 1972. The program, administered by NOAA's Office of Ocean and Coastal Resource Management, now includes coastal management programs in 31 U.S. states and territories, covering 97.2 percent of the U.S. shoreline. The program uses incentives (in the form of grants to the states and the "federal consistency" provision) to assist states in the preparation and implementation of coastal management plans. These state efforts have been multifaceted and have addressed, through a variety of means (regulatory, planning, public awareness raising), all uses of coastal areas. Three management practices under the Coastal Zone Management (CZM) program are especially important for ensuring sustainable tourism development: (1) provisions for the management of coastal development; (2) provisions to improve public access to the shoreline; and (3) provisions to protect (and, where necessary, to restore) coastal environments.

Management of Coastal Development

All CZM programs have elements which, in effect, help manage coastal development. Two of these are especially relevant to tourism development: (1) encouragement of water-dependent uses in the coastal zone and (2) the appropriate siting of new facilities in the coastal zone.

Encouragement of Water-Dependent Uses

State CZM programs actively encourage and facilitate the use of land adjacent to the shoreline for those purposes which require such a location. This policy helps ensure that proposals for tourism and marine recreation projects receive appropriate consideration in the government review process. It also helps ensure that meritorious coastal tourism developments are not crowded out of the coastal zone by uses that do not require a shoreside location.

Appropriate Siting of Facilities

Construction of new facilities in the coastal zone must meet the setback requirements of state CZM programs. While states differ in their requirements, the trend is to relate setback lines to annual erosion rates and, thus, to require the greatest setbacks from the high tidemark in those areas having the largest erosion rates. Facilities siting policies also help ensure that new tourism construction is not located in hazardous areas from the standpoint of coastal storm damage and flooding.

Improvement of Public Access to the Shoreline

A strong emphasis in the federal Coastal Zone Management Act relates to the importance of ensuring adequate public access to the nation's shorelines for recreational pursuits. All 31 state programs are actively pursuing this goal. Recognizing the limitations of simply planning for access, Congress added section 306A to the CZMA in 1980 to allow states to acquire land and fund low cost construction projects to provide public access ways to the beach and coastal waters.

Since 1980, for example, the California Coastal Program has acquired over 2,300 public access ways along the coast while the San Francisco Bay Conservation and Development Commission has increased public access around the perimeter of San Francisco Bay from 4 miles in 1977 to more than 96 miles in 1990. Under the CZM program, states and localities use grant funding and regulatory tools to secure improved public access for recreational purposes.

Protection of Coastal Habitats

The existence of healthy coastal habitats (wetlands, beaches and dunes, sea grass beds, mangroves, coral reefs, estuaries) is important to coastal recreation and tourism. State CZM programs represent one of the important management avenues in obtaining this protection. Within specified coastal zone boundaries, states and/or their local governments regulate activities which could adversely impact these habitats. Other federal programs, such as those under the Clean Water Act's Section 404 (dredge and fill program) and Section 320 (National Estuary Program), the Marine Protection Research and Sanctuaries Act (which controls ocean dumping), the Coastal Barrier Resources Act, the National Seashore Program, the Endangered Species Act, and the Marine Mammal Protection Act, also serve to protect coastal habitats. Furthermore, a national system of estuarine research reserves aimed at providing a representative system of natural field laboratories for management-related research and monitoring also exists as an adjunct to the national CZM program.

Management of Clean Water and Healthy Ecosystems

Clean water and healthy coastal ecosystems are essential to the maintenance of coastal tourism and recreation. Foreign tourists and the recreating domestic public stop going to areas where the waters are polluted, beaches are closed, or fish are tainted. For example, it is reported that the State of New Jersey lost $800 million in tourism revenues following reports that medical wastes had washed up on some of its beaches. According to EPA estimates, coastal and marine waters support 28.3 million jobs, generate $54 billion in goods and services, contribute $30 billion to the U.S. economy through recreational fishing, and provide a destination for 180 million Americans to recreate each year.

In the past 25 years, there have been extensive efforts made by federal agencies, especially EPA and NOAA, in association with the coastal states, to improve coastal water quality. Under programs authorized by the Clean Water Act of 1972 (as amended) and administered by EPA, significant improvements in water quality have been realized. Point sources have been largely controlled under the National Pollution Discharge Elimination

System (NPDES). Significant challenges remain regarding the control of non-point sources of water pollution (resulting from such sources as agricultural practices, urban and storm water run-off, and air deposition), especially in coastal areas abutting agricultural lands. EPA's non-point source program (under Section 319 of the Clean Water Act), and NOAA's program under Section 6217 of the CZM Act, have been used in combination in a number of coastal states to begin more effective measures to control non-point sources of pollution.

Protection of the marine environment is one of the critical services provided by the U.S. Coast Guard. This includes prevention of environmentally threatening marine accidents and responses aimed at minimizing adverse effects should accidents occur., This also includes protection of living marine resources and marine sanctuaries. The implementation of the Oil Pollution Act of 1990 is resulting in safer ships entering U.S. ports, safer vessel operators, and hence, cleaner coastal waters. NOAA's National Ocean Service provides safe navigation services, such as nautical charts, and information on water levels and currents, that help prevent marine accidents. It also performs hazardous material spill response activities. NOAA's role in pollution monitoring (National Status and Trends Program) and damage assessment are also important aspects of managing clean water and healthy ecosystems.

In addition, special planning and management efforts, largely directed at improving water quality and habitats, have been made in many of the nation's estuaries under the aegis of EPA's National Estuary Program (NEP). Under the NEP, 28 estuaries, designated as estuaries of national significance, have been the beneficiaries of substantially increased research and management attention. Management conferences convened in each estuarine area are used to oversee the characterization of each estuary, and the preparation and implementation of Comprehensive Conservation and Management Plans (CCMPs). These include resource and water-quality related goals and the action plans necessary to meet these goals. An enduring commitment from NEP stakeholders at all levels is vital to the successful implementation of the CCMPs and the long-term health and sustainability of these estuarine resources. This commitment must include the acquisition and leveraging of sufficient funds by state and local governments, follow-through on commitments agreed to by the implementors, and the full use of appropriate authorities. The continuing involvement of the federal government, notably the EPA, in the oversight and support of the NEP is also likely to be critical to the long-term success of the program.

The direct contribution to coastal economies made by cleaning up coastal waters is often not fully recognized. A recent report by the EPA indicates that in seven estuaries alone[1], tourism and beach going activities generate economic benefits of more than $16 billion to their respective regions (EPA, 1997). Clearly, these benefits depend on the maintenance of clean coastal waters and attractive ecosystems. While substantial progress has been made in improving coastal water quality since 1972, much remains to be done. Meanwhile, reauthorization of the Clean Water Act has been stalled for several years, the national policy framework for dealing with non-point source pollution remains somewhat unclear, and funding levels for water quality improvement programs are inadequate. Furthermore, the nation needs to decide if the current largely voluntary approach to non-point source pollution will be sufficient, especially for dealing with agricultural run-off problems.

Management of Coastal Hazards

In siting coastal resorts and other facilities, there is understandably a predilection for locating in beautiful but high-risk zones that are as close as physically possible to the edge of the sea, or otherwise take advantage of scenic views and proximity to beaches and ocean recreation. Of course, it is precisely these areas that are most vulnerable to both long-term and episodic coastal hazards: such as erosion, storms, and floods.

While government cannot be expected to protect individuals from their own recklessness, it does have a responsibility to provide the information necessary to permit informed decisions to be made with regard to the kinds and degrees of risk associated with living in various parts of the coastal zone. Furthermore, coastal areas that are clearly hazardous as building sites should be reserved for other uses. Government also has the responsibility to provide adequate warnings of impending storms or other hazardous conditions, and to develop plans for coping with such emergencies. Several government programs exist to meet these needs as discussed below.

At the federal level, FEMA's National Flood Insurance Program (NFIP) and the Coastal Zone Management Program exist, in part, to address these problems. The NFIP offers flood insurance to coastal landowners in communities that have met government standards for building in coastal areas (elevating structures above a designated flood level, designation of high hazard areas where no building is allowed, etc.). FEMA is also responsible for supporting and facilitating the work of state emergency preparedness offices in the preparation of coastal evacuation plans and plans to deal with disasters such as hurricanes both during the event and during the clean-up and reconstruction phases. NOAA's National Weather Service devotes considerable resources to the job of providing timely "state-of-the-art" forecasts and predictions of hurricanes and other coastal storms.

Through the federal CZM program, coastal states build in their own regulatory approaches such as construction setback lines, storm-resistant building codes, acquisition programs for hazardous areas, and the like. Recognizing the connections that should exist between the planning and management efforts under CZM, and cognizant of the lessons being learned during storm events by the emergency management programs, NOAA and FEMA are initiating a series of workshops to strengthen the coordination between these programs.

Advanced planning and follow-up are required to maintain a safe and secure environment for visitors. Tourists take their safety for granted when they go to the beach or visit a coastal resort or even rent a sailboat for the day.. Yet the coast is inherently a place with real risks, even under good weather conditions. Swimmers can drown and boats can collide or go aground, poisonous jellyfish can sting. And, of course, episodic large storms and hurricanes can have devastating consequences in coastal areas heavily populated with visitors.

Increasing numbers of Americans find themselves on the nation's waterways in connection with recreational boating, fishing, travelling to and from coral reefs for snorkeling and diving, and so on. Maintaining an adequate level of safety and accident prevention requires properly marked channels, rescue services, oversight of boating safety requirements (e.g., life jackets and other emergency equipment), and monitoring and enforcement of boating operations, including so-called "thrill craft." While some of these duties can be performed by local and state authorities, the maintenance of safe and well-marked waterways and maritime safety in general has traditionally been a federal government responsibility. In any event, the federal government is in the best position to ensure than an adequately comprehensive safety program is in place in coastal areas. The U.S. Coast Guard is the primary federal agency with responsibility for coastal search and rescue, enforcement of maritime laws, and maintenance of a national waterway marking system. The Coast Guard is also the coordinator of the national recreational boating safety program aimed at ensuring the safety of boats and associated equipment, and their safe operation by boaters. Through the production of accurate nautical charts and related products, NOAA provides essential information for navigating the nation's coastal waters.

Beach Restoration Programs

The federal government, acting through the U.S. Army Corps of Engineers, has long played an important role in the maintenance and restoration of the nation's beaches and shores. Experience in shore protection efforts has shown that soft solutions involving beach re-nourishment have produced better, more economical results than hard solutions such as seawalls and groins in many circumstances.

Seawalls and revetments first developed as the field of coastal engineering emerged., While these measures are often successful at protecting the development and infrastructure behind a beach, they do not address the real cause of beach erosion, which is a lack of sediment in the system. As understanding of coastal systems has grown through research and data collection programs, solutions to such problems has progressed. Today, beach re-nourishment represents a sound engineering solution that is economically feasible and environmentally sensitive. Only in areas with very high erosion rates and substantial shoreside facilities to protect are hard structural solutions considered.

The shift of population to coastal counties and the increased demand for coastal tourism destinations has exacerbated many existing beach erosion problems. Development in areas with high erosion rates and building on or in front of sand dunes, rather than behind them, are major factors contributing to increased beach erosion problems. Relative sea-level rise caused primarily by subsidence is another major factor in some areas. The interruption of sand flowing along the coast by natural or stabilized inlets is also an aggravating factor.

The Corps has conducted assessments of many of the nation's important beaches and has assisted coastal communities in the funding of beach nourishment projects. The bulk of the costs of these projects have been borne by the federal government with the local share generally being about 30 to 35 percent of the total cost. Just as the federal government is reconsidering its policies in this regard, coastal erosion and increasing relative sea-level rise in some parts of the country (notably the middle Atlantic and Gulf coasts) are increasing the need for beach replenishment projects.

As statistics cited earlier show, America's beaches are an important element in this country's attractiveness as an international tourist destination. A case in point concerns Miami Beach which virtually had no beach left by the mid 1970s as a result of erosion. Beach re-nourishment (at the cost of $52 million) in the late 1970s rejuvenated Miami Beach and enabled its beach to be reopened to the public. Beach attendance subsequently increased from 8 million in 1978 to 21 million in 1983. Annual governmental revenue obtained from foreign tourism in Miami Beach alone is about 40 times the cost of the beach re-nourishment project that has lasted over 15 years.

Given the role played by beach tourism in the nation's balance of payments and its impact on government revenues and regional and local economies, it is crucial that these assets be maintained at levels that promote and enhance their recreational use. If budgetary constraints make it necessary to reduce federal assistance for beach restoration and maintenance, a gradual and predictable approach should be adopted and states and coastal communities assisted in developing viable alternative funding arrangements.

Coastal Tourism and the need to Coordinate Federal Policies and Programs

While the issues discussed above are usually considered separately, all are of central importance to sustainable coastal tourism. Any one, be it poorly planned development, poor coastal water quality, unsafe or hazardous conditions, or eroding beaches, could seriously impact the tourism potential of a coastal area. Furthermore, policies and programs in each of these areas need to be developed and implemented in an integrated fashion, each taking account of the others. Failure to do this can result in such undesirable outcomes as erosion control structures that impair the recreational experience, or poorly designed development that causes water pollution or beach erosion.

Management of Ecotourism

Ecotourism or nature tourism is: "Tourism that involves travelling to relatively undisturbed or uncontaminated natural areas with the specific object of studying, admiring, and enjoying the scenery and its wild plants and animals, as well as any existing cultural areas."[2] While still relatively small, ecotourism is one of the fastest growing segments of the tourism industry and presents special management challenges.

Internationally, ecotourism is growing at a moderate rate with the financial impacts greatest in rural areas near important ecotourism activities. In 1988, international ecotourists numbered 236 million worldwide, with an estimated economic impact of $233 billion (U.S.). In 1994, the number of international ecotourists rose to 317 million with direct economic impact of $250 billion (U.S.). Although specific data on coastal ecotourism are difficult to obtain, market surveys in the United States show good prospects for ecotourism growth. In 1992, a U.S. Travel Data Centre survey indicated that 7 percent of U.S. travellers had taken at least one trip that they considered ecotourism and 30 percent claimed they would take one within the next three years.

In the United States, some coastal states have begun promoting ecotourism and nature-based tourism through the preparation of guides to ecotourism attractions and other publications. For example, the Marine Advisory Service of the Delaware Sea Grant

College Program produced a guidebook to ecotourism sites in the state. In 1996, the State of South Carolina, with the collaboration of the South Carolina Sea Grant Consortium, produced a handbook entitled *Guidelines and Recommendations for Nature-Based Tourism Planning and Practice in South Carolina.* Yet another example is the California Coastal Conservancy, which devoted its Summer 1997 issue of *California Coast & Ocean* to nature tourism.

Ecotourism in association with marine and estuarine protected areas, especially the National Marine Sanctuary Program and National Estuarine Research Reserve Program, has a great potential. However, for ecotourism activities to be sustainable, they must be managed properly and with special care. Unless properly managed, the impacts of ecotourism (for example, to remote pristine areas) may be worse than those of tourism to clearly defined and confined resorts.

In the United States, for example, concerns have been raised about the impacts of ecotourism on marine mammals, which are protected under the Marine Mammal Protection Act.

Commercial cruises to observe and "feed wild dolphins" operating in such areas as Texas, South Carolina, and Florida, were found to harm dolphins by making them reliant on accepting food from humans and decreasing their ability to survive in the wild. Threats to the marine mammal populations and to humans in these situations include: (1) substantially altering the natural behaviour of marine mammals, including foraging for food and migration, (2) the loss of wariness by humans, which places the animals at increased risk of injury or death from interaction with vessels, (3) animals receiving inappropriate or contaminated food, and (4) increased injuries to humans as the habituated animals become predictably more aggressive when they lose their wariness of humans and compete for handouts.

Management of Coastal Recreation Activities

The last decade has seen a great increase in the nature and magnitude of coastal recreation activities, which as has been shown, generate billions of dollars in economic activity. Recreational uses of a consumptive nature include hunting, fishing, shellfishing, shell collection, and the like, while non-consumptive uses include swimming, surfing, sun-bathing, boating, wind-surfing, jet skiing, bird watching, snorkeling, diving, glass-bottom boating, and many more. As coastal recreation activities have proliferated, the need for active management has increased as well.

At least three sets of concerns related to the management of coastal recreation activities must be dealt with, namely, environmental/resource concerns, amenity concerns, and safety concerns. Environmental/resource constraints include the maintenance of good water quality, and habitats and living resources which are free of health hazards, and which have good air quality, healthy coral reefs, healthy shellfish areas, etc. Amenity concerns include adequate controls on congestion, noise, landscape degradation, and the like. Safety concerns include adequate lifeguard systems, first aid facilities, telephones, codes of conduct for beach users, and notice systems for beach and water hazards and for weather-related risks.

In most cases, the responsibility for meeting these concerns is divided between the beach "owner" (often a local government or state government, but sometimes federal or private), resort and/or recreation facility operators, and state environmental or health departments. In general, nationwide standards for recreational beach operation do not exist, even with respect to beach closings. This would appear to be an area where additional attention at the national level is needed.

A promising start in this area is a new program recently launched by the EPA and designated the Beaches Environmental Assessment, Closure, and Health (BEACH) Program. This program is designed to encourage government agencies at all levels to strengthen beach water quality standards and testing methods using predictive water pollution models, to better inform the public about beach water quality conditions, and to make information about the risks associated with swimming in contaminated beach water available to the public.[3]

Emerging Tools and Techniques

Although coastal tourism constitutes a strong force (both positive and negative) in shaping coastal communities and local, regional, and national economies, coastal tourism is generally not seen as a specific sector requiring policy, planning, and management attention and resources. This is due, in part, to the fact that data and information tend not be gathered and aggregated under this heading. Hence, the magnitude and importance of leisure and recreationally motivated development in the coastal zone tends to be understated, understudied, and under-managed.

However, certain aspects of this situation may be changing. Since the Earth Summit in Rio de Janeiro in 1992, a number of new initiatives for sustainable tourism practices have appeared. For example, in 1993, a new periodical entitled *Journal of Sustainable Tourism* appeared, focusing on applying the principles of sustainable development to the tourism field. In 1997, on the occasion of the five-year review of the implementation of Earth Summit agreements, three organizations: The World Travel and Tourism Council, the World Tourism Organization, and the Earth Council; jointly published *Agenda 21 for the Travel and Tourism Industry: Towards Environmentally Sustainable Development* (WTTC et al, no date).

This report presents a summary of Agenda 21 (one of the main outputs of the Earth Summit), and the role that travel and tourism can play in achieving the goals of Agenda 21. It also outlines a program of action. Planning for sustainable tourism development is one of the priority areas of the program, which calls for complementarity between tourism and coastal development by adopting suitable policies such as the Global Blue Flag Program (WTTC et al.). The Blue Flag Program is a European campaign started in the 1980s which encourages local authorities to provide clean and safe beaches for local populations and international tourists. Blue Flag awards go to beaches that achieve certain standards in water quality, beach management and safety, and environmental information and education.

A guide for tourism managers has also been developed by the World Tourism Organization (WTO, 1996) on the formulation and use of indicators of sustainable tourism. Indicators signal unacceptable levels of impacts or stress, and these can in turn lead to the development of standards to govern tourism activities. Core indicators developed by the WTO include use intensity (persons per meter of accessible beach), species counts (number of species, change in composition), pollution levels (fecal coliform, heavy metal counts, etc.), and accident rates (WTO, 1996).

New tools are also being developed in connection with coastal tourism and natural disasters, such as hurricanes. The University of Florida, for example, in cooperation with the Florida Hotel and Motel Association, has prepared *The Hurricane Preparedness Handbook for Hotels and Motels.*

In a slightly different direction, Clemson University has prepared a handbook to guide communities and their tourism industries through crises of various types including those associated with natural hazards such as hurricanes. As outlined in its introduction, this guidebook "is intended to serve as a guideline to facilitate tourism recovery by protecting or rebuilding a local area's image of safety and attractiveness; reassuring potential visitors of the safety of the area; reestablishing the area's functionality and attractiveness; and aiding the local travel and tourism industry members in their economic recovery efforts").

Findings

As detailed above, coastal tourism and recreation involve major economic activity in U.S. coastal and ocean areas, and must be planned and managed with special care to insure that the environmental quality on which coastal tourism and recreation depend is maintained and enhanced. Major findings and areas of future work are summarized below:

1. Economic importance of coastal tourism and recreation. Coastal tourism and recreation provide a huge positive economic benefit in the United States, both in terms of jobs and earnings and in terms of balance of payments and governmental revenues. As discussed, over 90 percent of foreign tourism spending is concentrated in coastal states where beaches are the leading tourism destination. For example, Miami Beach reported more tourist visits (21 million) than were made to any National Park Service property. The federal government, moreover, receives about 6 times as much tax revenues annually from foreign tourism spending at Miami Beach than it spends to restore beaches in the entire nation. Yet, these values often go

unrecognized, and are not the subject of concerted attention by federal, state, and local policymakers.

2. There is little information on marine and coastal tourism. There is no systematic collection of data and information on the magnitude, nature, and economic and social impacts of tourism and recreation in the nation's coastal zone. This is, in part, responsible for a general under-appreciation of this set of activities and for the failure to devote adequate planning and management attention to the relevant issues that are raised for coastal tourism and recreation. To properly guide coastal tourism in a sustainable development manner, better data focused on coastal and marine areas will be needed. The types of information needed include:
   - Systematic collection and interpretation of coastal tourism data on a coastal county basis;
   - Collection and interpretation of data on coastal and marine recreation activities;
   - Expansion of existing databases, such as, for example, the Sea Grant Coastal Recreation and Tourism web service (organized by Oregon State University, in collaboration with many other Sea Grant programs);
   - Conduct of studies on the dynamics of tourism in coastal and marine areas. For example, what constitutes an optimal type and scale of coastal tourism? Who gets what, when, and where from expanded tourism? What is the distribution of benefits from tourism?.
3. U.S. promotional efforts to attract foreign tourists to U.S. coastal areas lag significantly behind those of other nations. Foreign tourists use U.S. coastal areas very frequently and contribute significantly to jobs, earnings, and tax revenues in coastal communities. Foreign competition in marketing other world coastal destinations, however, is increasing. In contrast to many other governments, the U.S. government spends very little in tourism promotion.
4. Federal policies and programs essential for the maintenance of healthy coastal tourism and recreation

(coastal planning and management, clean water, beach nourishment, management of coastal hazards and of coastal safety) are interrelated and should be treated as a whole. The economic viability and sustainability of coastal tourism and recreation are directly affected by at least four sets of federal policies and programs:

- Coastal planning and management (CZM) programs, especially in relation to the appropriate siting of tourism development and in ensuring public access, are of central importance in sustainable coastal tourism.
- Clean water and healthy ecosystem programs are vital to sustainable coastal tourism.
- Programs to ensure a safe coastal environment, especially with reference to natural hazards such as hurricanes and storms and to the maintenance of safe marine recreational and boating conditions, are essential for sustainable coastal tourism.
- Programs to maintain recreational beaches, by means of beach re-nourishment to combat erosion and relative sea-level rise, are also of central concern to sustainable coastal tourism.
- Programs to protect wildlife and coastal habitats are also essential to sustainable coastal tourism.

While a variety of federal efforts are focused on different programs of importance to coastal tourism, these have not been successfully coordinated. To remedy this situation, consideration could be given to the creation of an interagency initiative devoted to coastal tourism among the major federal agencies with programs in this area (e.g., NOAA (NOS [OCRM, NMS, NERRS], NMFS, OAR), the Department of Interior, EPA, FEMA, Army Corps of Engineers, Coast Guard, etc.). Related options could entail the mobilization of a public-private partnership to work in conjunction with the federal inter-agency group (involving such entities as state coastal programs, state tourist offices, aquaria, and waterfront redevelopers), and the development of a public awareness and outreach program focused on the determinants of successful coastal tourism.

5. Little guidance (in the form of standards, codes of conduct, manuals, etc.) is currently available to states and communities for guiding appropriate tourism development in coastal areas. While individual coastal communities and coastal states have taken initiative in preparing guides and codes of conduct related to coastal tourism and recreation, many others have not yet done so. The federal government can play a useful role here in providing guidance to states and communities in their attempts to manage coastal tourism and recreation appropriately. Useful activities include the development of standards, guides, and manuals for managing coastal tourism, in cooperation with relevant non-governmental organizations, the private sector, and international entities working on these issues. Also, management standards for recreational beaches, for example, those developed for the European Blue Flag program, could play a valuable role in improving conditions at some U.S. beaches

Importance of Coastal Tourism

The Welsh Coast is vital to the tourism industry in Wales. In 2006, spending associated with an overnight visit to the coast amounted to around £648million nearly 40% of total tourism spending in Wales.

It attracts around 4 million staying trips (16.9 million nights) each year together with an estimated 25 million tourism day trips. The greatest bulk of seaside tourism is for leisure and holiday purposes although cities and resorts such as Cardiff, Swansea and Llandudno also attract business and conference tourism. Visits to the coast account for 41% of all overnight trips in Wales-a much higher proportion than in England and Scotland where visits to the seaside only account for 20% and 13% of trips. Within the regions, seaside tourism is particularly important for North and South West Wales where it accounts for half of all activity (57% and 48% of tourism spend respectively). Seaside tourism is least important in South East Wales where it accounts for 12% of all tourism spend.

The direct impact of tourism amounts to an estimated 3.2% of whole – economy value added in Wales. The economic impact of tourism is much higher in many rural and coastal areas that, in relative terms, are more dependent on tourism.

Coastal Tourism Employment

Recent research has indicated that just under half of all full time jobs associated with the marine and coastal environment are in tourism related activities. The North Wales marine and coastal economy is predominantly, though not exclusively, tourism based. In West Wales, tourism accounts for over a third of direct coast and marine employment and in South East Wales it accounts for over half of coastal and marine sector direct jobs.

The Coastal Tourism Environment

The coastal environment is a major attraction to visitors who are drawn by the quality of its landscape, wildlife and sea water. The environmental quality of the Welsh coastline is reflected in the wide range and large number of designations and protected sites that cover the coastline of Wales. Some 70% of the coastline has been designated for its environmental quality.

In terms of EU and international designations, many parts of the coastal and marine environment are designated as Special Areas of Conservation and Marine Special Areas of Conservation. These areas are chosen for being the best examples in the UK for containing habitat types and species listed in the EU Habitats Directive. Other parts of the coast are designated as Special Protection Areas to conserve the habitats of certain rare or vulnerable birds and regularly occurring migratory birds. The Dyfi Estuary is the only designated Biosphere Reserve in Wales. The Biosphere reserves are areas nominated by national governments and designated under UNESCO's Man and the Biosphere (MAB) programme. In addition, vast sections of the coastline are designated under UK wide designations including:

- National Parks-Pembrokeshire Coast and Snowdonia
- Areas of Outstanding Natural Beauty at Anglesey, Lly^n and Gower
- Heritage Coasts at Great Orme, Anglesey, Lly^ n, Cardigan Bay, Pembrokeshire, Gower and the Vale of Glamorgan
- National Nature Reserves

- Marine Nature Reserves
- Sites of Special Scientific Interest

Important sites of archaeological and historic interest are also found along the coastline ranging from pre-historic sites to the Edwardian castles of Beaumaris, Caernarfon, Conwy, Harlech and Flint. Registered historic landscapes, parks and gardens make a significant contribution to the distinctiveness of the Welsh coast and to its appeal to residents and visitors.

Current trends in Coastal Tourism

Over the past 15 years, it is apparent that visitors are undertaking less trips to the Welsh seaside, with a decline in the number of trips and nights spent by UK visitors overall on the Welsh coast. The seaside share of the UK holiday market in Wales has fallen from 61% in 1991 to 41% in 2006.

The seaside sector has been particularly affected by the continuing rise in the number of long holidays taken abroad by UK holidaymakers. The number of long holidays taken at the Welsh seaside declined in number from over 2.7 million in 1991 to 1.76m in 2006. This decline, however, has been off set by a growth in short breaks which rose from a low point of less than 1m in 1993 to a high of over 2.2m in 2006.

Visitor Profile

In terms of visitor profile, figures suggest that in 2006, almost 24% of staying trips to the Welsh coastline originated in Wales. The North West (25%) and the West Midlands (23%) were the two main sources of staying visitors from England. Visitors to the North and Mid Wales coast tended to come from the North West of England, while visitors to South West and South East Wales came from a more varied origin base. Staying visitors to the seaside were more likely than the average holidaymaker to Wales to be travelling in large groups, with accompanying children and to be from lower socio-economic groups. Caravans and camping, particularly static caravans, were the preferred form of accommodation for tourists staying at coastal locations, accounting for 44% of all trips in 2006. Staying in self catering flats and cottages was also moreprevalent than the average while a smaller proportion of trips stayed with friends and relatives or used serviced accommodation. The coast attracts a higher proportion of long holidays compared to other types of location, with 45% of seaside trips involving a stay of over 4 nights, compared to 37% of all trips to Wales.

Seasonality

Seaside holidays show a greater seasonal peaking with 49% of trips being taken in the peak season (June, July, Aug) compared with 36% and 42% for small town and countryside trips respectively. The high seasonality reflects the relative importance of family holidays, many of which are governed by school holiday periods, as well as a preference for warmer weather for water based activities Only 19% of spend for coastal tourism occurs in the shoulder season (Oct – Mar) compared to 33% for tourism overall in Wales. In terms of occupancy, the seaside hotel sector has similar occupancy levels (57%) to that of small towns (57%) and country/ village (53%) whilst the highest levels of occupancy are found in city/large towns (71%).3 Room occupancy rates in the hotel sector across most locations have remained relatively constant during the 1998 – 2006 timescale with any differences typically only a few percentage points. Levels of occupancy in self catering units at the seaside average at 57% over the year. Static caravan parks at coastal locations have a relatively high level of occupancy at 67% whilst the lowest levels of occupancy are found in touring parks (41%).

Day Visitors

In terms of day visits, the last day visitor survey, undertaken in 2002, showed that family groups with children also accounted for a higher proportion of tourism day visits to the coast than for tourism day trips overall. In addition, a higher proportion than average of people over 55 years undertakes day trips to the coast.

Activities

Whilst the proportion undertaking an activity as the main purpose of their holiday has not increased greatly over the last 15 years, the number taking part in an activity, as part of their visit, has almost doubled with 80% of staying visitors taking part in an activity whilst staying on the coast. The most popular activities are shopping, walking, visiting heritage sites and swimming.

Information on activities undertaken by overseas visitors was collected in a visitor survey undertaken in 2003. The survey suggests that overseas holiday makers undertake a wide range of activities and have a higher propensity to visit heritage sites and museums than UK holidaymakers.

Tourism day visitors were much less likely to be involved in individual activities than staying tourists. For day visitors to the coast, the main activity was beach related including sunbathing and paddle. Future drivers and trends in Coastal Tourism

Drivers

As with general tourism activity, future changes in visitor activity on the coast will be influenced by a number of common factors. These are likely to include:

Available Leisure Time

Holiday entitlement has remained relatively stable over the last decade but the future will see increases in statutory holiday entitlement to 24 days in October 2007 and to 28 days from April 2009. This could lead to an expansion in the number of trips and nights spent away from home. However competition for consumers' free time is becoming more intense with the choice of things consumers can do in their spare time becoming increasingly diverse. There has been an increase in the number of retired people as a proportion of the total population. This sector has therefore experienced a growth in the total volume of available leisure time, but may in the future have fewer resources to significantly increase holiday taking.

Disposable Incomes

Until recently, incomes for those in work have grown faster than inflation although we are now experiencing a reverse in this trend. Expectations about retired incomes are uncertain given the changes in pension schemes in recent years.

Demographic Change

The older age groups will increase both absolutely and as a proportion of the population. Children under 16 will increase in number but the proportion of family households will decrease.

Socio-economic Change

There is likely to be an increase in the upper socio-economic groups with some decline in the proportion of DE groups. The proportion of the population benefiting from higher education is also increasing.

Lifestyle Changes

A growth in interest in personal health and fitness and in nature conservation has been apparent over the last decade. These trends are likely to continue, reinforced by concerns about climate change.

Information Technology

The growth and take up of the Internet has had a major impact on customers' ability to research and book tourism trips at home and abroad. It is essential that the tourism industry on the coast maintains a strong presence on the Web to compete with other destinations at home and abroad, although the proliferation of sites will also underpin other forms of marketing activity such as word of mouth. Information technology will also impact on information provision and distribution at the destination, through mobile phones and freestanding interactive panels extending the reach of traditional tourist information networks.

Ethical Consumerism

Consumers are becoming more ethically aware. In 2004, UK consumers spent a total of £25.8 billion on ethical goods, an increase of 15 per cent on the previous year. Over the same period, UK household expenditure increased by only 3.7%.

Market share of ethical consumerism had increased by 40% in the previous Other research indicates a growth in awareness amongst holidaymakers of the environmental dangers of tourism, whilst increasing numbers of people believe that travel companies should do more to protect the environment and support local people.

Climate Change

There is some anecdotal evidence that concerns about climate change may deter people from taking as many short breaks abroad, and that they will switch to taking more breaks in the UK. There is little evidence currently to suggest that UK visitors will be prepared to give up their main holidays abroad in favour of destinations in UK.

Transport Issues

Rising car ownership and use is likely to be reflected in growing road congestion both in destination and origin areas, which could inhibit any growth in tourism day trips in particular. The volume of traffic on roads in the UK has increased by 22% over the past decade according to the Department for Transport.

The continued growth in budget air travel will ensure fierce competition from overseas destinations both for long holidays and short breaks. The potential imposition of a fuel tax to meet climate change considerations could slow or reverse such growth.

Structure of the Industry

Tourism infrastructure provided by the private sector is very fragmented and often disadvantaged by limited resources and/or skill bases. This factor may inhibit the private sector from playing a full role in taking up opportunities unless innovation and business development advice is available.

Future Demand

In terms of future demand for holidays on the coast, our available research indicates that the long term trends that have impacted on coastal tourism over the last fifteen years are likely to be sustained. Long main holidays by UK residents to Wales are likely to be static in volume and are more likely to decline. Being relatively more dependent on the long main holiday, the seaside is likely to be more affected than other locations.

Tourism data shows that there have been significant increases in the number of UK residents choosing to take short breaks in the UK. We are therefore likely to see sustained growth in the short breaks and additional holidays market, although the growth may be slower as a result of competition from overseas destinations. Demographic and income changes are likely to stimulate growth in higher value activities which are attractive to older age groups including yachting, motor boating in the sea cruising and golf. The same drivers will raise expectations of standards and quality of accommodation.

Socio-economic and demographic drivers are likely to increase interest in arts, culture and heritage opportunities, whilst lifestyle and income growth are likely to sustain the growth in food, local products and eating out. Activities appealing to most age groups, such as walking, will continue to dominate in terms of the volume of participants. Adventure sports such as kite surfing, sub aqua diving and similar activities will continue to grow and attract the younger active age groups, although there may be some displacement from older established sports.

Key Challenges for Coastal Tourism

The Tourism Market

One of the main challenges for many parts of the coastline and particularly noticeable in coastal resorts is the continuing need to adapt in line with changing visitor expectations. The traditional two week 'bucket and spade' holiday has changed, visitors' needs and demands are now much more diverse. The tourism industry needs to continuously improve and develop new products to meet the evolving tastes and needs of consumers, in particular the needs of growth markets such as the short break market. In addition, a number of coastal resorts in Wales are suffering from social and economic problems. These stem from a number of sources including:

- seasonality of employment
- a higher number of elderly residents
- poor accessibility in some cases
- out of date and ageing tourism infrastructure
- imbalances of housing stock

Accommodation

Many resorts are dominated by caravan accommodation. Much of the caravan stock is used by individual families and their friends rather than being available for holiday letting. The larger sites often provide shopping and recreational facilities on site, which reduces local spend, although owners of caravans tend to spend more in the locality. A broader range of serviced accommodation would allow more choice for the visitor and appeal to the growing short break market Similarly, high quality accommodation, in all sectors, will attract visitors with a higher purchasing power. Consumer expectations are rising, making it imperative to invest in the quality of accommodation in order to attract and retain visitors to the coast.

Lower occupancy rates within the seaside accommodation sector overall have a detrimental affect in terms of attracting private investment. Any public sector support should not only be directed towards investing in the quality of accommodation itself, but in stimulating demand during the quieter off peak season.

Skills and Labour Resources

The seasonal nature of the tourism industry on the coast, together with the small scale nature of most tourism businesses poses challenges in retaining and equipping staff with the appropriate skills. In the short term, labour gaps, particularly in low paid jobs are being filled up by workers from other countries with lower wage levels. However, as these countries develop, the source of labour is likely to decrease, increasing the importance of recruiting and retaining staff locally through improved working conditions and career prospects. Local people sometimes feel excluded from new establishments set up by entrepreneurs from outside the area. There is a continuing need to stimulate entrepreneurship within the local population and to adopt an integrated approach to stimulating and supporting business start ups and business growth.

Access

The strategic access via the M4 and A55 has significantly improved journey times to many parts of the Welsh coast. However, there are still many areas of the West Wales coast perceived as difficult to access due to journey times and the nature of the road network. Public transport access by rail to the coast is also relatively good with regular services along the North Wales and South Wales coast. However, services become less frequent further west and throughout Mid Wales. Many coastal locations are accessed by narrow country lanes which can suffer from congestion during the summer and cause safety issues for walkers and cyclists. While the private car is likely to remain the main mode of travel for staying and day visits, the challenge is to develop innovative forms of public transport, to move people around local 'hot spots', and to make it easier for visitors to walk and cycle around destinations. There are a number of good examples already in Wales. In considering forms of public transport, consideration needs to be given to the specific needs of people undertaking outdoor activities both in terms of the equipment that will need to be transported and in relation to the frequency and times of transport.

Coastal Erosion

All coastlines are subject to change over time due to tidal and wind effects which can result in coastal erosion. Coastal erosion and falling sand levels have become an increasing concern around some parts of Wales. If such erosion continues, it could have a major impact on both the environment and the economy and on tourism in particular. Coastal erosion takes place over many years, so it can often be perceived as stable on a human timescale. However, how we deal with the consequences of coastal erosion will be an important consideration in taking forward the Coastal Tourism Strategy.

Climate Change

Climate change is likely to have significant impacts on the coast. Figures from the UK Climate Impacts Programme (UKCIP) and the Met Office indicate that:

- Globally temperatures could rise anywhere between 1.5 and 5.8 by 2080 –between 2 and 8 times the rise already seen since 1990. In the UK, an average rise of 2 – 3.5c is anticipated.
- Winters will become wetter (20-30% wetter by 2080) and summers may become drier (35-50% drier by 2080). Heavier rainfalls will become more frequent.
- Relative sea level will continue to rise around most of the UK.

The potential impacts of climate change are likely to be various.

An example is the possible increase in extreme weather events such as storminess which may have the effect of increasing flooding in low-lying areas, and increase erosion rates that could lead to a loss of beaches.

A rise in sea level would have implications for low lying lands and coastal infrastructure. Tourism is also a contributor to climate change. The tourism industry and visitors alike are becoming more aware of the need to reduce their carbon footprints-this may well lead to an increase in demand for domestic holidays.

Managing and Developing the Coastline

There is increasing pressure on the coastal resource, and a growing recognition that the coastline should be managed in a more strategic and coordinated way. The impact of visitors on sites around the coast result in additional management costs to land owners and local authorities in terms of sustaining the quality of the environment and providing facilities for visitors to enjoy a safe experience.

While some revenue costs can be recovered through car parking and other charges, much of the management costs arise in respect of public goods and spaces, with the costs having to be borne by the host authority. Resources required to cover the management costs arising from visitor activity are often under pressure from other spending priorities. Without appropriate management, there is potential for activities to spoil the peace, tranquillity and quality of the environment that many visitors to the coast are seeking.

Conflict Between Activities

The potential conflict between specific activities is another challenge facing the coastline. The beach can be used for a variety of different activities ranging from sun bathing to physically demanding sports such as parakiting. The challenge is to manage the coastal area to the maximum benefit of all potential users. Conflicts between activities exist not only on land but also at sea. Activities such as bathing, windsurfing, surfing, sailing, angling, and the use of powerboats and personal watercrafts need to be properly managed. The pursuit of such activities will undoubtedly have an effect on the natural environment. The challenge is to instil a sense of responsibility for the coastline Analysis amongst stakeholders.

Second Home Ownership

There is continued concern in some areas as to the degree to which second home ownership within coastal communities is adversely affecting capacity in terms of visitor accommodation and the affordability and availability of housing to the local workforce. In terms of absolute numbers, higher concentrations of second homes and holiday homes are found along the coast at Penarth, St Brides Major, Gower, the Pembrokeshire coast, along Cardigan Bay, the Lly^n peninsula and Anglesey.

The Assembly Government recognises that in-migration and the purchase of second homes has influenced community structures in some rural and coastal tourist areas of Wales. The issue of the Welsh language being lost from rural communities is also one that has taken on increasing importance owing to the increase in net in-migration and pressures that this has placed on local housing markets in Wales.

Partnership and Integration

The challenge for the Coastal Tourism Strategy will be to achieve a consensus on the way forward and to foster a collaborative approach to delivering the strategy. A range of organisations and interested parties have different responsibilities for the coast. Within Local Authorities alone, coastal related responsibilities are carried out by a wide range of departments including beach cleaning, coastal defence, licensing, tourism, countryside and recreation and some local authorities are also Harbour Authorities.

Initiatives such as the Green Sea Partnership involving the public, private and voluntary sectors are already achieving coordinated action to improve the quality of Welsh beaches. The Partnership has finalised a Green Sea Development Strategy to cover the period 2006 to 2015 which aims to achieve a target of 100 blue flag/green coast award beaches and 9 blue flag marinas by 2015, the year of the introduction of the new Bathing Water Directive. This is an example of successful partnership working on the coast which has involved the pooling of resources to deliver a set of agreed outcomes.

Developing the Strategy

In this chapter, we set out the strategic context and outline the key policy objectives that the strategy will need to address. We outline a vision for the strategy and establish the aims and key outcomes that the strategy will seek to achieve.

Policy Objectives

The One Wales document agreed by the Welsh Assembly Government presents the Assembly Government's priorities and programme for the next four years. It sets out a vision for a prosperous Wales where there is a strong an enterprising economy and full employment based on quality jobs. Tourism is regarded as being vital to economic prosperity and job creation in all regions of Wales.

The priorities for tourism are:

- Promote Wales actively in external markets, drawing on our unique markets, culture, history and environment
- Strategic investment in facilities and employee skills
- Support for the tourism industry as the market moves increasingly towards shorter and activity based breaks

The Coastal Tourism Strategy will also help to deliver the following key One Wales commitments:

A Sustainable Environment

Tourism is an activity that can have a truly major impact on sustainable development, due to the unique relationship that tourism, compared with other economic activity, has with the environment and society. Tourism is highly dependent on a quality environment and cultural distinctiveness-qualities which can be destroyed if badly planned or managed. However, tourism can be a driving force for the preservation and promotion of these qualities through raising awareness and income to support them, and indirectly by providing an economic justification for the provision of such support by others.

There is strong emphasis in One Wales on protecting the environment including commitments to support local authorities and voluntary action to improve the quality of the local environment and the creation of an all Wales Coastal Footpath.

Creating Jobs

The tourism industry is well-placed to provide important employment opportunities throughout Wales, even in the most sparsely populated and peripheral regions. The industry needs to increase profitability and productivity so that earnings and the quality of jobs supported by the industry can improve. Initiatives that contribute to extending the tourism season will help to support more year round jobs within the industry and increase productivity.

Improving Health and Activity Levels

Clear advantages can be gained from linking the tourism and recreation agendas. It is therefore highly appropriate to link planning for leisure and tourism together and to develop approaches that ensure that local people are also able to benefit from facilities which visitors come to enjoy. Tourism businesses can also promote health and well-being amongst their own employees.

There is a specific commitment in One Wales to fostering a public sense of ownership in relation to the countryside, urban green spaces and our coastline, recognising that many socially excluded groups do not currently enjoy their social, cultural and health benefits.

Regenerating Communities

Tourism is often a catalyst for wider economic and local regeneration activity. Spending by tourists can help support local services, shops and community amenities that would not otherwise be viable thereby enhancing quality of life and creating a greater range of opportunities for all sectors of the community. The tourism industry can provide entry-level jobs and offers employment opportunities for economically inactive people or other returners to work, with the right support and training. Community based initiatives that support tourism can also act as an entry point for people into the paid workforce.

Equality

The Assembly Government has a statutory duty to promote equality and is committed to promoting gender equality, good race relations and tackling discrimination on the grounds of age and disability. Tourism is a major employer of women in Wales – with women representing nearly 60% of the workforce within the tourism, hospitality and leisure sector. This raises specific issues in relation to providing suitable training and working arrangements for women working in the industry. In addition women and men will undertake different activities on holiday and catering for women, men and families will be increasingly important for tourism providers. It is also essential that the tourism industry in Wales meets the needs of disabled visitors and other disadvantaged groups in society.

Strategic Context

We have reviewed in the technical report all the key documents at national, regional and local level that will affect to some degree the development, use and management of the coast of Wales. The following have been identified as being of particular relevance to the development of coastal tourism.

Achieving our Potential – mid Term Review

The mid term review of *Achieving our Potential,* the national tourism strategy for Wales has set five strategic challenges for developing tourism in Wales. These are:

- Distinctive branding
- Higher quality
- Easier Access
- Better skills
- Stronger Partnerships.

A series of priorities and individual actions have been identified for each of these challenges to describe what needs to happen differently to ensure that sustainable growth is achieved within the industry. While all of the five challenges outlined above are important, arguably it will be the achievement of higher quality that will be the most critical and crucial. Tourism businesses which are most likely to succeed will be those that deliver a high quality experience to visitors, understand their markets and communicate effectively with them, invest in their products and staff and attract and retain a motivated and skilled workforce.

Catching the Wave

Catching the Wave (2004) is the Welsh Assembly Government's tourism watersports activities and facility development strategy. The strategy states that few UK destinations can match the diversity and all inclusive nature of the Welsh coastal offer in the watersports market. The strategy is underpinned by a number of targets for 2010 including:

- to grow the number of UK watersports trips and nights by 20% to just over one million trips representing around 5 million bed nights
- to grow the value of UK watersports tourist spending by 40% to over £200 million
- to grow the numbers of trips taken by the higher spend overseas market by 50% and to increase overseas visitor spend by 40% to £15 million.

To support the 'Catching the Wave' initiative the Welsh Assembly Government, in partnership with local authorities and other organisations, have prepared local maritime studies. To date, two studies have been prepared to investigate opportunities for investment in coastal regeneration and watersports in Cardigan Bay (St David's to Trefor) and an action plan for increasing the economic benefit of the Mon a Menai coast. A similar study is currently underway in Conwy and Denbighshire and a Waterfront Masterplan has also been prepared in the Swansea Bay Spatial Plan area. The Coastal Tourism Strategy will build on this work, and will link the opportunities that have been identified for watersport development with the wider tourism product on the coastline.

Assembly Government has produced a strategy for Integrated Coastal Zone Management *Making the most of Wales' Coast* 10 which aims to provide a management framework to facilitate integrated working on the coast by the different interests involved in managing our coastal assets. It also sets out the links that must be made between diverse national and local policies and strategies so that people involved in managing and using the coast can do so in a way that takes into account the needs of others. A key objective of the ICZM process is to help ensure that all sectors and organisations successfully integrate ICZM management principles into the development of relevant policies.

Transport Strategy

The Welsh Assembly Government has recently published a Wales Transport Strategy *Connecting Wales*. The Transport Strategy will have a key role in improving accessibility to and within Wales and in helping to achieve a more sustainable tourism industry. The tourism sector will need to work closely with the four Regional Transport Consortia to ensure that tourism related solutions and innovative ideas are properly identified and prioritised. It will be important to consider the role of public transport and non vehicle modes in reducing the reliance on the private car.

Marine Bill

The proposed Marine Bill is likely to have a major influence on coastal tourism. The aim of the Bill will be to help develop the UK Government's vision for clean, healthy, safe, productive and biologically diverse oceans and seas.

Proposals include developing a more integrated management regime for the marine environment through introducing the concept of marine planning. Marine Planning would develop a much wider strategic approach to considering the needs, aims and possible locations of sectoral activities for the marine area as a whole. It would also look at the potential of cumulative effects of many different activities together, and the compatibility or conflict between activities, or between activities and environmental protection.

In addition, the Marine Bill White Paper outlined several proposals to protect Marine Biodiversity in UK Waters. These include a proposal to set up Marine Conservation Zones to provide protection for species and habitats considered of national value that cannot currently be protected by EU habitats designations. The Bill is also likely to introduce powers to manage unregulated activities (such as tourism and recreation) where these might have an impact on a Marine Conservation Zone or on important marine wildlife outside protected areas. The Welsh Assembly Government will be responsible for deciding how the Bill's proposals are implemented in Wales.

Health Challenge Wales

The Welsh Assembly Government's approach to improving health recognises that the way forward lies in adopting an integrated approach in which different policies and programmes add value to each other. The Health Challenge Wales programme has been developed to provide a new national focus and a way to drive forward all efforts to improve health. It means that government at all levels, organisations in all sectors and individuals can be challenged to do more to take action to improve people's health. The Assembly Government has outlined its aim of increasing the numbers of Welsh people using the Welsh natural environment for outdoor activities in its Sports and Physical Strategy Climbing Higher.

Better Place to Play

The Environment Agency-Wales published a Strategic Plan for Water Related Recreation in Wales that provides a set of priorities and opportunities for the development of water-related recreation. The plan is aimed at encouraging more people in Wales to take part in water related recreation and identifies new opportunities for water recreation at the coast and inland.

Vision, Aims and Outcomes

This strategy sets out the following vision for coastal tourism:

'An integrated year round coastal tourism industry, based on an outstanding natural environment and a quality tourism product that exceeds visitor expectations, whilst bringing economic, social, cultural and environmental benefits to coastal communities'.

The Strategy

The following strategy has been developed to meet the vision, strategic aims, policy objectives and challenges identified in previous chapters.

It has been presented under five themes. The final theme, Coastal Management, covers areas relating to the whole coastline while the other themes concentrate on particular locations or activities. Inevitably, there is some overlap between the themes, which reflects the integrated nature of activities and responsibilities along the coast.

The themes covered are:

- Coastal Towns and Resorts
- The Rural Coast
- Coastal Activities
- Coastal Culture
- Coastal Management

Coastal Towns and Resorts

Towns and cities around the coast of Wales vary greatly in size and character from the capital city to small resorts and fishing ports. Tourism's contribution to local economies will vary with seaside resorts being particularly dependent on visitor spending.

Cities and Towns on the Coast

Larger cities and towns on the coast such as Cardiff, Swansea and Newport have a tourist offer that embraces a wide range of shopping, eating out, cultural, recreational and leisure attractions, as well as specific opportunities related to the coast for water and land based informal recreation. They also have a range of serviced accommodation to support business tourism and the short break leisure market. In Swansea and Cardiff (45%) and (60%) respectively of accommodation demand comes from business travel. Smaller towns such as Aberystwyth and Bangor also benefit from local economies which include a university sector as well as other services. The wider local economy provides a stronger base to support shopping and catering activity than those towns dependent primarily on tourism. As a result, they provide a focus for day visitor activity from home and holiday accommodation in the surrounding areas. In addition, Aberystwyth, due to its location between North and South Wales, its increasing importance as a national centre and the new location of the Welsh Assembly Government regional office, has the potential to strengthen its accommodation base. Initiatives to regenerate the town and to develop its tourism role are emerging from the masterplanning work that has been undertaken which will enhance Aberystwyth's role as a coastal tourism town.

There are other coastal towns which have a distinctive appeal relating to their history, townscape and setting, such as Caernarfon and Conwy. Some other coastal towns such as Llanelli and Burry Port have not traditionally attracted much tourism activity, but the development of their coastal resources such as the Burry Port Harbour Development, Pembrey and the Millennium Coastal Parks provide opportunities for attracting a wider day visitor market as well as stayingtourists.

Holyhead, Swansea, Pembroke and Fishguard provide points of entry for visitors using the ferry services from Ireland, as well as catering for UK visitors to Ireland. Apart from regular ferry services, there is potential to develop cruise ship facilities particularly at Holyhead and Swansea to meet the growing market for this form of tourism. Milford Haven also has potential in relation to the cruise market.

Coastal Resorts

Coastal resorts are those towns on the coast where the local economy is dominated by tourism. They include Prestatyn, Rhyl, Llandudno, Beaumaris, Pwllheli, Porthmadog, Barmouth, Tenby, Saundersfoot and Porthcawl. They vary greatly in terms of their size, character and accommodation base. Apart from staying tourists, many of the resorts attract substantial numbers of day visitors from home, particularly those located on the South East and North East parts of the Welsh coast. While coastal towns such as Colwyn Bay, Aberavon and Barry may have a wider economic base, tourism is still important.

Resorts will continue to be a major focus for visitor activity at the seaside. However, there will continue to be competition, not only from other seaside destinations at home and abroad, but also from city and countryside destinations in Wales and elsewhere. Moreover, many resorts have been adversely affected by changes in tourism activity, remaining over dependent on long family holidays and having limited appeal to the younger generation and overseas markets.

As a result, the tourism season in most resorts is short, with a high proportion of employment being seasonal and often poorly paid. Coupled with other economic difficulties, this has led to some of the most deprived economic and social wards in Wales being found in coastal resorts. While leading resorts such as

Llandudno and Tenby provide an attractive living environment for residents and visitors, others suffer from a poor or run down appearance reflecting low levels of investment and confidence by the private sector.

The future prosperity of resort communities will depend not only on tourism activity but also on strengthening the local economy to provide additional employment and income opportunities for residents. This will best be achieved by diversifying the local economy to provide a greater choice and range of employment opportunities, and by adding value from tourism activity. Successful regeneration schemes will depend on the public, private and voluntary sectors delivering a concerted package of projects tailored to meeting the needs and opportunities of individual resorts. They will need to build on the Assembly

Government's approach to regenerating disadvantaged communities which focuses on building capacity within communities and engaging with all groups of residents to help understand the root causes of the problems that face individuals and households within the community. This process will help ensure that communities within resorts are empowered to take up the economic and social opportunities that are created. Some resorts have already benefited from regeneration programmes, which can provide lessons for future initiatives.

In supporting regeneration initiatives, priority at national level should be given to those areas where:

- the local economy is particularly dependent on tourism activity.
- existing tourism infrastructure is not well adapted to changing market needs.
- there are opportunities for new development to meet emerging market demand.

Deprivation in Coastal Communities

The prosperity of the different settlements varies widely depending on local circumstance, as do the levels of multiple deprivation in local communities. In some cases, such as Cardiff, areas of relative prosperity can be found in close proximity to areas of multiple deprivation. Coastal settlements with communities falling within the top 10% of communities suffering from multiple deprivation include:

- Major settlements with a varied economy including Cardiff, Swansea, Newport, Aberavon Llanelli and Barry
- Resort towns, including Barmouth and Rhyl
- Smaller towns where tourism contributes to the local economy, including Holyhead, Amlwch, Conwy, Caernarfon, Pwllheli, Aberystwyth, Pembroke Dock.

These wards are included in the Assembly Government's Communities First Programme which supports the establishment of Communities First Partnerships and helps to deliver capacity building projects.

It will be important to engage with the Community First Partnerships that have been set up within these areas when undertaking regeneration initiatives and other projects outlined in the implementation plan to ensure that local communities are involved in identifying local needs and solutions for regenerating their areas. The Community First model may also be appropriate for other areas where significant regeneration programmes are undertaken. The Welsh Assembly Government is committed to developing Communities First into Communities Next from 2009.

Providing an Attractive Environment

A crucial objective for resorts will be to improve and maintain the public the natural and historic environment to ensure that they are attractive to residents, investors and visitors. The appearance of the approaches to the resort, the sea front and the town centre are crucial in forming the visitor's initial impressions of the resort. An environment which is shabby, ill kept with ugly and poorly sited street furniture will detract from the visitor's enjoyment of the resort.

Resorts therefore need to ensure that they set high standards of design and landscaping for their public areas, including the provision of street furniture on the beach and adjoining areas. High standards of design, including innovatory architectural approaches should be encouraged for new development and redevelopment schemes while conserving the best of the resort's heritage, which contributes to the unique character of the place.

The private sector can also play an active part in maintaining public frontages in good order, and contributing towards the costs of landscaping and planting in the town centres and promenades. The existing public and partnership initiatives already being undertaken to improve the urban seaside environment need to be strengthened and expanded. The objective is to provide an attractive urban and seaside environment for the enjoyment of residents and visitors alike, which contributes to the unique character of each resort.

Beaches and Seaside

The beach and adjoining sea areas provide the unique attraction of seaside resorts. The Blue Flag and Resort Seaside Award schemes set standards for beaches used by the public including criteria relating to water quality, management of land and water recreation to avoid conflict between incompatible activities, safety and first aid provision, toilets, fresh water, litter and refuse disposal and environmental and safety information. A high proportion of resort beaches have attained these awards. However, a number of beaches continue to be affected by diffuse pollution and there are also indications that average beach litter density in Wales is increasing year on year.11 The beach and sea provide opportunities for a wide range of informal and active pastimes including swimming and sun bathing, sailing and beach games and more adventurous water based activities such as personal water craft and water skiing.

The enjoyment of the beach experience can be enhanced by good management and provision of facilities such as launch points, fresh water showers and organised children's play provision during the peak periods for family holidays. Good design and landscaping of beach facilities, promenades and street furniture can also add to the experience. The management of intensively used resort beaches is a complex task involving health, safety and environment issues, conflict resolution between different beach and water users, and coordination and liaison with private operators on an adjoining the beach.

The use of innovative management approaches could assist in enhancing the beach and seafront as a primary focus of visitor enjoyment. City and Town centre managers provide a possible exemplar. Beach masters or resort managers could be appointed with similar responsibilities and powers to manage and enhance the visitor enjoyment of the beach and immediate onshore and offshore areas, whilst involving the private, public and voluntary sector stakeholders in a coordinated approach to facility provision and maintenance.

Accommodation

The quality, scale and type of tourist accommodation varies greatly from resort to resort. Many establishments were first developed over 50 years ago and struggle to match customer expectations and aspirations in the 21st Century. If resorts are to continue to attract staying tourists in competition with other destinations, then it is essential that the accommodation provided meets or surpasses their expectations. No accurate figures currently exist for the coastal accommodation stock in Wales although a national audit of all bedstock is currently underway. It is possible to obtain some proxy indication of the quantity of accommodation by type, by relating tourism nights to occupancy data. On this basis, there are over 100,000 bedspaces in commercial accommodation located around the Welsh coast, of which half are in static caravans, either owned or available for holiday letting.

Serviced accommodation capacity is estimated to account for around 12% of the stock and self catering around 8%. There are, however, concentrations that mask the real picture. Llandudno has a substantial stock of serviced accommodation whereas the lack of similar facilities on the Lly^n Peninsula can cause problems when the area is hosting national and international events. Similarly, there are a number of high density caravan/camping sites along the North Wales coast, but a lack of quality camping on certain stretches of Cardigan Bay. In order to adapt provision to the changing needs, a multi-pronged approach will be needed including:

- investing in existing establishments to develop higher quality standards appropriate to their category and type, including serviced accommodation, caravan and camping sites and hostels

- the redevelopment or conversion of existing establishments which are not physically capable of being improved to appropriate standards to more viable uses
- the development of new establishments particularly where new opportunities and activities generate additional demand

Visit Wales has commissioned several serviced sector accommodation supply and demand studies to identify any shortfalls in the range and quality of accommodation provision in specific areas of Wales.12 These studies, in particular, identify whether deficiencies can be met by the extension/improvement of existing operations or through the provision of new facilities. A number of coastal locations are covered by these studies.

In terms of accommodation trends, a definite growth sector within the accommodation sector has been the rise in importance of 'boutique', 'designer' or 'townhouse' hotels. Key characteristics of this type of accommodation include high quality design fittings, central locations and limited size, targeting the upper end of the market at high room rates.

Many four star commercial hotels and country house hotels in the UK have now developed health/beauty/relaxation spas of varying size and quality. Such spas are emerging as a 'must have' facility to meet the demands of the short break market at the upper end of the market, though these also need local demand.

In terms of static caravan stock, a high proportion is individually owned with only a quarter available for commercial letting. While there are individual sites of high quality, many sites have standard layouts with varying quality of central facilities.

In some cases, it may be appropriate to allow expansion of existing sites in order to encourage operators to reduce density and to provide more imaginative and landscaped surroundings without incurring a potential loss of income. Towns and resorts should also encourage active networking between accommodation establishments to provide exchange of experience, mentoring, general business support and referrals.

Visitor Attractions

In addition to the beach, resorts need to provide a wide range of activities and attractions for the visitor if they are to continue to attract and increase the volume of staying and day visitors. The coast already has a range of visitor attractions including the world heritage listed Edwardian castles in North Wales, the National Waterfront Museum in Swansea, steam railways, local museums and other sites.

However, resorts offer opportunities for developing additional activities and specialist attractions drawing on the concentration of visitors to resorts without displacing visitors from existing attractions. In particular, there should be opportunities to:

- increase the number of opportunities for visitors to try new water and land based activities ranging from boat trips for wildlife watching to sports such as water skiing, dinghy sailing, paragliding and other activities.
- provide additional wet weather facilities such as indoor play areas, climbing walls, bowling greens and alleys and other recreational and leisure facilities.

There may also be opportunities to develop new attractions related to the heritage, culture or physical characteristics of the coast. However such developments will need a robust business plan including a consideration of the impact on existing attractions.

Retail and Catering

Two thirds of visitors enjoy shopping, and even more enjoy eating out while at the seaside but the retail and catering offer in many seaside resorts is limited, reducing the potential level of expenditure by visitors. The development of a wider range of specialist shops offering local arts and craft products together with high quality local produce could widen the retail offer and attract greater visitor spending.

While there are individual restaurants which offer high quality cuisine in some resorts; there are no comparable concentrations of eating out opportunities in any of the Welsh resorts. Visitors (including day visitors) are looking for a quality food experience in a variety of hospitality establishments. There are opportunities to raise the quality and choice of all types of catering establishments, using local Welsh produce particularly fish and shellfish and traditional Welsh recipes. Resorts should make special efforts to encourage a wider range of shops, particularly specialist shops selling local arts and crafts.

Visitor Access

Most visitors to resorts come by car. While staying visitors can be accommodated within the resorts, day visitors from holiday accommodation outside the resort or from home can cause congestion and pressure on parking facilities within the resort, particularly during the peak holiday season. Pressure within the resorts can be eased by promoting alternative methods of travel such as cycle routes and public transport, or by establishing seasonal park and ride systems. The provision of dedicated land trains or bus services connecting car parks and the main attractions within the resort can also assist in reducing car movements while helping to distribute visitors to the range of destinations.

Traffic management schemes can help to reduce congestion particularly at 'hot spots'. Advanced variable electronics signing on key approach routes can assist in directing traffic, as well as 'in car' traffic information or information from the Traffic Wales web site. Development in real time traffic information will be particularly relevant in dealing with peak seasonal traffic demands. Similarly pubic transport users (rail/bus/sea) require an integrated timetable and customer information system to provide them with 'real' information. There is a need to extend interactive tourism information points to include public transport hubs and tourist locations remote from TIC's.

The Rural Coast

The rural coast of Wales is a magnificent resource for residents and visitors to enjoy, offering spectacular coastal scenery, attractive small towns and villages, opportunities for informal land and water based recreation and a wildlife environment of exceptional diversity and interest. The coast is also valued for its unspoilt scenery, peace and quiet. A balance needs to be struck on the rural coast between tranquil areas and areas supporting a large number of people and a range of activity.

Coastal Settlements

Coastal towns and villages were often established as fishing ports or commercial harbours. Inshore fisheries remain an important function in some settlements and can add interest for the holiday visitor. While the commercial use of many harbours has declined, they often offer potential as safe havens for visiting boats, as well as bases for leisure activities such as sea angling, diving and leisure boat trips to watch wildlife as at Aberdovey, Aberaeron and New Quay. Other small coastal resorts include Tywyn and Borth. Tourism is an important contributor to the local economy, with villages attracting both staying and day visitors, as well as acting as service points for the surrounding rural areas. Most have an attractive environment and ambience for the visitor as well as specific heritage attractions, cultural or historic associations such as Conwy, Caernarfon, Beaumaris, Criccieth, Harlech, St Davids, Pembroke, Laugharne and Llansteffan. The establishment of the Wales Coastal Path, as well as rural cycle and riding routes, should help to underpin and develop existing tourism activity, while the combination of coast and countryside coupled with specific leisure or cultural activities should provide opportunities to attract niche and short break tourism markets.

Rural Accommodation

There is already a substantial amount of holiday accommodation along the rural coast. Much of the rural accommodation is in self catering cottages and static caravan sites, together with individual owned and managed hotel and guesthouse accommodation.

The development of the Wales Coastal Path, as well as water and land based activities along the coast, will provide opportunities to expand the accommodation base to cater for the changes in demand. In particular, there should be potential for camping sites, bed and breakfast and hostel accommodation serving younger and more active visitors.

Rural Beaches and the Rural Environment

The Welsh Coast is blessed with many attractive coves and beaches outside the main resort areas including: Red Wharf Bay, Newborough, Black Rock, Morfa Harlech, Morfa Dyffryn,

Aberdovey, Newgate, Broad Haven, Barafundle, Freshwater East, Rhossilli, Oxwich, Pendine, Pembrey. Many of these sites attract substantial informal use for both passive and active recreation and leisure uses, but their management poses problems and costs for local authorities, the National Trust and local communities. Charging for car parking, voluntary donation schemes and other initiatives can help to offset such costs.

The high quality of the coastal environment is recognised by the large number of environmental designations covering the bulk of the coastline. The quality is a major attraction for visitors to the coast, and it is vital therefore that development and visitor pressures are controlled to ensure that the resource is not inadvertently damaged or degraded. Where damage is occurring as a result of overuse, then positive management measures should be taken to match the capacity of the site to the user pressure, and restoration measures taken to make good damaged areas. Because of their rural character, the criteria for Blue Flag designation are not always appropriate for rural beaches. In order to provide a quality standard for such beaches, the Green Coast Award has been developed by Keep Wales Tidy, setting out a set of criteria designed to sustain the conservation value as well as visitor enjoyment of these areas. Wales is unique in developing the Green Coast award, thereby reinforcing the strong image of an unspoilt coastline for visitors to enjoy.

In addition to meeting the provisions set out in the criteria with regard to management, safety, information and conservation measures, local communities are also encouraged to set up local support groups to monitor and assist in the management of the beaches. The principle of involving the local community in the management and conservation of the local coastal environment should be encouraged through support for a range of possible organisations from voluntary associations to local trusts and companies. The Keep Wales Tidy Clean Coasts initiative encourages community participation through the establishment and operational management of voluntary Coastcare Groups. There are currently 98 voluntary Coastcare groups. Tourism businesses can also play their part, through encouraging their employees to participate in volunteering schemes on the coast.

Access

While access to the rural coast in many parts of North and South Wales is afforded by the M4 and A55 as well as the main rail routes, local access to individual rural sites is often reliant on narrow lanes and minor roads. As a result, congestion often occurs on routes providing access to popular sites during peak visitor periods. The heavy use of cars to reach those sites adds to pollution levels, as well as detracting from the visitor's experience of the visit.

There are a number of innovative public transport initiatives around the coast which provide visitors with alternative ways to enjoy the coastal experience. These include dedicated coastal bus services linking sites along the coast, and boat excursions along the coast and to islands off the coast. Such alternatives can help to reduce traffic pressures as well as adding interest and opportunities for the visitor.

The proposed development of the Wales Coastal Path will provide enhanced opportunities for walking along the coast, while the extension of existing cycle and riding trails, including the National Cycle Trail will also provide additional facilities to enjoy the coast in an environmentally friendly way.

Coastal Activities

There is considerable variation in volumes of participation, demand trends and spending for outdoor activities around the coast of Wales. By far the largest demand is for walking, (69% participating whilst on holiday). Adventure (8%) sailing (5%), sea angling (6%) and (wildlife watching (5%) have 'medium' levels of participation. Other activities include golf (3%) and cycling (4%).

The spatial distribution of activities along the Welsh coast is a function of the physical geography, the distribution of suitable terrain and attractive landscapes, and the location of infrastructure, transport networks, accommodation and other facilities.

It will be important to consider the needs and requirements of disabled people when developing and promoting coastal activities. Wales is establishing a good track record in encouraging equal opportunities for all participants. Where such facilities are provided, they need to be adequately publicised via, for example, the Disability Wales or the Visit Wales website. Whilst information on the types of activities undertaken by men and women on holiday is currently unavailable, it will be important for the strategy to strike a balance between developing activities that appeal primarily to men such as golf or fishing and activities that have more appeal to women.

In relation to the provision of opportunities for coastal activities, both land and water based, consideration needs to be given to strategic planning through the use of appropriate methodology, such as the Recreation Opportunity approach. This will enable consideration to be given to providing for the full range of desired activities in the most appropriate locations whilst retaining more tranquil areas.

Coastal Footpath

Of all the activities undertaken at the coast, walking is by far the most popular. Walking, for the vast majority of visitors to the coast, will be one amongst many activities undertaken during their holiday.

There is also a smaller niche market for walkers who undertake specific walking holidays. Growth in niche walking holidays is likely to be strongest for independent centre-based walking breaks. Such holidays already account for the bulk of walking holidays in Wales, and are likely to continue to do so in the future.

There are already a number of coastal paths, including the Isle of Anglesey Coastal Path, the North Wales Path, the Lly^n Coastal Path, Ceredigion Coastal Path, Carmarthen Bay Coastal and Estuaries Way, Glamorgan Heritage Coast Path, as well as the Pembrokeshire Coast Path, providing around 1000kms of footpath around the coast. 60% of the coast currently has public access. Some areas will always be inaccessible, for example, ports, industrial sites and areas of nature conservation.

The Welsh Assembly Government has announced a new coastal access programme to increase public access to Wales' coast. A key aim of the programme will be to eventually link all existing coastal paths to form an All Wales Coastal Path. As part of the programme, there will be opportunities to provide links and loops from the spine path and to improve access to cyclists and horse riders in the coastal zone. The creation of circular routes from the spine route will enable local attractions and local communities near the coast to benefit from the Coastal Path, maximising the economic benefits from the investment.

It is envisaged that the coastal access improvement programme will last four to five years. The programme will aim to deliver enhanced public access by maximising existing path infrastructure. A number of key interests will be involved including the coastal local authorities, the National Trust, Countryside Council for Wales, Farming Unions, RSPB and the Ramblers Association.

It will be important to develop appropriate accommodation linked to the walking and cycling opportunities, including quality accommodation across all types from bunkhouses and Bed and Breakfasts to three and four star serviced accommodation.

The Visit Wales Walkers and Cyclist Welcome scheme provides guidance and accreditation to accommodation providers that specifically cater for walkers and cyclists and provides information on the additional facilities that are required, including drying areas and secure cycle storage.

Wildlife Tourism

The coast of Wales has some of Europe's best landscapes and an abundance of maritime habitats, making it an attractive destination for visitors wanting to explore the natural environment and its human imprint.

The dramatic cliffscapes and stacks of Holy Island and Pembrokeshire are prime bird nesting areas, the mudflats of the Dee and the Severn hold massive invertebrate populations; the estuaries of the Conwy, Mawddach, Dyfi and Tywi harbour a variety of saltmarsh dwellers, while the unique unglaciated via landscape of Milford Haven offers further marine and freshwater sanctuary.

All the above invite wildlife and coastline exploration, and while it is difficult to assess the potential scale of the market, the Scottish Executive in 2002 estimated that the wildlife tourism market in Scotland was worth £57m and employed some 2000 people. The number of wildlife tourism operators in Scotland grew by 37% between 1997 and 2002. It is also estimated that wildlife watching is growing by some 10% a year across the world. The 'Wildlife Economy Wales' 13 study highlights the considerable potential of developing wildlife tourism in Wales in terms of:

- Extending the tourism season in specific locations where there is an opportunity to do so.
- Securing an increase in visitor spend at sites which are currently popular, where appropriate.
- Improving the links between wildlife activities/interests and other activities such as general outdoor visits, tourism and agriculture.
- Developing new attractions and attracting new people to new and existing sites. A coastal wildlife tourism development programme could include elements of the following:
- wildlife and birdwatching events with wildlife organisations such as CCW, RSPB and the Wildlife Trusts in Wales.
- seawatching from the shore and from a series of specially designed and constructed coastal hides and viewpoints, with information on different species.
- a programme of coastal boat trips – seal and dolphin watching (although it will be important to observe Codes of Conduct)
- island explorations – e.g. Anglesey, Bardsey, Skomer and Skokholm, subject to environmental carrying capacity of the Islands.
- a series of seashore safaris – exploratory events for children, using interpretation techniques developed at Ynyslas and Oxwich NNRs.

It is critical, however, that any further wildlife related tourism development is appropriately managed to ensure that the wildlife resource is protected and wherever possible enhanced. Visitor management, particularly at the more sensitive locations, will be an important consideration as will consideration of the degree to which there is capacity for expansion in certain locations.

Other Coastal Land Activities

In addition to the walking and cycling activities mentioned, some parts of the coast are particularly renowned for certain land-based activities, namely golf, climbing and kite sports. Participation in climbing is growing steadily whilst participation in kite sports is growing rapidly from a small base. There would appear to be limited opportunity to further promote climbing or to provide additional facilities.

Kite sports on the other hand are an opportunity to attract a new, younger market to traditional resorts, though management will be needed to avoid conflicts with other beach users. Golf is already being promoted by Visit Wales as a niche activity. However, to take full advantage of the interest in golf which will be generated by the Ryder Cup in 2010, there is a need to increase the amount of high grade accommodation located close to premier golf courses and to consider the case for additional golf course provision.

Coastal Activities-Water

Levels of participation in water–based activities are relatively low in comparison to land-based activities such as walking. However, water-based activities have significant localised economic impacts where there are harbours or marinas or natural conditions suitable for specific activities such as surf beaches, dive sites or angling locations.

Angling in particular is an important contributor to a number of local coastal economies. Fishing Wales has demonstrated the high value of recreational fishing to the Welsh economy. The 2004/05 marketing campaign generated an additional £27m into the economy, contributing to the estimated £100m+ of angling tourism revenue. Coastal fishing pays an important element with 48% of angling visits being to the coast. Of these 69% are shore based anglers and 31% boat anglers. There are some 70 charter boat skippers operating from Welsh ports. Boating and sailing generates significant economic impacts and helps to create a distinctive atmosphere. The economic impacts of boating tourism can be increased by building new marinas or improving the facilities at existing harbours and marinas to meet the growing demand for berths.

In other locations, new slipways or all-state-of-the tide landing stages could facilitate access to the water for sport use, nature cruises, coastal kayaking and angling boats. Other relatively minor improvements such as the provision of trailer parking and showers would bring additional use and the potential for local economic benefits. It should be borne in mind that facilities require maintenance and use can be very seasonal. It is, however, feasible to provide some facilities from May to September (temporary pontoons) and remove them for the winter.

While there are locations where new slipways or pontoons are required, there is also a need to improve and increase the use of existing slipways. There is a need to review the capacity, condition and current management of the entire coastal network of launching and landing facilities to identify whether investment is warranted. Much work has already been done in some areas with the preparation of coastal recreation audits.

There are water activities that are particular to parts of the Welsh coast. Not only does this generate significant economic impact, sports such as surfing and wakeboarding provide a distinctive atmosphere. It is important to safeguard those markets by providing good quality facilities at key locations and increase numbers and spending where there is the opportunity to do so. There is also potential to initiate 'try it' opportunities to develop an interest, in particular, in watersports.

Various visitor surveys conducted around the coast have all highlighted that one of the main attractions of the Welsh coastline is its unspoilt scenery, peace and quiet. While boating and watersports are important, there should be a focus on activities that are less intrusive.

Enjoyment of coastal or offshore waters for recreational boating need not conflict with conservation initiatives or lead to environmental degradation. Initiatives such as the Green Blue Project set up jointly by the British Marine Foundation and the Royal Yachting Association aim to provide information to the marine industry and users about potential environmental impacts of recreational boating and promote effective mitigation measures.

Most complaints arise from the use of personal watercraft (PWC's) – including noise and safety concerns. However, the use of PWC's is a legitimate leisure activity if appropriately managed.

Local authorities in Gwynedd, Conwy, Denbighshire and Anglesey have already instigated a registration scheme for PWC users. The registration scheme is valid for all four areas and requires users to register with one of the councils with proof of identify and insurance before being able to use any of the beaches/slipways in the area. This offers the advantage of an ultimate sanction against those who do not comply with bylaws and local regulations by withdrawing their registration for the whole region of North Wales. There is a need to explore whether a regional zoning and management system for the use of PWC's could be introduced and implemented on a Wales wide basis. With regard to developing watersports, the following have been identified as opportunities:

- Provide access to water-based activities for new participants within harbours
- Safeguard the markets in specific water activities and in the following activities increase numbers and spending: Pembrokeshire (improve slipway access and management) and develop the potential for Gelliswick as a Dive Centre – Surfing – Lly^n, Pembrokeshire, Porthcawl, Gower (provide better beach facilities, including showers and changing)
- Climbing – Holyhead, South Pembrokeshire (continue to manage noclimbing agreements to ensure continued participation at important nature conservation sites), Conwy
- Kite sports
- Anglesey, Lly^n, Conwy
- Sea angling
- Coast-steering
- Sea kayaking
- Windsurfing.

There may also be additional longer-term opportunities to develop or increase existing activities by the provision of artificial reefs to improve surfing, diving or sea angling activity. In addition, the Environment Agency's water recreation action plan identifies the following areas as possible hubs for general coastal watersport activity – Swansea, Cardiff, Milford Haven, Anglesey, Colwyn Bay, Cardigan and the Teifi Estuary, Aberdyfi, and Barmouth.

Marinas and Harbours

Catching the Wave identified eleven marinas around the coast of Wales and some twenty three harbours (plus six commercial harbours and fifteen yacht stations). In addition to the above, the Swansea SA1 marina is now a commitment. An audit undertaken in 2003/4 by the British Marina Federation identified over 7500 moorings along the Welsh coastline with active proposals at different stages of development for a further 3500 permanent new berths.

The technical report has identified some 16 schemes relating to potential marina/harbour developments which are at various of stages of consideration, including new marina developments and improvements to existing marinas. A key objective within *Catching the Wave* is to increase the supply of long stay and visitor berths and moorings. The need for this is strongly supported by waiting lists for berths at a number of locations. For example, Pwllheli has a waiting list of some 450 names.

In the past, in the UK and other European countries, most notably Spain and Portugal, marina developments have been supported by residential development in order to fund the cost of the infrastructure eg seawalls, pontoons and onshore facilities. Without such provisions, marina development is rarely financially viable without public sector support.

In many of the potential marina locations in Wales, significant marina related housing would not be appropriate and therefore public sector support towards the capital costs could be required. The scale and type of marinas most appropriate to the majority of the Welsh Coast is more on the lines of the Brittany experience in France ie marinas of a scale that do not require major residential development, but development that is restricted to marine related commercial development, some commercial leisure and limited ancillary housing.

The size of the marinas will need to be sufficiently large to be able to generate sufficient income from mooring and related fees to cover the ongoing revenue costs arising from the management of the marina. This is thought to be in the order of 350-400 berths. Smaller harbour schemes, including the use of temporary berths or smaller scale summer moorings can also provide an alternative to larger marinas. Various fact finding missions to Brittany have been undertaken where the following main lessons learnt have been:

- that any marina strategy is a long term strategy.
- that marinas and other watersports can be developed in tandem.
- that there are definite benefits to rural hinterlands from marina developments.
- marina and watersports should be linked to other tourism opportunities – such as heritage and golf.
- there needs to be local support from the outset.
- the incorporation of visiting berths are important eg. Kernaval marina at Lorient has 680 berths with 100 reserved for visitors and generated 12000 yacht night visitors per year.
- events play an important part of establishing profile and reputation.
- getting children onto water for fun and experience as early as possible is important. 9000 Breton children per year receive boat lessons through schools.
- Innovative building methods and materials used in marina construction.
- facilities for boat waste disposal and drainage systems are important as are proper shower and toilets. EU regulations are increasingly setting higher standards.
- dual use of space – winter storage areas used as food markets in the summer.

Experience has shown that marinas and ancillary facilities can provide significant local economic benefits both in terms of jobs and spend. A recent study by the University of Glamorgan on the economic impact of Pwllheli Marina indicated that the direct income generated by the development in 2005 was £19m with a further £8.9m spent by berth owners outside the immediate area.

With regard to jobs, the study estimated some 260 direct and indirect jobs were supported by the income generated. While the demand for berths currently exceeds supply, it would not be practical or desirable to build or improve all the marina opportunities that have been identified especially as many would require sizeable public funding.

Therefore, it is necessary to evaluate schemes in order to determine best value for money, local benefits and fit with the wider environmental, economic and social policies of the Welsh Assembly Government and other national organisations.

It is recommended that possible new marinas and existing marinas and harbours that would benefit from improvement works are assessed by the Area Spatial Plan Groups to determine the most appropriate location for investment within their region.

The location and development of marinas will also need to be considered from a marine planning point of view as well as from a terrestrial and spatial point of view.

Assessment Criteria

The assessment should consider the following:

Policy and Strategic

- Compatibility with the Wales Spatial Plan and other national environment and economic strategies
- Compatibility with regional, local and marine planning policies
- Demonstrate strategic approach in relation to other coastal initiatives (including other marinas).
- Environmental and Wider Conservation Interests
- Compatibility with the environmental policies of national organisations (CCW, EA etc.)
- Subject to satisfactory geophysical, sediment movement, wave/wind analysis and coastal/estuarial survey and modelling

- Subject to a comprehensive Environmental Impact Assessment
- Commitment to attaining Blue Flag accreditation
- Subject to compliance with WAG flood risk policies
- Consideration of impact and relationship to environmental designated areas (including the need to screen for potential impact on SAC and SPA sites under the EU Habitats Directive
- That sufficient land is available for initial operation and potential future development (including winter boat and trailer storage)
- Consideration with regard to access – both in terms of vehicle and pedestrian access and navigable boat access during much of the tidal period
- Safety of operation
- Where appropriate, should compliment existing harbour and shoreside facilities
- Consideration of visual impact on the character of the wider built and natural environment and
- Consideration of impact on water quality (in accordance with provisions of the Water Framework Directive).

Economic and Business

- A robust business case should be prepared including a cost plan, outputs/outcomes and a marketing strategy
- Must demonstrate proven user demand, proximity and accessibility to markets
- Should have a local employment policy and demonstrate level of local commitment
- Should identify appropriate training and skills development and local business support
- Should not be in direct and immediate competition with existing facilities, thus avoiding economic displacement
- Should demonstrate added economic value including direct and indirect tourism multiplier effects

- Should enhance or maintain land and water opportunities where feasible.

Social and Community

- Demonstrate significant local support
- Provide a consultation strategy that addresses a community engagement plan
- Should be able to demonstrate local community benefits.

Marina Development

Whilst it has not been possible to undertake a detailed financial viability or market demand assessment of the proposals to build new marinas or extend existing marinas within the context of developing the strategy, a review has been undertaken of existing reports. Taking into account locational considerations, local support and a preliminary view of the criteria above, the following locations have been identified as having a number of attributes that merit further consideration by the Area Spatial Plan Groups.

* Rhyl (new) Pwllheli (extension)
* Swansea SA1 marina (new)
* Beaumaris (new) Fishguard (new)
* Holyhead (extension) Burry Port (extension)

Some of the above are well advanced with regard to obtaining planning permission and the required maritime approvals, but have certain land or dredging issues to resolve, while others are at the feasibility/business planning stage. The development of the above marinas would provide the Welsh coastline with 18 purpose built marinas in addition to a number of other mooring locations (ports/harbours and yacht stations). Where funding is not already committed, Welsh Assembly Government funding will be dependent on them meeting the criteria outlined above. Other potential sites, which are longer term opportunities for new marina or extended marinas include:

* Pont Penrhyn Porthcawl
* Pembroke Dock Cardiff
* Newport Barry

* Colwyn Bay/Llandudno

The development of these sites will need to be considered against the criteria established, the capital cost, the balance between public/private sector involvement, any impact from new marinas (on both side of the Bristol Channel) and the wider regeneration benefits.

Locations where major works may not be appropriate, but certain limited improvements to increase the number of moorings and/or facilities which could bring significant local benefits include:

* Caernarfon Aberaeron
* Porthmadog Cardigan
* Barmouth New Quay
* Aberdyfi Milford Haven

The types of improvements envisaged include improved public space eg promenade enhancements, improved parking, identified trailer parking areas, improved slipways, additional fixed shoreside moorings, pontoons to give 24 hour shore access from drying out harbours, toilet and shower facilities. A full list of marina/harbour related facilities are included in the technical report.

It will be important that any new provision or upgrading of existing facilities are made to a high quality and standard. This also applies to any ancillary activities related to accommodation, eating and drinking. Improved facilities will enable Wales to further develop its high profile with regard to international and interregional sailing and watersports events.

Visiting Berths

It will be important to ensure that any new mooring facility includes the capacity to provide an adequate supply of visiting berths, to encourage visits to other areas around the Welsh coast. Visiting berths are also very important for events, competitions and regattas. It is appreciated that visiting berths which are only used occasionally (but frequently during the peak season) do not generate the same income levels as the annual renting of berths and that they require additional management.

However, there are examples around the coast of Wales where proactive management of berths has made regular berths available to visiting boats whilst the regular user is away. It is important that there are opportunities for sailors to sail around the coast in the knowledge that visiting berths are available. These facilities would also provide 'safe haven berths' for any boats requiring refuge due to the weather, tide or mechanical failure. Marina operators and harbour master have however emphasised that boats would never be turned away. Over time, the interest in travelling around the coast of Wales could become as popular as the current cross Irish Sea ventures.

Cruising

Cruising is one of the growth sectors in international tourism. Passenger departures from British Ports rose from 50,000 in 1990 to over 270,000 in 2003. While the bulk of the cruises were to the Mediterranean, Atlantic Islands or Scandinavia, an increasing number of operators cruise around the British Isles, with the Irish Sea increasing in popularity particularly Dublin and Belfast. The east coast Irish ports are receiving up to 70 cruise liner visits per year. In Wales, there were 15 calls in 2005 and 12 in 2006. Any liner calling at an Irish port could also call at a Welsh port.

There are a number of sub markets within the cruising market, including:

* Capitals of Europe – which could include Cardiff, Dublin and Belfast plus ports en route
* The four Country Round Britain cruise
* Short Irish sea cruises
* The Celtic Fringe – taking in northern Iberia Bay of Biscay, the Irish and North seas.

The size of the vessel also varies-from ships accommodating 600/700 passengers to the typical 2600 passenger liner. The trend is for larger vessels, with the largest liner (new liner for Royal Caribbean) having a capacity of 6400 passengers. The new larger liners will be for the international market, in particular America and the Caribbean, but it will mean that existing cruise liners will be cascaded down to other market areas. The four ports in Wales with potential for developing the cruise liner market are Holyhead, Milford Haven, Swansea and Cardiff. Proposals are at an advanced stage, particularly at Holyhead and Milford Haven. In order to maximise potential, shore side disembarkation is generally required, as this is preferred by cruise liner operators and passengers. Supporting facilities, including covered walkways, coach/taxi areas, information points and general reception areas are also desirable. The importance of alongside facilities and the provision of a cruise liner terminal cannot be overstated. The Port of Seattle, a major port for the Alaska cruise market, is an example of where providing these facilities has had a significant impact on passenger numbers. In 1999, 6,615 passengers sailed from the Port. Since the opening of a cruise terminal in 2000, passenger numbers have increased to 686,000.

Spending from cruise passengers and crew can benefit the port and immediate area, in addition to the income generated from port fees. There are various estimates for average spend by passengers and crew. Assuming that each passenger spends £50 and each crew member £30, a 600 capacity vessel would typically result in £25,000-£30,000 spend per docking.

The Cruise Wales partnership was established in 2004 and involves the Welsh Assembly Government, the ports, local authorities and tourism operators. The partnership has achieved some success in attracting new cruise calls to Wales and in identifying the potential that is presented by the cruise liner market. A Wales Cruise Action Plan for 2006 – 2013 has been prepared. Due regard will need to be given to environmental considerations (such as dredging) when choosing locations for potential new facilities. Coastal Culture The coast has been the muse of writers and poets from the mediaeval story telling of the Mabinogion to Dylan Thomas's *heron priested shore*. Today the coast is home to many different settlements and communities, each with its own distinctive historical and contemporary cultural identity. The Welsh language is still the living, working language in many of these areas and events and festivals such as those held at Aberdaron and Fishguard present a vibrant modern cultural life.

Cultural tourism can attract visitors at all times of the year to established and new places of interest. It can help address seasonality and extend the offer beyond the usual destinations and is attractive to the short break market. It can also enhance the more established types of tourism, by adding an extra dimension to beach and resort holidays. It will be important to ensure that the coast makes the most of its cultural offer and that this is linked to activity and other coastal products in order to broaden visitor appeal and stimulate demand in the off peak season. A review of the cultural tourism strategy has been undertaken14 and its recommendations will need to be taken into account when developing projects that support the delivery of this strategy.

Food

Food is an essential part of the tourism offer for Wales. In recent years, we have seen significant improvements and additions to the food offer, both in terms of local produce and its preparation and presentation in cafes, restaurants and other eating establishments around the coast. Restaurants such as those at Portmeirion in Gwynedd, the Harbourmaster in Aberaeron and St Brides in Saundersfoot are showing a modern confidence in local and regional cuisine.

There are a number of ways that support for regional and local food can be achieved, including:

- awareness campaigns using television, radio and website media, joint marketing with local supermarkets, production of recipe books and other publications.
- working with local growers, suppliers and others to develop local supply chains.
- promoting particularly distinctive Welsh coastal foods, e.g. salt marsh lamb, Lly^n and Pembrokeshire lobster, local shellfish.
- working with hotels, restaurants and cafes to develop quality seafood menus.
- the development of sea food trails

There is also potential to develop the 'slow food' concept-building on the idea originally developed in Italy of quality ingredients cooked with love. Wales could develop a series of coastal town 'Convivia' which run courses, tastings, dinners, food and drink events, and local campaigns. Food and seafood festivals also have an important role in celebrating and raising the profile of food from the sea and local area. There is scope to develop a high profile Seafood Festival that could attract visitors from further afield and which could also play a useful role in raising the profile of Wales as a quality seafood destination. It could be held at different coastal locations each year or build on existing seafood festivals such as Pembrokeshire Fish Week, Cardigan Bay, Anglesey and Lly^ n Seafood festivals. Care needs to be undertaken to avoid the over exploitation of food and fisheries and to foster an understanding of limits and capacity – the Assembly Government's fisheries strategy provides guidance on these issues.

Events

Activities are an important part of the coastal tourism experience in Wales and special events and festivals can add an extra dimension and provide an incentive for visitors to visit and importantly participate. Hosting special events during quieter times of the year is another successful measure that destinations can adopt in order to ensure more uniform flow of demand across the year, in particular where an event would generate an overnight stay.

An events programme could have a number of distinct advantages:

- It is an attractive way of presenting an active and dynamic destination to visitors who are looking for participatory holiday opportunities.
- It can provide interesting contact opportunities between residents and visitors.
- It can help to test and develop thematic ideas best suited to the interests of residents and visitors.
- It is a flexible way of market testing, if effective monitoring and feedback mechanisms are included.
- It can assist an area to develop a strongly themed identity.

In order to be viable and offer consistently high quality of information and provision, a degree of coordination and management would be required. It would also have to demonstrate an element of financial independence. Welsh Ministers have decided that a major events unit will be set up within the Welsh

Assembly Government that will develop an events strategy in support of wider Assembly Government strategic objectives.

This unit will develop an overseeing/coordinating role, working closely with the Regional Tourism Partnerships. In order to develop an events programme the following will need to be addressed:-

- collecting and collating relevant events information.
- developing and introducing a suitable vetting scheme.
- providing minimal standards and guidance to event providers.
- developing and maintaining an events database.
- liaising with participating organisations on effective marketing and promotional activities.
- seeking, wherever possible, areas for joint working and synergy between events.
- providing meaningful feedback to organisers and main sponsors.
- securing longer term financial support, especially from the private sector.

An audit of current provision indicates a patchy and sporadic spread of events along the Welsh coast. The most obvious are those run by local sailing clubs, such as regattas and competitive races. Other coastal events may or may not reflect a marine or maritime theme. In order to address this, a coastal events programme should be developed, which would:

- place events into a common accessible database which could be the basis for a coastal events website, or a dedicated page on a wider coastal tourism website for Wales, linked to an accommodation offer
- filling the gaps (in space and time)-a strategic look at what's missing and the opportunities presented for new activities in different places at certain times of years
- local celebrations of related themes – developing events based on maritime history, trade, food, culture, possibly under the banner of Sense of Place

- a coastal cultural dimension, featuring literature, music, theatre and language
- develop events celebrating the link between art and the sea, featuring traditional and contemporary work, involving public and private galleries and public art spaces
- a series of high profile local or regional maritime festivals, combining the best of local activities such as sailing, watersports, food and drink and related entertainment
- a coastal ecotourism or green tourism activities programme
- introductory and non-competitive events on all aspects of watersports, from primary school level to lifelong learning
- national and international level competitive sailing and watersports
- build on Cadw's events programme at coastal properties and educational interpretation of sites especially World Heritage sites.

The logistics, time and costs of coordinating an events programme should not be under estimated. It will be important that the following criteria is taken into account in developing an events programme. Events also require appropriate infrastructure to effectively cater for them.

- Will the tourism season be extended?
- Is there potential for generating additional bed nights?
- Will there be wider tourism benefits?
- Is the tourism infrastructure adequate to cope with the event?
- Is there potential media interest?
- Are there local benefits?
- Is the event of strategic importance?
- Is there appropriate infrastructure in place to cater for transportation to and from events?

Coastal Heritage and the Arts

Visiting a heritage site is amongst one of the most popular activities undertaken by visitors to the Welsh seaside. Virtually every mile of the coast of Wales bears the traces of Welsh history from prehistoric burials and forts to the coastal defences of the Napoleonic Wars and World War II. Some of the most enduring and iconic coastal images owe their drama and magic to the historic environment – from prehistoric Carreg Samson in Pembrokeshire, to Harlech Castle and Llandudno Pier. The castles of Edward I in North Wales are one of only two World Heritage Sites in Wales and are visited by half a million people a year. The Victorian period brought engineering such as the Telford and Stephenson bridges and the distinctive architecture, piers and promenades of many seaside towns.

The traces of prehistoric settlements and burials are part of what can be discovered when walking the various Coastal Paths (for example in Anglesey). National and local museums hold many of the physical artefacts of Wales' seafaring tradition – fish traps and shipwrecks are monuments to fortune and misfortune.

Opportunities for promoting coastal heritage include marketing Wales' coastal history and heritage as part of the coastal tourism offer and improving the availability of information to visitors about coastal heritage in publications and websites, including website links to Cadw and other historical bodies.

High quality interpretation at coastal and heritage sites is also key in terms of attracting visitors. The setting out of overarching themes that can link together different properties by type, period, activity and locations can help encourage people to visit other sites in the area. It is also important to offer a choice of interpretation, depending on the audience and character of the site. Both traditional and more innovative technological techniques can be used to communicate a site's significance, sense of place and welcome.

The historic environment can, however, be vulnerable to damage from inappropriate leisure activities – the grass banks of a prehistoric settlement may be a new challenge for BMX or trail bikes and a coastal fort may seem an attractive location for a summer evening bonfire or drinking session. Interpretation, information and local interests need to be aware of these dangers and be a positive force for considerate enjoyment.

Arts, Museums and Galleries

There have been key developments over recent years at the coast that provide an important platform upon which to build. These developments include:

- The National Waterfront Museum in Swansea
- Oriel Mostyn, Llandudno
- Visitor and conference facilities at the National Library, Aberystwyth
- Venue Cymru, Llandudno
- Galeri, Caernarfon
- Theatr Mwldan, Cardigan

Museums and Galleries, including local museums, provide a valuable contribution to interpreting the sense of place and history of an area. There are opportunities for museums to develop a more integrated approach through the development of themes and through signposting to other associated museums and attractions. Museums should also be encouraged to schedule key exhibitions outside the peak season that will attract visitors at times of the year that would otherwise see modest customer flows.

The arts, including the visual and performing arts also provide a stimulus for tourism. A new landscape gallery for Wales is currently being built at St David's that will provide opportunities for tourists to appreciate the artistic interpretation of the Welsh landscape across the centuries. Public Art schemes can help to create a Sense of Place, reinforcing the character of our towns and villages, whilst individual businesses can display the work of local artists helping to create a distinctive, local environment.

Welsh Language

The Welsh language remains the everyday language of most communities along the western seaboard of Wales. It can be encountered in shops, on signposts and in many other day-to-day situations. It can add a real sense of local identity to a place or a situation. *Iaith Pawb*, a national action plan for a bilingual Wales, outlines the Assembly Government's aim of promoting Wales' modern bilingual nature. This work should be further supported in order to make the Welsh coast a truly bilingual holiday destination, helping to give it its unique selling proposition. Bodies such as the Welsh Language Board and Mentrau Iaith (county-based language bodies) are actively promoting the use of Welsh in tourism, through introducing initiatives that encourage tourism businesses to make more use of Welsh, adding a valuable dimension to the coastal tourism experience.

Tourism and other relevant economic activity can help to maintain the viability and sustainability of many of our traditional Welsh speaking communities. The Assembly Government recognises, however, that large scale developments can affect the linguistic balance within communities. Planning Policy Wales and the accompanying Technical Advice Note 20 on the Welsh Language affirm that policies for the location of such development should take into account which areas could best accommodate them to secure economic benefits whilst not eroding the position of the Welsh language. The One Wales agreement includes a commitment to review and reissue TAN with a view to allowing authorities to use Language Impact Assessment for planning purposes in areas of housing pressure.

Coastal Management

The Welsh coastline is diverse in character ranging from urban seaside resorts, working harbours and ferry ports, to small rural communities and isolated stretches of coast. There are a number of landowners, including local authorities, the National Trust, Ministry of Defence, private owners and the Crown Estate together with a number of bodies with management or regulation responsibilities. These include the Local Authorities (various departments), Harbour Authorities, Sea Fisheries Committees, Crown Estate, Environment Agency, Countryside Council for Wales, Welsh Assembly Government and various UK Government Departments. Coastal Management needs to consider issues surrounding the management of coastal destinations/resorts, environmental management, visitor management and people management.

The ICZM strategy advocates a broad holistic approach to coastal management that will enable coastal planning and management to look at the big picture and view coastal issues in the wider context.15 Partnership working that involves agreeing and delivering common goals for coastal areas is key to effective management. There are many examples of partnership working at national and local levels in Wales, including the Wales Coastal and Maritime Partnership, the Green Sea Partnership and local forums such as the Pembrokeshire Coastal Forum and the Severn Estuary Partnership. In North Wales, CCW is taking forward the 'Straight to Head' initiative which is considering how the economic, social and environmental assets of the Menai Straits can be maximised through better coordination of activity. It is imperative that tourism and regeneration interests are fully engaged in such partnerships where they exist. The ICZM strategy also advocates the need to explore opportunities for similar coordinated action elsewhere on the coast.

Visitor Management

Much of the natural coast already benefits from positive countryside management through the efforts of the National Park Authorities, Areas of Outstanding Natural Beauty organisations, Countryside Council for Wales, local authorities, and voluntary organisations such as the National Trust, the Wildlife Trusts and the RSPB.

Whilst it is recognised that a strong policy framework is in place for the development and protection of the Welsh coastline, there is a need to strengthen visitor management at the coast to meet rising visitor expectations. Studies for DEFRA by the Institute of Estuarine and Coastal studies of Hull University have identified that in coastal areas, unregulated activities – such as recreation and tourism-have the potential to cause adverse impacts on conservation in terms of the risk they present for the marine environment.

At some sites, there may be conflict between a group of activity users and wildlife interests in particular areas or at particular times, for instance, climbing on the sea cliffs at Holyhead during the breeding season, or the harassment of dolphins and seals by overenthusiastic pursuit by visitor boats. Disturbance to wildlife as a result of coastal tourism activity is not solely restricted to water-based recreation. Larger numbers of visitors to rural coastal areas could potentially damage coastal habitats and wildlife such as sand dunes, salt marshes, coastal heath and rocky shores. The provision of better coastal access could result in disturbance to previously untouched areas.

In some areas, voluntary agreements and codes of conduct have been agreed between user groups and operators to limit any environmental disturbance.

These initiatives have value in raising awareness of the potential damage/disturbance that certain activities can cause. There is scope to seek to agree other similar arrangements at other sites with existing or potential conflict. Accreditation schemes have also been developed for operators that have signed up to follow various codes of conduct. The WiSe (Wildlife Safe) scheme for example has been set up to deliver training and accreditation for operators of registered passenger and charter vessels who wish to view marine wildlife. All WiSe operators have agreed to abide by appropriate Codes of Conduct for the animals that they view, created to ensure that their operations are safe and sustainable.

Coastal Recreation Areas

There are a number of locations around the Welsh coast which because of their character, the recreational opportunities they offer or their location, attract substantial numbers of visitors. They range from popular resort beaches to country parks areas with wildlife and archaeological interest.

These sites are a vital resource for coastal tourism, absorbing pressures which might otherwise fall on more sensitive areas, and have a major impact on visitors' experience and enjoyment of the Welsh coastline. However, the popularity of these areas generates additional management costs over and above those which would otherwise be incurred by the land manager in meeting local demand.

While some organisations such as the National Parks and AONBs receive support from the Welsh Assembly Government, resources for visitor management in other cases have to compete with other revenue expenditure priorities. Some areas are able to recover management costs through car parking or launch fees, or the provision of catering and retail facilities on a franchise or self operated basis.

However, the ability to recover costs is often limited by the costs of collection or the commonality of facilities such as beaches and open countryside where public access is freely available. The consultation highlighted the fact that many coastal managers are struggling to find the resources to maintain existing facilities and sites, let alone consider exploiting potential opportunities to provide improved facilities and new recreational facilities within a safe and well managed environment.

These costs arise from the need to:

- Provide visitor facilities such as toilets, freshwater showers at beaches and car parking for visitors. These involve capital costs as well as on-going revenue costs in maintenance, cleaning and supervision
- Increased land management costs in providing and maintaining footpaths, styles and other access, which because of the heavy use require stronger provision and increased maintenance to avoid damage, erosion and other adverse effects
- Water management costs including buoys and signage to separate different water use areas as well as enforcement costs of safety regulations and by laws
- Cleaning and litter clearance from beaches and countryside areas
- Safety provision ranging from lifebelts and first aid facilities to lifeguards and safety boats for water activities
- Information and interpretive provision to increase visitor enjoyment of the site
- Preparation of activity management policies.

To address the issues outlined above, it is proposed that consideration is given to identifying coastal recreation areas that provide informal recreation opportunities for a substantial number of visitors.

The management of these areas would be given a high priority with regard to a beach/coastal warden or, if appropriate, lifeguards. They would also be areas where minimum standards with regard to the range and quality of facilities would be set.

In the first instance, it is proposed that two pilot areas are identified. The pilot coastal recreation area's principal aims would be the integration of resource planning and visitor management and the consideration of innovative but practical and fair ways of raising revenue from visitors. One pilot area would be chosen to reflect visitor pressure from a range of beach/water sport users, and another where the main issue is visitor pressure and environmental capacity. The pilot areas could consider whether the income from car parking, use of slipways or franchising of refreshment facilities could be directly used to improve general facilities, cleaning, life guard or beach wardens provision.

There is also potential for the pilot recreation areas to explore in more detail issues surrounding the carrying capacity of the area. The results could then be used to develop a methodology that management bodies could apply in their particular circumstances. Capacity should be considered to encompass the environment, the effects on users, the needs of local communities and the limits of existing infrastructure. They could also take into consideration how different management approaches could limit or extend the capacity of an area. Potential pilot areas will be decided by the Welsh Assembly Government and funds identified for a 2/3 year pilot study.

Environmental Management

Water Quality

Bathing water quality and beach cleanliness is fundamental when looking to maintain or achieve standards. Substantial investment has been made over recent years to improve water quality around Wales, resulting in 98.8% compliance of Mandatory, and 88.8% of Guideline Bathing Water Standards being achieved at EU designated bathing waters around Wales in 2006. At non-EU identified bathing waters 92.6% complied with the mandatory standard whilst 45.3% complied with Guideline standards. In 2006, 43 beaches were awarded a Blue Flag, 4 marinas were awarded a blue flag and 50 beaches were awarded the Green Coast Award. Such quality standard compliance and presentation of awards enhance the offering and attract tourists, particularly for family beach holidays, water sports and other water related activities.

There are challenges ahead with tighter bathing water standards coming into place by 2015, together with the introduction of the Water Framework Directive requiring nearly all inland and coastal waters to achieve 'good status' by 2015.

Climate Change

Climate change is likely to have a huge impact on tourism and on coastal tourism in particular. Climate is an essential resource for tourism, especially for beach, activity and nature tourism segments. Changes in our climate are likely to present opportunities for the Visitor Economy in Wales, as well as posing potential threats that will require adaptation measures to manage their impacts. Our understanding of these threats and opportunities are at present limited, and it is therefore proposed that further research is undertaken in this field. Some of the key issues that will need to be addressed include:

Rising Sea Levels and Coastal Erosion

UKCIP predicts that sea levels around the UK will have risen another 26 to 86 centimeters by 2089. Extreme high tides and severe storms will occur more frequently. Shoreline Management Plans, prepared by Coastal Defence groups, comprising representatives of maritime local authorities, the Environment Agency, Countryside Council for Wales and other interested bodies, set out a strategy for sustainable coastal defences. These are currently being revised to take account of the latest evidence available and will map areas at risk of coastal erosion in greater detail. Planning policies identify areas on the coast at risk of flooding. Any tourism developments will need to take account of these plans.

The Welsh Assembly Government is currently refreshing its policy with regard to flood and coastal risk management and moving away from the traditional approach of building sea defences to one which focuses on the overall management of the flood risk. This approach could include adopting measures such as:

- allowing areas to flood to create saltmarshes for wildlife or restoring sand dunes that can provide natural coastal defences

- relocating buildings/ facilities
- refurbishing buildings to accommodate flooding.

This new approach, while placing much greater emphasis on managing the consequences of flooding will nonetheless continue to rely on the effective maintenance and improvement of the sea defence infrastructure. This will inevitably require significant investment in existing infrastructure in the future in a climate where funds will be in short supply. The Welsh Assembly Government will need to maximise benefits from such investment through, for example considering the potential of incorporating tourism and regeneration considerations into coastal defence schemes. Tourism considerations could cover visual aspects, effects on access, the current use of the coastal area and importantly whether there can be additional 'new' benefits/uses for the local community and the visitor economy. This may require innovative approaches with regard to evaluation and cost/benefit analysis.

In addition, rising sea levels may well alter the wave configuration around the coastline, thus impacting on water sport activities.

Environmental Capacity

The natural landscape is a key attraction for most visitors to the Welsh coast. Climate Change is likely to put pressure on vulnerable landscapes and is likely to further impair their ability to accommodate visitors. Responding to this challenge will require measures that sustain the environmental capacity of these landscapes whilst developing new opportunities in less vulnerable locations.

Visitor Trends

Climate change is likely to lead to a significant change in visitor patterns to Wales. Drier summers could attract more visitors to Wales, while an increase in temperatures and shortage of water could displace tourism from established destinations in southern Europe. A recent study by the Hadley Centre has suggested a major revival of the British seaside holiday as a result of destinations such as Greece and Spain becoming too uncomfortable in the summer. Other research has claimed that there is little evidence to suggest that we would automatically give up our holiday abroad to become domestic tourists, rather than switching to other foreign destinations. Conversely, wetter and stormier winters could reduce tourist volume and value outside of the peak season. The increased seasonality of tourism could place a strain on business profitability and lead to full time jobs being replaced by seasonal jobs thereby reducing the quality of jobs in tourism.

If the mitigation of climate change leads to a reduction in air travel as a result of taxes on aviation fuel, international visits to Wales may suffer but visits to Wales from within the UK are likely to increase. Forward planning for an increase in visitor numbers to Wales would be necessary to ensure that capacity is in line with summer demand. There will also be pressures from other mitigation measures such as renewable energy developments adjacent to coastal resorts.

Managing Coastal Destinations

The visitor experience is made up of a wide range of individual elements provided by many different businesses, public organisations and individuals. It only requires a weakness in one or two of these elements to undermine the whole experience. If a destination can meet and even exceed the expectations of its visitors then it will have an advantage over prospective competitor destinations. In order to do this, destination stakeholders need to understand their market and its needs. They also need to understand and meet – even exceed – the expectations and needs of local residents. This can only be achieved through partnership working with tourism businesses, the voluntary sector and the community to ensure an integrated approach.

One technique that can help deliver an integrated approach to destination management is Integrated Quality Management (IQM) which the European Commission's Tourism Unit has sought to encourage destinations to adopt.

Integrated Quality Management is an approach to managing a tourism destination which focuses on an ongoing process of improving visitor satisfaction, while seeking to improve the local economy, the environment and the quality of life of the local community. It is a tool which can be used by destination stakeholders to understand their markets and the communities living within the destination. It can help them identify needs and expectations, assess how the destination is performing against these needs and expectations and identify ways in which they can be met. An important part of the process is the monitoring of the impacts of tourism on the local economy, community and the environment.

Managing Coastal Facilities

Resource Management

The Welsh Assembly Government's Environment Strategy outlines the importance of achieving a more sustainable pattern of consumption and production in order to reduce the impact that economic activity has on the environment. Tourism businesses have a key role to play through improving the way they manage their resources, through for example, reducing waste and water use. It is recognised that smaller and medium sized businesses have limited technical and managerial capacity to improve resource management and a range of environmental management schemes have been developed to assist these businesses. One such scheme is the Green Dragon Environmental Standard, which is an environmental management system designed to meet the specific needs of Welsh organisations. It has, in recent years, been applied to the tourism sector and has been a condition of Visit Wales tourism grant support. Better environmental management can increase profits, improve efficiency, mitigate carbon footprints, reduce waste, improve local supply chains and provide a key marketing edge.

Some of the main future challenges are:

- ensuring greater sign-up to environmental management schemes by tourism businesses
- ensuring a high retention and progression rate through schemes
- further adaptation of the Green Dragon scheme to meet the specific needs and characteristics of the tourism sector
- championing exemplary projects and businesses, illustrating clear actions and benefits

- appropriate siting of tourism facilities that takes account of the availability of water resources.

Quality Assurance

Accommodation standards are another consideration with regard to enhancing the visitor's experience. Customers demand high standards in tourism accommodation, and their expectations are continuously rising as their own standard of living rise at home and abroad.

It is essential that operators provide high quality accommodation if coastal tourism in Wales is to compete successfully with other destinations. Visit Wales, together with other national partner bodies, operate quality assurance schemes for different types of accommodation, attractions and activity provision. Only accredited accommodation is promoted nationally and internationally by Visit Wales.

In compliance with the Disability Discrimination Act 1995, tourism businesses are required to make reasonable provisions to meet the needs of disabled people in terms of equality of access and employment.

The UK population is ageing and this will have further implications for facility provision and employment structures. The industry must be prepared therefore to invest in new facilities and promotional tools to cater for the needs of all visitors. Specialist advice and financial assistance is made available to tourism businesses to prepare accessibility statements and to provide adequate facilities for people with special needs.

Managing People

Tourism like other industries needs a skilled and experienced workforce and it is therefore crucial that the tourism industry in Wales invests in its people to ensure profitable businesses are developed and a high level of service is provided. Training and skills development will offer more rewarding and clearer career development opportunities, which are essential for retaining staff. Developing an appropriate qualifications structure for the industry will also help to professionalise the industry. The majority of tourism businesses in Wales are self employed operations or small businesses employing less than five people, which means that training and skills development is often difficult to fund and accommodate within working practices. Innovative training opportunities therefore need to be supported and developed that fit business needs. To support the successful development of tourism at the coast, appropriate skills will be required not only in the hospitality sector but in other related areas including:

- Marine Environment and Conservation Management
- Management of coastal public sector resources
- Ecotourism development and delivery
- Watersports management and marketing
- Management, Customer Service and communication skills
- Craft Skills Development (particularly chefs)
- Interpretation and information provision, including Web-based services and wireless technology
- Marine engineering relating to the maintenance and repair of boats
- Coastal Heritage interpretation and promotion.

It is also important to ensure that opportunities are provided for local people to gain relevant skills and knowledge, in particular, to undertake specialist roles such as watersports instructors or to undertake management roles. Providing opportunities for local people, especially young people, to experience activities that visitors come to enjoy will increase employment opportunities for local people in coastal tourism related jobs and will provide associated economic development opportunities in the longer term.

The skills required to support the effective delivery of the strategy identified above fall under the remit of the following Sector Skills Councils:

* SkillsActive: Active Leisure and Learning-sport and recreation, health and fitness, outdoors, playwork and caravan industries.
* Lantra: land management and production; animal health and welfare; environmental industries.
* People 1st: hospitality, leisure, travel and tourism.

Skillsmart Retail Retail

* Creative and Cultural Skills advertising, crafts, cultural heritage, design, music, performing, literacy and visual arts.
* Semta: Science, engineering and manufacturing technologies sector (including marine sector, covering shipbuilding and repair, boat building and marine equipment manufacturers).

These Sector Skills Councils (SSCs) are part of a network of 25 Uk-wide employer-led bodies that have been established by Government to ensure that the needs of employers form the starting point for future education and training.

The SSCs, as part of the Sector Skills Agreement (SSA) process, have analysed each sector's skills needs and provision and have mapped out the skills needed by employers in these sectors.

Action plans have been agreed within the SSA between the SSCs and the Welsh Assembly Government, JobCentre Plus, Careers Wales, the Higher Education Funding Council for Wales (HEFCW) and Wales TUC that will seek to fill any skill gaps and shortages through influencing the Assembly Government's mainstream learning policies and programmes. Details on how the Assembly Government is addressing skills development in these areas are contained in these action plans.

The new school curriculum, published in October 2007, also places a greater emphasis on outdoor learning. The new Physical Education curriculum will encourage schools to offer pupils the opportunity to acquire skills in adventurous activities such as watersports, which may be pursued in curriculum time, after school, or as part of an out-of-hours residential experience in new and challenging environments. 60% of the workforce employed in the tourism, hospitality and leisure sector in Wales is female. Many women are attracted by the part time opportunities offered by the industry, but part time working can have certain draw backs, including fewer advancement opportunities, lower pay per hour and less formal training.

There are also implications for tourism employers in terms of providing flexible training and working arrangements and addressing childcare and elder care issues. Unemployment in Wales is at a 30 year low.

However the Welsh Assembly Government's, Skills and Employment Strategy, *Skills that Work for Wales* demonstrates that the employment rate is still lower that in many other parts of the UK, due to higher levels of economic inactivity in Wales. Latest figures indicate that 24.5% of the working age population is economically inactive compared with an unemployment rate of just above 5%. There is therefore a potential pool of indigenous labour which, with appropriate support and targeted training, could benefit the tourism industry.

Jobcentre plus is currently looking to roll-out the successful Pathways to Work pilot – an initiative aimed at helping claimants moving onto Incapacity Benefit to find work. A partnership between the Welsh Assembly Government and Job Centre plus is now extending the Pathways to Work pilot to other parts of Wales through a wider Want2Work initiative.

The initiative involves providing financial incentives and flexible trial periods to encourage the economically inactive and employers to work together to their mutual advantage. There are opportunities for the scheme to be tailored to the needs of tourism and leisure employers.

Businesses also have a role in tackling the root causes of inactivity through promoting employee health. The two most common causes of sickness absence are stress and back pain. Much of this is preventable and can be addressed by workplace health promotion programmes, such as the Corporate Health Standard which is being promoted by the Assembly Government as part Health Challenge Wales. Tourism businesses should be encouraged to adopt this Corporate Health Standard.

Delivering the Strategy

The strategy has identified a wide range of opportunities that need to be considered and acted upon in order to realise the full tourism potential of the Welsh Coastline.

A three year action plan has been prepared which presents the recommendations and identifies a series of actions necessary to implement or move forward the recommendations. It also identifies the most appropriate lead authority/organisation and other possible partners.

The action plan will be available in electronic format only to allow for regular updating. In developing the delivery strategy and proposed actions, we have been mindful of the vision set out in Chapter 2. As well as considering the vision, account has been taken of the strategic aims of the strategy, the practicality of the proposals, and possible sources of funding.

Delivery of the framework will depend upon cooperation and developing a partnership approach between a number of authorities/organisations. The resources required to implement the strategy are significant but reflect the importance and opportunities presented by the coast of Wales.

The availability of funds cannot be guaranteed at this stage in the process, but will need to be considered by the various stakeholders. It is likely that many of the coastal economic and regeneration projects will be eligible for EU Convergence funding under the Spatial Regeneration Frameworks. There are also a number of other budgets that could be involved for different elements of the strategy.

The implementation of the strategy will only be achieved by the key players working together. We will seek to engage all groups involved in developing the economic, social and environmental aspects of the coast in the private, public and voluntary sectors, using existing structures and partnerships wherever possible. Visit Wales, within the Department of Heritage, will chair a steering group within the Welsh Assembly Government that will coordinate the implementation of the strategy at the national level.

Other divisions and departments within the Welsh Assembly Government will also have a crucial role to play, in particular, the Department of Environment, Sustainability and Housing and the regeneration teams based in the regional offices of the Department for the Economy and Transport. There are also a number of external partners who will have an active role in the delivery of the strategy including the local authorities, the Countryside Council for Wales, the Environment Agency, the National Trust and the RSPB. In particular, Local Authority Local Development Plans, which will form the basis for future planning consents, will have a key role in providing the statutory framework to guide development to implement the strategy.

The role and potential of the coastline of Wales will feature in all six Spatial Plan Areas and detailed below are some of the elements that will need to be considered. In addition, the regional collaborative boards announced as part the Making the Connections proposals for improving public services in Wales could have an important role to play in implementing the strategy, in particular for areas that call for collaborative activity between authorities.

Geographical Considerations

The action plan includes actions that are relevant to all areas. The following actions have a specific geographical dimension that will need to be considered in future funding proposals, regeneration plans and spatial plan area documents.

North East Wales – Border and Coast

The coast includes a number of traditional seaside resorts which have suffered from a changing market and rising visitor expectations. There is a need to diversify their local economies and to improve their image and tourism offer as they still provide quality beaches.

Elements to Consider in North East Spatial Plan Area

- to continue regeneration of the coastal resort of Rhyl and Colwyn Bay to diversify and strengthen the local economy
- improvements to the coastal defences and the enhancement of the physical links between the town and the promenade at Colwyn Bay
- to ascertain the financial and market viability of developing further berths at Rhyl (Foryd Harbour)
- to consider further redevelopment of conference tourism facilities at Llandudno based on the enhanced facilities at the North Wales Conference centre and physical improvements to support the development of conference hotels and business tourism.

North West Wales – Eryri a Môn

North West Wales has a strong sense of identity and an outstanding coastline. The quality of the coastline is recognised by its various environmental designations. The coastline provides quality beaches, popular marinas, potential for increasing nature tourism and a backdrop of Snowdonia National Park. There are a number of coastal towns where the local economy is dominated by tourism and service towns, some with heritage attributes, such as Bangor and Caernarfon.

Elements to Consider in the North West Spatial Plan Area

- to consider the potential for developing nature tourism and heritage within the environmental capacity of sensitive sites eg. Newborough Warren, Holyhead Mountain
- to implement coastal resort and town centre physical improvement programmes to diversify and strengthen local economies at Holyhead, Caernarfon and Bangor
- to consider how the accommodation stock in the Lly^n Peninsula and Bangor area could be improved
- to improve the facilities for watersport participants on Anglesey and on the Lly^ n Peninsula (for diving, surfing and kite sports)
- the creation of a sailing academy and events facility at Pwllheli
- to explore sustainable forms of visitor transport across the Menai Strait and to consider opportunities to enhance the summer bus service on the Lly^n peninsula
- the provision of visiting berths at marinas, harbours and yacht stations around the north west coast
- to consider the benefits (for users and the local economy) of improving boating facilities and access at Caernarfon and Porthmadog and the development of further facilities at Bangor
- to consider the improvement of facilities for cruise liners (including alongside berthing) and for passengers in Holyhead

- to work with Nant Gwrtheryn to invest in cultural/business tourism on the Lly^n Peninsula
- to continue to develop the tourism potential of the heritage of Caernarfon and Conwy, in particular their Castles and Town Walls
- to develop the heritage tourism potential of Anglesey.

Central Wales

Central Wales has an extensive coastline from south of Porthmadog to south of Cardigan. There are a number of coastal settlements, Aberystwyth and Cardigan being the main service centres, with smaller settlements with a tourism role such as Barmouth, Aberdyfi, Aberaeron and New Quay. The coastline has a number of environmental designations including the Dyfi Valley which is a designated Biosphere Reserve. While there are perceptions with regard to accessibility of the area, the area does have significant potential with regard to nature tourism.

3

Sustainable Tourism Management

It is almost impossible, with a title for a paper such as this, to avoid getting into a discussion on definitions, and debate about the merits and shortcomings of Eco-tourism as a tool for or component of sustainable development. There are many critics of Eco-tourism, who see it as a form of environmental opportunism that allows continued exploitation of natural environments by mass tourism. Mass tourism cloaked in a green name. Eco-tourism is certainly a buzz word, and is becoming as ambiguous as the word 'natural' on the supermarket shelf. Here is another definition of Eco-tourism:

> *"A form of tourism inspired primarily by the natural history of an area, including its indigenous cultures. The ecotourist visits relatively undeveloped areas in the spirit of appreciation, participation and sensitivity. The ecotourist practices a non-consumptive use of wildlife and natural resources and contributes to the visited area through labour or financial means aimed at directly benefiting the conservation of the site and the economic well-being of the local residents. The visit should strengthen the ecotourist's appreciation and dedication to conservation issues in general, and to the specific needs of the locale. Eco-tourism also implies a managed approach by the host country or region which commits itself to establishing and maintaining the sites with the participation of local residents, marketing*

them appropriately, enforcing regulations, and using the proceeds of the enterprise to fund the area's land management as well as community development." Ziffer, K., 1989: 6.

This is a tough definition of Eco-tourism but we believe it is appropriate and necessary in order to highlight the special nature of genuine Eco-tourism-what Eco-tourism should strive to be. Further, it is important to emphasise that Eco-tourism does not equal nature tourism, rather it is a distinct niche/segment of the more general nature tourism sector.

The Nature-based Tourism-Eco-tourism Spectrum

One of the reasons for continued debate on the merits of Eco-tourism to achieve sustainable development is that there is no blueprint for successful Eco-tourism development in all of its facets. Rather, there are examples of different projects in which particular components are innovative or well-implemented. Sites and potential projects need to be considered on a case by case basis, as many local factors-environmental, human, political, economic, social, cultural etc will work for the benefit of, or to the detriment of, an Eco-tourism project.

In some cases it will be very hard to 'develop' Eco-tourism. For example, in Cuc Phuong National Park mass tourism is already well established and the Park has developed facilities, hardened sites, opened up areas, to cater for these tourists. It will be very hard for Eco-tourism to be developed, unless the Park is able to restrict the number and movement of visitors, unless it can create specific Eco-tourism zones to direct ecotourists away from the present built up areas. But this may place even more environmental pressure on the Park.

Despite the lack of a blueprint, the last few years have seen a number of Codes of Sustainable Practice, Codes of Responsible Behaviour, Guidelines for Eco-tourism and Sustainability etc developed for tourists, tour operators, national park managers, policy makers alike. These have been developed by environmental NGOs; NGOs dedicated to raising awareness of the negative impacts of tourism and striving to make the tourism industry more responsible and sustainable; national parks and nature reserves; and, within the tourism industry itself, international or regional tourism organisations; tour operators; outdoor equipment suppliers....

Carrying Capacity and Limiting Numbers

Eco-tourism markets are expanding faster than any other tourism market segment. Eco-tourism is inherently limited in the extent to which it can be developed and promoted, given that it cannot support large numbers without setting in train a process of succession and change which destroys the reason for its existence.

A big difficulty for Vietnam and other countries wishing to embrace Eco-tourism is the idea that in order to achieve a sustainable Eco-tourism industry planners/managers/policy makers must impose limits.

How difficult is it to impose restrictions on the number of visitors to an area...when there is the lure of expansion, as people queue up at the gate? And in a country with a huge domestic population...the concept of limiting numbers appears almost ludicrous and is certainly controversial. It is natural that there will be concerns about equity and elitism, especially if fees or charges are used as a means to limit numbers.

The Principles for Sustainable Tourism (Tourism Concern/ WWF)

1. *Using resources sustainably:* the conservation and sustainable use of resources-natural, social and cultural-is crucial and makes long-term business sense;
2. *Reducing over-consumption and waste:* reduction of over-consumption and waste avoids the costs of restoring long-term environmental damage and contributes to the quality of tourism;
3. *Maintaining Diversity:* maintaining and promoting natural, social and cultural diversity is essential for long-term sustainable tourism, and creates a resilient base for the industry;
4. *Integrating Tourism into Planning:* tourism development which is integrated into a national and local strategic planning framework and which undertakes environmental

impacts assessments, increases the long-term viability of tourism;

5. *Supporting Local Economies:* tourism that supports a wide range of local economic activities and which takes environmental costs and values into account, both protects those economies and avoids environmental damage;
6. *Involving local communities:* the full involvement of local communities in the tourism sector not only benefits them and the environment in general but also improves the quality of the tourism experience;
7. *Consulting Stakeholders and the Public:* consultation between the tourism industry and local communities, organisations and institutions is essential if they are to work alongside each other and resolve potential conflicts of interest;
8. *Training Staff:* staff training which integrates sustainable tourism into work practices, along with recruitment of local personnel at all levels, improves the quality of the tourism product;
9. *Marketing Tourism Responsibly:* marketing that provides tourists with full and responsible information increases respect for the natural, social and cultural environments of destination areas and enhances customer satisfaction;
10. *Undertaking Research:* on-going research and monitoring by the industry using effective data collection and analysis is essential to help solve problems and to bring benefits to destinations, the industry and consumers.

How to decide when enough is enough, when restrictions need to be imposed? The management tools of 'limits of acceptable change' and carrying capacity are very important management tools to assist in achieving sustainability NOT ONLY for Eco-tourism or nature tourism, but for the tourism industry as a whole. However their application is far from easy and unfortunately there exists a lack of understanding and awareness of the concept as applied to tourism.

Carrying capacity has four branches: physical, biological, psychological, social. All are related to the number of visitors/ tourists to a site or area:

- Physical is the actual number of visitors a site can hold;
- Biological is the point at which environmental degradation occurs to the extent that it is irreversible or unacceptable;
- Psychological is the point at which the tourists feels the quality of their experience is damaged by the number of other tourists and/or their behaviours, and
- Social is the level at which the local inhabitants of the site (possibly the tourist attraction themselves) feel disrupted, intruded upon etc.

As carrying capacities include qualitative as well as quantitative aspects, there is consequently no 'correct' or empirical figure for an area. Nevertheless it is vital that an attempt is made to arrive at some estimations of the carrying capacity of each site, using the best methods and knowledge available. This research will assist in management decisions. Putting such work in the 'too hard' basket is counter to the principles underlying sustainable development. The target audience/market needs to be carefully considered in establishing carrying capacity. Eco-tourism does not cater for all and any type of tourist, just as a beach-side resort holiday does not appeal to all.

There is a cultural component relating to carrying capacity that may be obvious but is important to highlight: An Australian will have a different concept of psychological and social carrying capacity and even physical and biological carrying capacity from their Vietnamese or Asian colleague. At the most basic, the perception of and tolerance towards crowding will be very different.

The Target Market(s) and Managing for the Target Market(s)

The above leads to some questions:

- WHO, WHAT TYPE of tourist does Vietnam want to cater for?
- high, middle or low income;
- short stay visitors, long stay visitors, high spenders, low spenders;
- those seeking relaxing beach resort holidays away from it all;

- those seeking physical challenge and close encounters with locals in remote areas, e.g.: trekkers;
- those interested purely in cultural and artistic features of Vietnam who also like to travel and stay in comfort;
- those who travel in tours on the major routes, or those who travel independently;
- those who want to travel to natural, undisturbed areas and learn about the environment;
- those who stay in small hotels and guest houses, those who prefer large;
- visitors from the region ie: ASEAN, China, Japan, Korea, or Europeans or Australasians;
- domestic tourists...
- Can Vietnam target and successfully cater to all these categories?
- Does Vietnam, in developing Eco-tourism, want to provide 'add on attractions' for tourists already coming to Vietnam or does it want to try to attract a new market?
- What are the implications for achieving genuine Eco-tourism when the domestic tourist often acts as though the environment is a resource to be 'exploited and developed'-exemplified in the consumption of wildlife for food and medicine?
- Is the Vietnam domestic tourist compatible with the international visitor to natural areas or the international ecotourist?
- Is there a difference between Asian tourists and Western tourists?

If Vietnam wishes to bring the international ecotourist to visit its protected areas, then this decision will have considerable implications for how it handles the domestic tourist and manages those areas.

It is important to match the numbers and types of ecotourists/ nature tourists with the characteristics of the destination. This requires the monitoring of nature/ecotourists. Understanding customer groups, their motivations and characteristics, is essential for promotion, marketing, planning for improvement of facilities and services including information needs, controlling impacts via restrictions on numbers or zoning of protected areas for different types of use and different types of visitors.

The Recreational Opportunity Spectrum (ROS) developed by Clark and Stankey is a useful management tool to assist here. The ROS is an integrating framework for resource management, its underlying rationale being the assumption that providing a diverse range of recreational opportunities will best assure quality recreational experiences as it will provide for the many tastes and preferences that motivate people to participate in recreation.

Division of the resource into zones with certain biological, social and managerial characteristics helps establish objectives and guidelines for their management, regulations and limits on activities, and enables assessment of optimum and maximum carrying capacity conditions and the level of change tolerated (Koeman 1989). Inadequate data collection on the market can lead to decision makers developing an area in such a way that they lose their market.

Numerous studies of visitors to national parks around the world have shown that nature tourists are generally more accepting of conditions different from home than are other types of tourists, that they do not demand international glamour, but are satisfied with or want to use local goods and materials and eat local foods....and that they are more demanding in seeking information about their destination.

Nature/ecotourists are also generally willing to spend more, to make an active contribute to conservation causes or community development by their visit or during their visit. Part of the attraction to the ecotourist or dedicated nature tourist is the ability to experience an undeveloped area which is in stark contrast to the urban existence of many travellers from the industrialised world. They are looking for something new and meaningful.

Thus Eco-tourism can be promoted without excessive capital requirements and infrastructure developments. Though this may mean there is no need to build a concrete hotel inside a park with air-conditioning and TV, it does not mean that nothing needs to be done to cater for ecotourists. It is very important that a quality experience be offered.

Quality includes considerations such as the amount and type of information and interpretation, the environmental and cultural sensitivity and skills of guides and park managers, the level of professionalism, dedication and hospitality exhibited by all involved, the degree of local community involvement, the direction of fees paid by the ecotourists to conservation and local community development projects...

There is an inherent risk, however, in assuming that everyone calling themselves an ecotourist is environmentally sensitive and aware. Amongst those included in the definition of ecotourist are those persons who visit a natural place for a few days, unlikely to ever return...they may not care of the long-term repercussions of their activities, especially if they have paid a considerable amount for their travel. The phenomenon of affluent tourists jet-setting the world to visit famous natural sites has been coined the "this year the Galapagos, next year Antarctica" syndrome.

Environmental Education and Awareness

There are initiatives underway in Vietnam to improve environmental education in schools in Vietnam, however it is still obvious that lack of environmental education and information for students (from preschool level up), the general public, tourists and local communities alike is a major problem in developing sustainable Eco-tourism. Environmental education and information dissemination is of prime importance to the realisation of genuine, sustainable Eco-tourism or nature tourism in Vietnam. We need to educate the tourists, both present and potential, both domestic and international.

- Where are all the interpretative and environmental information centres in national parks and nature reserves in Vietnam?
- Investing in such centres is investing in the future, investing for sustainability. Should they be given greater priority than the purchase of vehicles, or even the building of large new park headquarters?

- Is it not essential that every new park HQ have an interpretive/environmental information centre included?

Allocating the space is not all however; the centres need to have extensive materials developed, staff trained in management, hospitality skills, language, culture of local communities, environmental education and sustainable tourism.

There is the very real danger that any Eco-tourism initiative/ project in Vietnam will be overtaken, overrun, swamped by mass tourism to natural areas, or general nature-based tourism (that has none, or only some of the principles of Eco-tourism). A problem not only of lack of environmental awareness but also simply because of sheer numbers!

"The National Parks in North America are being "loved to death" by almost 400 million visitors in 1991 "trampling over the fragile habitat, ruining the flora with the pollution from their cars, scaring the animals, destroying the wilderness..." In Kenya, the central circuit of Amboseli National Park has been reduced to semi-desert by visitors' vehicles, while in the Maasai Mara, which receives 200,000 visitors a year, the construction of a large number of lodges outside the controlled area threatens to overload the system."

Supply-oriented Management

It is important to note that Eco-tourism CAN be, but is NOT automatically, a form of sustainable tourism. To achieve sustainable Eco-tourism involves balancing economic, environmental and social goals within an ethical framework of values and principles. Eco-tourism faces considerable challenges, not least is the challenge to keep foremost a supply-oriented management perspective. A supply-oriented management perspective has as its primary considerations the nature and resilience of the resource, cultural or local community preferences, and interpretive and conservation programmes. Essentially a supply-oriented management perspective puts the resource-national park, protected area, local culture and community-before the demands of tourists. Growth can only go so far, and not nearly as far as with other forms of tourism given the dominance of ecosystem and ecological considerations.

Who is Responsible for Eco-tourism?

Eco-tourism/nature tourism cannot be solely developed by the Ministry or government agency of tourism or by the national park department as tourism crosses over many sectors. There is a need for strong interagency cooperation and linkages. This could be achieved through a Sustainable (Eco) Tourism Taskforce. The Task-force could be responsible for working towards the development of a national Eco-tourism or nature tourism strategy for Vietnam, which could have as goals the establishment of a Sustainable (Eco) Tourism Association and Sustainable (Eco) Tourism Commission. Further, Eco-tourism needs cooperative, collaborative arrangements between Govt. at all levels, parks, NGOs, local communities, tour operators. In developing a national Eco-tourism strategy, these stakeholders need to be fully included in the process.

National Eco/Nature Tourism Strategy for Vietnam

If Vietnam wants to promote nature tourism; tourism to both protected areas and NON protected natural areas, then it needs to develop a national Eco-tourism or nature tourism strategy. We recommend that a Think tank on the Development of a National Eco-tourism Strategy be convened as a first step. The objectives of the Think-tank could be to gather together key decision makers and implementers from the tourism, planning, environmental, educational, socioeconomic sectors in Vietnam to:

1. discuss the need for a National Eco-tourism Strategy (NES) or Nature Tourism Strategy (NNTS) for Vietnam;
2. clarify where or to what extent tourism and Eco-tourism can occur in protected and non-protected natural areas in Vietnam, by clarifying what use rules apply to the different categories of protected areas ie: nature reserves, national parks, marine/coastal zones etc;
3. learn about Eco-tourism, alternative tourism and sustainable tourism principles and management tools, actions/strategies...;
4. learn about the development and composition of National Eco-tourism Strategies from other countries, their implementation and component activities or programmes;

5. consider options for a national definition of Eco-tourism;
6. suggest key elements of a NES or National Nature Tourism Strategy (NNTS);
7. draft a methodology and timetable for the development of a draft Strategy;
8. call for recommendations/nominations for working groups or agencies to be responsible for actively developing key elements of the Strategy according to the agreed timetable;
9. call for recommendations/nominations for the body responsible for carrying forward the initiative ie: 'tying it all together', and
10. consider the areas in which Vietnam/the above bodies require capacity strengthening/training/technical advice to assist in the development and implementation of the NES/NNTS.

Tour Operators

Tour operators are an extremely important component of successful Eco-tourism. The way they function, their choice of destination, the way they package and sell trips, the type of support services they provide, and their cost structure, are all important factors to understand how to make changes in the way nature tourism impacts host countries.

It is important that the role of private small business in the tourism industry be recognised and encouraged. Private operators (or guest houses or guide services etc) are often smaller than government owned operations. They have the potential to be more efficient, flexible and innovative...in a carefully controlled and regulated Eco-tourism market. Small is supposed to be beautiful in Eco-tourism.

It is also essential that cases of Eco-Exploitation: using 'green' or 'eco' to falsely sell a tourism product that is far from ecologically responsible or sustainable, are exposed, whether the culprits are state or private operators.

A quote: "You don't become an ecotourist operator by just having nature as your destination…what do you do with waste? What do you do with hazardous chemicals? How do you transport?

Do you buy locally?...Are you encouraging wildlife? What are you doing with your sewage?

It is these kind of nitty gritty things that will make the difference between Eco-tourism being a force for the environment or simply being another threat."

A good step, if Vietnam wants to promote sustainable tourism, would be to develop, adopt and disseminate National Codes of Conduct or Practice for Sustainable Tourism and Eco-tourism. A formal system of accreditation-such as a 'green stars' system could be considered and worked on for Eco-tourism operators. Non compliance to such a 'green stars' system by those proclaiming to be Eco-tourism operators would mean they are required to disassociate from (not use) the term Eco-tourism.

Ideally, these activities should be undertaken in co-operation and consultation with all tourism stakeholders, not decided by government alone, in order to ensure acceptance of the measures. How to get such a consultation process going? How about looking at allowing the establishment of a non-government body to bring together all operators in Vietnam-a Vietnam Sustainable (Eco) Tourism Association? Could the Chamber of Commerce and Industry's proposed *Business Council for Sustainable Development* play a valuable role?

This Association could work together with the Sustainable (Eco) Tourism Task-force to establish an independent Sustainable (Eco) Tourism Commission to be responsible for assessment, certification and policing of the industry. The Commission could have broad representation from the various stakeholder segments e.g.: government; protected area managers; hotels; tour operators; travel agents; guides; foreign tour operators; airlines; transport firms; local authorities; conservation organisations; NGOs. The Eco-tourism Society has produced *Guidelines for Nature Tour Operators,* which our Project is going to translate into Vietnamese, hopefully for distribution nation wide. In the future, such guidelines could be adopted by managers of protected areas as rigorous standards as part of a supply-oriented management regime. Though this may undermine freedom to practice for all and any tour operator, and incur considerable additional costs, operators, whether state or private, would have to comply.

The challenge is for host countries, regions and national parks to enlist the support of operators, for the purposes of conservation, education of tourists, appropriate behaviour etc., not simply rely on imposing restrictions from above. Cooperative partnerships need to be formed.

Tour Operators Segmentation

Practices need to be established that prevent the doers-those operators who are proactive and eager to cooperate on constructive conservation and community development projects, who are active in conserving and improving the areas they visit-from being placed at a competitive disadvantage in the industry.

Pro-active "Doers" in the Tourism Industry: Sharing Responsibilities

Boo (1990) notes that small companies visiting national parks seem to be contributing more to conservation than large ones. She provides an example of a responsible operator, 'Journeys' in the US, which donates a portion of the land costs of their trips to a non-profit conservation organisation and offers 'active conservation tours' such as a cleanup of the Machu Pichu trail.

Multatuli Travel in the Netherlands establishes relationships with local NGOs in Indonesia, Philippines and elsewhere and brings tourists to visit and contribute to their development projects.

Tour participants of such tours are likely to make contributions of their own. There are many more examples...

Such operators should not be placed at a disadvantage in the competitive tourism industry for being so environmentally aware, responsible and proactive, rather they should be acknowledged and in doing so the level playing field would be raised for the entire industry, so that others will also become active doers.

Local, Community Participation

- What is the main reason for developing Eco-tourism?
- Is it purely economic ie: is it to be used for generating foreign currency for national or provincial general revenue?

- Is it for developmental purposes ie: to provide local, rural communities with the opportunity to raise their standard of living and quality of life, increase their participation in natural resource management and conservation?
- Is it for conservation, ie: to provide national parks with the opportunity to strengthen conservation capabilities through increased income, and community participation in Eco-tourism?

Tourism to protected/natural areas can benefit rural, remote regions when other industries are centred on cities and towns, ports and transportation routes. There is a growing gap between the rural and urban areas in Vietnam, the former are missing out on many of the benefits and advancements of a more open economy...Eco-tourism can assist in spreading the benefits of development, stimulating economic activity and growth and provide an opportunity for diversification of the economy (Boo, E. 1990).

Eco-tourism can be a tool for conservation and rural development, but this will only materialise:

> *"if a concerted effort is made to incorporate local populations into the tourism industry. Involvement with local people and consequent rural development will not happen automatically. In some cases [including Vietnam] tourism to protected areas is not benefiting the surrounding population. Nature [eco] tourism will not contribute to rural development unless rural people are brought into the planning and development of the industry".*

The Galapagos Islands of Ecuador, a UNESCO natural heritage site, have suffered considerable social conflicts (in addition to severe environmental problems) due to tourism.

"Competition between the wealthier tourism sector and others is producing direct cultural conflict, aggravated by the fact that most of the tourism labour force is brought in from mainland Ecuador. Newcomers now outnumber those who grew up with and learned to value the special, fragile nature of the islands". Careful consideration should also be made to the distribution of benefits of Eco-tourism amongst local populations-does the project benefit the local poor, often ethnic minority population, or is it controlled by local elites and hence reinforce long-standing inequalities between the majority and minority groups?.

In elephant conservation projects on wildlife reserves in Zambia, local people, including former poachers, have been provided stable jobs and incomes as guards and tourist and hunting safari guides through training initiatives. This has raised the quality of safari tours.

What is the extent of participation? Eco-tourism projects are often directed by expatriates who are not necessarily familiar with local conditions and needs. Training local people to manage their own projects can avoid misunderstanding and possible hostility. Training should thus not only be for low paid and low status jobs, but for higher level management jobs.

Local resentment to being cut-off from the benefits of tourism can be explosive. An oft-cited case is the Maasai in Kenya. Widespread resentment exists amongst the Maasai nomadic pastoralists over the inadequate compensation paid to them for their displacement from traditional grazing lands with the establishment of national parks. The Maasai have resorted to killing wildlife in the parks in protest. Experience shows that with local people fully integrated into tourism projects, and receiving the benefits, infringements such as tree felling (Nepal) and poaching of wildlife (Zimbabwe) reduce markedly.

It is important to be aware of the abuse of the term "participation". Participatory approaches have been used in some cases to increase acceptability of tourism projects and as a means to detect potential conflicts and mitigate 'local threats' early on, rather than being truly committed to fostering democratic decision-making and empowerment of local people. Participation means different things in different societies and political structures. The level of participation will influence the sustainability and success of Eco-tourism in Vietnam.

"Quite clearly, employment is no substitute for sustainable access to resources. The 'hire the natives' approach to compensation also tends to create a small salaried class of locals at the same time that exclusionary policies are negatively impacting the economic situation of the remainder of the community and for relations between the park and the local community".

In 1997 an interactive conference-*Eco-tourism at a Crossroads: Charting the Way Forward*-was held by the Kenya Wildlife Service, The Eco-tourism Society of Kenya and The Eco-tourism Society (US). The conference's primary purpose was to use Kenya as a case study for other nations to examine, as Kenya's tourism industry is almost at a crisis point and requires urgent action. Participants-300 in all-were from government (38%), private sector (35%), NGOs (185) and local communities (9%). One of the recommendations that came out of the conference was the need for a Community Eco-tourism Association to represent communities seeking to create Eco-tourism projects; assist them with any land use and tourism revenue distribution problems, as well as with questions of business, legal, and market plans for Eco-tourism (Elper-Wood, M. 1998).

Economic Values, Revenues and Management Systems

The magnitude of benefits countries receive from nature tourism/Eco-tourism depends in large part on the scale of the tourism, the size of the country, and the complexity of the country's economy. The same can be said at the regional and local level.

Too much reliance on tourism renders an area susceptible to seasonal, economic fluctuations and changes in tourist tastes. It is best for tourism to be one of several activities, and to fit in with traditional activities e.g.: to compliment agriculture rather than competing with it or causing its decline.

Care also needs to be taken to not place excessive emphasis on the economic (tourism) value of parks as this can lead to decision makers believing that parks exist primarily for economic profit. If tourism then fails to meet economic expectations, other more damaging economic activities could be taken up.

"What will happen when forests, wildlife and other natural assets are increasingly valued in monetary terms? For instance, the visitor-attraction worth of each lion at Kenya's Amboseli Park has been estimated at US$27,000 per year and each elephant herd at US$610,000. To stress the profit-making potential of Eco-tourism, will the next step be to calculate the visitor attraction worth of a

Maasai, a Karen or an Igorot?" In Vietnam, as in other countries, a hindrance to developing sustainable Eco-tourism is the problem of 'general revenue'. That is, park tourism revenue becomes general revenue for the central government, and/or provincial government, and there is considerable uncertainly about how much will be returned to the park as its budget allocation each year.

This system can hinder conservation and also Eco-tourism:

- it makes the protected areas highly susceptible to government budget cuts during economic downturns;
- it does little to encourage local park personnel to develop and participate in Eco-tourism or improve training in tourism;
- it does little to encourage the park to provide or improve educational information for tourists;
- it does little to promote conservation and strengthen commitment to and pride in the park (Boo, E. 1990).

Development of Eco-tourism requires improved internal and financial management incentives. It requires a dedicated portion of park revenue to be controlled by park management to provide an incentive for efficient administration (with some still going to central government so that national support for the parks will be maintained) (Ziffer, K. 1989).

With such a system in place ecotourists will be satisfied as they generally like to know, or even demand to know, how the money they pay is spent on conservation and development projects. If they know it is not simply going to general revenue they are more likely to make voluntary contributions. It cannot be assumed that protected areas will be able to generate sufficient tourist revenues to be self sufficient. In many cases tourism should not be considered as a path towards self-sufficiency but as a means to defray the costs of operations. Eco-tourism will not be appropriate for all protected areas in Vietnam, nor for all parts of a particular protected area (Ziffer, K. 1989).

Nepal and the Annapurna Area: the Environmental Impact of Uncontrolled Tourism to Natural Areas

Tourism is one of the main sources of foreign exchange income for Nepal. Each year, over 36,000 trekkers and 36,000 porters visit the Annapurna region which supports 40,000 local inhabitants.

About 60 per cent of these trekkers come during four months of the year. They are concentrated in few places, resulting in devastating impacts on both local cultural and natural environments. Forest is cleared each year to construct hotels, lodges and furniture and to provide fuel for cooking, hot showers and campfires. 400,000 hectares of forest are cleared each year. This is a deforestation rate of three per cent per year. One hectare of cleared forests loses 30-75 tons of soil annually. This has led to devastating landslides and floods.

86 per cent of Nepal's energy comes from forests. In the Annapurna virtually everybody depends on fuelwood for cooking as there are no alternative sources of energy. The total daily wood consumption by and on behalf of each trekker equals the amount used by a Nepalese family of five for a week.

Tree lines have been raised and entire ridges previously cloaked in rhododendron (one of the attractions of the area and Nepal's national flower) denuded. Few trees are left within the Annapurna Sanctuary itself.

Virtually all food and housekeeping items have to be imported from Kathmandu and elsewhere, inflating local economies and introducing non-nutritious diets.

Inadequate sanitation facilities and indiscriminate practices by tourists and trekking groups have left virtual 'minefields' of human excreta and toilet paper. Toilets, if they exist at all, are often dangerously close to water sources. Non-biodegradable litter such as plastics, tins and bottles, used primarily by tourists, are disposed of in nearby streams or strewn in piles at the edge of the settlements.

Tourism, as a messenger of outside values and behaviours, has also affected local cultures. Village youths are easy prey to the seductiveness of Western consumer culture as tourists are laden with expensive trappings: hi-tech hiking gear, flashy clothes, cameras and electronic goods.

The Project, Implemented by the King

ACAP strives to ensure that the beneficiaries from trekking tourism and conservation activities will be the local people, at the same time making them the guardians of their resources. The approach is that of a grassroots philosophy that strongly discourages a handout philosophy. As a result traditional subsistence activities are woven into a framework of sound resource management, supplemented by small scale conservation and alternative energy projects to minimise the impact of tourists and upgrade the local standard of living."

In our recent visit to Ba Be National Park, we were upset to hear that the Park does not charge an entrance fee, rather this is collected by the local district authorities, with none of the revenue being given to the Park. It has also been said that both the Park and the district authorities are charging entrance fees for international visitors. Is this not bad publicity?

There appear to be tensions between the Park and district and provincial authorities. These tensions seem to be related to some extent to disagreement over the development of tourism in the Park and lack of clarity on the responsibilities for tourism in the Park.

The Park seems almost 'anti-tourism', or rather scared of it. This is not surprising if the Park feels powerless to exert any control over the development and growth of tourism, particularly if it is mass tourism.

The Park has the potential for small, controlled, low impact trekking Eco-tourism that includes overnight stays in villages within the park. The villages can hence benefit from tourism to the park by charging overnight and meal fees, as well as through the sale of agricultural produce (fruits, home cultivated NTFPs such as mushrooms and orchids and honey) and crafts. Residents from the villages can also be trained in language and guiding skills and employed by the park to lead the trekking tours. The present system of issuing permits for overnight stays needs radical change if local villages are to be allowed to benefit from Eco-tourism.

However, despite the potential, if the government's aim is to increase mass tourism (albeit nature-based tourism) to the area, and the Park has no control over tourism within its boundaries, any Eco-tourism initiative started could be overrun, in a short period of time.

For example, local authorities have begun to promote the Tay new rice festival as a means to bring in more tourists. Last year approximately 10,000 persons visited over a two day period. Naturally the lake is the major feature of the park, and over 100 diesel powered boats appeared to serve the crowds of tourists. The Park is very concerned with the use of diesel engines by locals, which are causing both water and noise pollution. Is this use compatible with an Eco-tourism experience and conservation of the park? Lack of co-operation and unclear management responsibilities will be detrimental in the long run to conservation of the area and the development of Eco-tourism.

Small and Local is Beautiful?

Eco-tourism is concerned with small scale, locally owned, built, managed facilities. Eco-tourism has three important benefits for developing countries:

1. facilities and infrastructure are simpler and less expensive than those demanded by conventional mass tourism;
2. being locally owned and operated Eco-tourism projects are not caught up in the need to conform to corporate Western multinational tourism concerns, and therefore can have a much higher input of local products, materials and labour. This means greater multiplier effects in the local economy, and also reduces import leakages and the remittances from expatriate labour which result from large-scale, foreign owned operations;
3. profits accrue locally instead of flowing back to the parent country.

BUT investing in Eco-tourism in developing countries is lucrative. In the face of foreign investors, try to think small and local. If foreign money is required, find the right partner, whether a company or an NGO, who has a more philanthropic bent, who understands the philosophy of Eco-tourism and has experience in Eco-tourism.

Vietnam is currently concerned with attracting foreign investment in tourism, in drawing up master plans for areas with large scale tourism and recreation projects to the sum of millions of USD dollars. Such scales and priorities are not appropriate for

Eco-tourism. The benefits of Eco-tourism to Vietnam can be lost due to:

- the international organisation of Eco-tourism (tours agents and other middlemen in host countries take their percentages);
- foreign investment in Eco-tourism (revenue is returned to the investor's country);
- inflationary pressures at a local level due to foreign involvement (demand for produce, materials, imported goods etc);
- loss of sovereignty with foreign 'take-over', and
- lack of participation of locals (in employment, training, management and operation etc). Locals may also be excluded from the natural attraction, their 'backyard', by price or other means.

A World Resources Institute report noted that Zimbabwe retains only an estimated 10% of nature tourism expenditures, while the Annapurna region in Nepal retains less than 10% (Ziffer, K. 1989). In Belize, 65% of the Belize Tourism Industry Association.

It is somewhat disturbing to hear that tourism developments (involving foreign investment) of Dan Kia resort near Da Lat, the Victoria Hotel in Sa Pa, the Dong Mo Cultural Village in Ha Tay are Eco-tourism developments.

Conclusion and Recommendations

There is no example of tourist use that is completely without impact. Eco-tourism does leave a mark on protected areas. It is a compromise that allows tourism but set limits, controls, strict management systems, monitoring feedback mechanisms etc. It is a compromise between the primary role of protected areas-protection and preservation of the environment-and providing local communities with development opportunities that can at the same time enhance conservation goals, if carried out properly. Eco-tourism can effect and influence mainstream mass tourism, and indeed it can help make the rest of the tourism industry adopt more sustainable principles and act more responsibly and sustainably. This phenomenon is observable around the world. However, I would argue that now Vietnam needs to be concerned with trying to make the entire tourism industry sustainable, not focus on Eco-tourism to achieve sustainable tourism development. In relying on, and waiting for Eco-tourism to reform the rest of the industry irreparable damage may be done and reforms, if they occur at all, will come slowly and may come too late. Eco-tourism and sustainable tourism principles need to be adopted together in a two-pronged approach.

Key Factors Required for Successful Eco-tourism

- Aim for strategic, holistic and detailed planning;
- Careful and integrated management:
    a. forging strong inter ministerial co-operation between the ministries of planning and investment, science technology and environment, tourism, education and training, agriculture and rural development, and
    b. being committed to management that facilitates and ensures input from all stakeholders: tour operators, protected area managers, government, NGOs, local communities etc;
- Establish a national Sustainable (Eco) Tourism Task force to develop a National Eco-tourism or Nature Tourism Strategy;
- Create an environment conducive to the establishment of a private sector Eco-tourism Association, independent Eco-tourism Commission and Community Eco-tourism Association;
- Intervene in the market e.g.: fees to protected areas, limits on numbers, regulations and Codes of Conduct for the industry (developed with the industry);
- Consider each natural area individually (eco and env impacts of tourism, what the area has to offer, local community needs and interaction with the environment, local infrastructure etc);
- Focus on the local and regional level-it is easier for nature tourism/Eco-tourism to be developed successfully at these levels;

- Start small and go slow;
- Believe that small is beautiful and quality is paramount;
- Invest in awareness raising, education and training for tourists, tour operators, local guides, protected area managers, local communities, local authorities;
- Aim to maximise local benefits for conservation and economic development;
- Aim to maximise local participation and involvement at all levels;
- Aim to maximise use of local products, materials;
- Aim to focus on recycling, waste management, alternative technologies and fuels. Manuals have been produced that provide practical information on such topics, we have a few and will be getting more;
- Constantly monitor and evaluate and develop a feedback mechanism for modifying growth and minimising impacts and setting limits.

The Impact of the Shadow State on Eco-tourism Policy

The shadow links that are ultimately responsible for decision making in Belize indicate evidence of a process that is more formalised than simply a matter of *ad hoc* or unco-ordinated corruption. Rather the links between the public and private sector, local elites and external capital constitute a shadow state, and this is nowhere more apparent than in the inability of the formal state apparatus to enforce environmental legislation in the Eco-tourism industry.

Unlike Sierra Leone, Belize—once dependent on primary commodities—is a major tourist destination for North America and Europe. Tourism is a relatively recent development that really began with the expansion of tourist facilities in the 1980s, but it is now Belize's single largest foreign exchange earner, and the Belize Tourist Board (BTB) estimated that in 1994 tourism earned the country Bz$150 million (US$75 million). According to BTB statistics, the three major tourist markets for Belize are the USA, Canada and Europe, and the number of visitors from the USA increased by 55% during the period 1991 to 1995.

However, the purpose of this article is to examine the similarities and differences between the Belizean and Sierra Leonean cases. This article will investigate the possible existence of a shadow state in Belize through an analysis of the Eco-tourism industry, its relationship with external capital, local elites and licit and illicit investment and trading networks. The existence of shadow links between the private sector, the public sector and criminal elements means that enforcement of environmental legislation is problematic in Belize. Since the country is promoted as an Eco-tourism destination, enforcement of regulations to ensure that tourism developments do not damage the environment is important. Belize has an extensive framework of environmental legislation, including the Environmental Protection Act, and it has established a Department of the Environment whose stated aim is to prevent and control pollution.

A common complaint among locally based tour guides and the conservation community was that, while legislation was in place, it was rarely enforced. Godsman Ellis, President of the Belize Eco-tourism Association, stated that policing was not carried out in the face of the country's low financial resources, limited manpower, inadequate technological and administrative resources, and its open borders, and that very few cases of environmental violations had been brought before the courts, despite the legislation that had been put in place.

One interviewee, who was involved in marine conservation in Belize, stated that, although environmental impact assessments were legally required for all new tourism developments, the government office responsible for monitoring such assessments was completely overwhelmed by requests for assessments because it was so poorly staffed. In addition, when conservation authorities have tried to press for prosecutions for breaches of environmental legislation, they have faced opposition from powerful sets of interest groups. One example of this was an Ambergris Caye, when there was debate between the resident 'gringo' community, the local community and conservation officers over the fate of resort owners whose catamaran ran aground in the Hol Chan Marine Reserve, causing extensive damage to the coral reef. The incident occurred against a background of highly publicised environmental breaches by 'live-aboard' dive ships owned by external investors. The most high profile incidents involved the *Fantome* and the *Rembrandt Van Rijn* in the marine protected areas, Glovers Reef and Half Moon Caye (respectively). The companies that owned the vessels were offered options to compensate for the damage they had caused or risk having their licences revoked, but the local press reported that there was a perception that the owners were not sufficiently punished because of their high profile connections in Belize. The catamaran incident also occurred against a history of local resentment against foreign land and property owners who had settled on Ambergris Caye. A Department of Environment Report detailed that several foreign-owned resorts or hotels were not abiding by the legal requirements for construction and management of piers. This was especially contentious because several residents had complained that, while the regulations state all piers must be open to the public, any Belizean who went to the pier would immediately be removed by the owners or managers of the establishment.

In the case of the catamaran in San Pedro, those involved in the conservation community, such as Mito Paz, the Director of Green Reef, were highly critical of the catamaran incident and felt that the owners should be taken to court. Those who opposed high levels of foreign ownership speculated that the catamaran ran aground because of the carelessness and general disrespect for the environment they associated with newcomers to the island. In contrast, external investors in the tourism industry in San Pedro were concerned that the incident was being used by local opponents to criticise the gringo community as a whole. One member of the gringo community, who had assisted in pulling the catamaran off the reef, vigorously argued that it was an accident that could have happened to any boat. In fact, the owners of the boat took the step of writing a public apology in the local *San Pedro Sun* in an attempt to quell rumours about negligence. In it they stated that the engine had failed and the winds had died, and so the boat ran on to the reef before the anchor could be dropped.

Despite the arguments between different interest groups in the tourist areas of Belize, it was clear that ultimately there was a perception among both sets of interest groups that a shadow decision-making process was underway and that this would determine the outcome regardless of the legislation. This indicated a perception that breaches of environmental legislation and wider problems with criminality among foreign and local elites were either overlooked, tolerated or actively supported and encouraged by key members of state agencies, because parts of the state apparatus had been co-opted by these powerful networks of elites. It is also important to provide the political context in which the shadow state operates. Within Belize it is essential to acknowledge the deep divide between supporters of the People's United Party (PUP) and those of the United Democratic Party (UDP). This division permeates local politics, can be exploited by foreign elites in the tourism industry and plays a central role in determining the coverage of certain issues in the Belizean press. In terms of the tourism industry it is important because key. gures in either party are able to offer significant levels of patronage to their supporters. The stakes became higher in 1997 because it was an election year when the opposition PUP were feted to win (and they achieved a landslide victory). Political opponents and economic competitors in Belize have pointed to the role of the current and former Ministers of Tourism and the Environment as major players in the tourism industry. The former Minister of Tourism and the Environment, Glenn Godfrey (PUP), has been able to utilise contacts in his own constituency, which covers the two prime tourist areas of Caye Caulker and Ambergris Caye. In particular, the construction of a new airstrip and condominiums on Caye Caulker have been credited to Godfrey. Indeed, one interviewee suggested that conservation organisations in Belize were. rm supporters of the PUP; political opponents of this party were keen to point out that conservation NGOs might have 'turned a blind eye' to his activities because they were PUP supporters.

The shadow state has also affected organisations that engage in lobbying on conservation issues, especially when they have fallen foul of the deep political divide between the PUP and UDP. The Lamanai Room Declaration of 1997, which detailed major environmental abuses in Belize and was signed by numerous local conservation agencies, including the Audubon Society and Coastal Zone Management Project, was criticised for political bias by those who supported the then UDP government. Victoria Collins, Editor of the *San Pedro Sun*, suggested that the Lamanai Room Declaration was perceived by UDP supporters as designed to strengthen the position of the PUP amid public speculation that an election was to be called.

The then Minister of Tourism and the Environment, Henry Young, accused the parties at Lamanai of trying to topple the UDP government. Over the course of the UDP government term, Young became a developer in Placencia, where large areas of ecologically important mangroves were cut to make way for tourism developments. Political opponents of such developments speculated that local business elites and external investors were able to seek protection from prosecution for environmental breaches because of their links with politically prominent. gures in Belize and with the ruling UDP. It is clear that, in accordance with Reno's model of the shadow state, local elites utilise informal networks to reward their clients. The Eco-tourism industry provides one example of the manner in which those elites can bestow political and economic favouritism upon their international and local supporters.

In promoting tourism as a development strategy, elites often aim to entice foreign investors and large international tour operators into the country to underwrite their own investments and patron–client networks. The involvement of foreign interests in the Belizean tourism industry has assisted the creation of a shadow state. The convergence of legal and illegal business interests with government interests is apparent in the development of coastal tourism. The dominance of foreign capital in the tourism industry is made possible by the compliance of and collaboration with local companies and the political and economic elite. This is especially the case in Belize, where there is a legal stipulation that international tour operators and investors must have a Belizean partner. In Belize a few key families own or are major. gures in the operation of a number of tourism-and transport-related businesses, and as a result tourists brought in by overseas operators can be funnelled through a series of businesses all owned by one family or elite group which is ultimately reliant on international tour operators. Historically, on Ambergris Caye three key families, Blake, Alamilla and Parham, who were also related through marriage, have been economically dominant. They held sway over the development of the island through gun running to the Santa Cruz Maya in Mexico during the middle of the 19th century, and later thanks to ownership of coconut and timber plantations, and other land. Furthermore, Gach Guerrero, Secretary of the conservation organisation, Green Reef, is also owner of Amigo Travel and manager of Island Air, a member of the Board of the Ambergris Caye Historical Society, an officer of the Belize Tourism Industry Association, and the 1997 and 1998 chairman of the International Sea and Air Festival. Similarly, the Vega family on Caye Caulker own the tour operator Belize Odyssey and the Vega Inn, are involved in environmental and tourism consultancy and a. shing business, and members of the family sit on the BTIA, the Protected Areas National Council and the Coastal Zone Management Programme. However, it is not unusual in a country with a relatively small population to. nd that certain individuals and families have a major role in the public and private sectors.

An examination of the ways that land for tourism development is sold and resold in the coastal zone reveals the extent to which external capital is involved in the expansion of Eco-tourism in Belize. For example, large parcels of land on Ambergris Caye are owned by a US-based company, Sunset Coves Ltd. The role of Sunset Coves on Ambergris Caye was the subject of some debate in the local press, specially the *San Pedro Sun*. Sunset Coves began as a San Pablo Town Board project, and the land was paid for by local islanders who were promised they would be full partners in its development. The scheme had support and assistance from the local MP (and former Minister of Tourism and the Environment) Glenn Godfrey.

However, Sunset Coves went into receivership in 1996 because of an unpaid debt of Bz$300 000 ($150 000), and as a result it was sold to Raymond Yusi of Western Caribbean Properties, based in California. This pattern of sale of land to external investors is common in the tourist dominated islands of Belize. The *State of the Coastal Zone Report* (1995) indicated that leased national lands were often sold to external investors or subdivided in joint ventures and then sold on to the highest bidders, who were primarily nonresidents. An examination of the tax and valuation rolls for Ambergris Caye revealed that there was a small number of US citizens, including Albert Dugan, Corrie McDermott, Gerry McDermott and Ian Ritchie, who owned or controlled the sales of large swathes of land on the island.

Ian Ritchie was formerly the owner of Southwinds Property, which facilitated the purchase of properties in Belize by external investors; he is also owner of a major resort (Captain Sharkey's) on Ambergris Caye and is beginning land speculation in Roatan in Honduras.

A Department of Environment Compliance Monitoring Site report for San Pedro states that: Several foreigners who live or own hotels/resorts along the beach prohibit people from using or passing through the beach reserve ... totally disregarding the 66 feet reserve as required by the National Lands Act ... these people do not even own the beach and yet they lay claim to ownership by not allowing anyone to use the beach.

In their election manifesto for 1998– 2003, *Set Belize Free*, the PUP claimed that tourism had decline thanks to corrupt practices that allowed 'unscrupulous foreigners to side step Belizeans' and that the BTB had been 'plagued by mismanagement and corruption'.

Caye Chapel (owned by a former mining millionaire from Kentucky) has proved to be a controversial tourism development that highlights the links between foreign investors, support from local political and economic elites and local perceptions of corrupt business practices.

The island was completely re-landscaped and artificially expanded to provide an exclusive tourist resort. The development of the island included building a beach and a golf course, and dredging for sand to build the beach and to allow larger boats to dock at the island. In the process, the dredging stirred up the sea bed, disturbed lobster, sheries and destroyed Caye Caulker shing grounds.

The island has been perceived in Belize as an example of an environment being totally remastered in the pursuit of tourism development. The alliances which form the shadow state in Belize ensured that the island could be overhauled to conform to the image of Cayes presented to potential visitors. There was a great deal of local speculation about the way in which the owner of the island appeared to be able to dredge around it and build a beach without proper permission.

Those who opposed the development of Caye Chapel speculated that the owner was allowed to undertake such activities because he was protected by the highest political authorities in the country in return for free trips to the island, and that the owner had been careful to pay the relevant officials in order to avoid environmental regulations.

For example, one interviewee stated that Caye Chapel was a glaring example of what happened to the environment in Belize when a corrupt politician and a foreign millionaire cooperated, and that it was all about money and there was no-one willing to stop it. Caye Chapel will have its own airstrip and casino to allow gamblers to direct from Miami to the island. Critics of such tourist developments have complained that while the USA and UK berate Belize for failing to tackle money laundering, drug trafficking and a possibly corrupt offshore sector, it is the citizens of these countries that are most likely to avail themselves of the facilities on offer in Belize.

Another example of the links between local elites and external property investors was the highly controversial plan to build a dolphin park called Cangrejo Caye. Aspects of the process to create the park indicate that common forms of public consultation were circumvented in order to push through a major tourist development despite local opposition.

Cangrejo Caye was to be developed by a Mexican company, Dolphin International, and it offered tourists an opportunity to swim with 'semi-captive dolphins', along the lines of the highly successful and lucrative dolphin park in Xcaret in Mexico. The residents of Ambergris Caye were first informed of the plans for the park when an advert appeared in *Destination Belize 1997* that encouraged tourists to visit it before it was even built.

As a result Dolphin International embarked on a public relations campaign, and local business people who were the promoters of Dolphin International ensured that donations to local charities received favourable coverage in the local press, including when the company sponsored the San Pedro football team and it was renamed the Dolphins in honour of its new backers.

In addition, Dolphin International, which also used the name Cangrejo Caye Educational Experience Ltd., invited a number of Belizean 'movers and shakers' to a free weekend at its dolphin resort at Xcaret in Mexico. Cangrejo Caye was part of a redevelopment programme for Ambergris Caye that included shrimp farming by Nova Shrimp Ltd., the construction of an airstrip and a new pier, all of which was to be developed under the auspices of the North Ambergris Caye Development Corporation (NACDC).

The dolphin park was opposed by some local tour guides who viewed it as unwelcome competition and as contrary to the spirit of Eco-tourism in Belize. Tour operators Daniel and Elodia Nunez openly opposed the park because they disagreed with the idea of keeping wild animals in a captive environment to satiate tourist desires. They stated that they believed that the dolphins at Xcaret were slowly dying, partly because dolphins like to swim freely over large distances in order to feed and so keeping them in pens would be cruel and detrimental to the environment, since the dolphins would eat out such a small area.

According to Daniel and Elodia Nunez, in 1998 the park was forced by local opposition to accept demands for a full environmental impact assessment before construction was begun. This strong pro-conservation lobby was identified by Victoria Collins, Editor of the *San Pedro Sun*, as a major factor in preventing the construction of Cangrejo Caye. Opponents of the development there were keen to speculate that the owners had failed to pay off the right officials in the opposition People's United Party (PUP), which was tipped to win the next election. Indeed, after the PUP had won the general election of 1998, the Urban Planning Officer for Ambergris Caye, Al Westby, remarked that the investors from Dolphin International had been invited back once more to Belize to discuss the future development of Cangrejo Caye further. The case of the dolphin park can also be viewed as an indicator of the extent of the shadow links between state agencies and the private sector.

National Tourism Policy

In order to develop tourism in India in a systematic manner, position it as a major engine of economic growth and to harness its direct and multiplier effects for employment and poverty eradication in an environmentally sustainable manner, the National Tourism Policy was formulated in the year 2002. Broadly, the "Policy" attempts to:-

- Position tourism as a major engine of economic growth;
- Harness the direct and multiplier effects of tourism for employment generation, economic development and providing impetus to rural tourism;
- Focus on domestic tourism as a major driver of tourism growth.
- Position India as a global brand to take advantage of the burgeoning global travel trade and the vast untapped potential of India as a destination;
- Acknowledges the critical role of private sector with government working as a pro-active facilitator and catalyst;
- Create and develop integrated tourism circuits based on India's unique civilization, heritage, and culture in partnership with States, private sector and other agencies; and
- Ensure that the tourist to India gets physically invigorated, mentally rejuvenated, culturally enriched, spiritually elevated and "feel India from within".

Scheme for Product/Infrastructure and Destination Development

The focus under this scheme is on improving the existing products and developing new tourism products to world class standards. For infrastructure and product development, the Ministry of Tourism has been providing Central Financial Assistance to the State Governments during the 9th Five Year Plan which resulted in strengthening of the infrastructure and product development in the country. The scheme has been restructured during the 10th Five Year Plan to meet the present day infrastructure requirements. The past experience had been that a large number of small projects had been funded under the Scheme, spreading the resources very thinly, which at times had not created the desired impact. The focus in the Tenth Plan has been to fund large projects of infrastructure or product development in an integrated manner.

Under the revised scheme, the destinations are carefully selected based on the tourism potential. Master planning of these destinations is undertaken so as to develop them in an integrated holistic manner. The master plan is suppose to tie up all backward and forward linkages, including environmental considerations. Realizing the importance of destination development, the total outlay for this sector has been increased substantially. Important tourist destinations in each State, in consultation with the State Governments, are taken up for development. This include activities ranging from preparation of master plans to implementation of the master plans. The destinations are selected in consultation with the State/UT Governments.

Scheme for Integrated Development of Tourist Circuits

Under this Central Financial Assistance scheme the Ministry of Tourism Government of India has been extending assistance to States for development of tourism infrastructure. Experience has shown that in the past funds under the CFA have been used to fund a large number of small isolated projects, spread throughout the length and breadth of the country resulting in the resources being spread very thinly.

Therefore, in order to provide quick and substantial impact, during the 10th Five Year Plan, this new scheme of Integrated Development of Tourist Circuits have been taken up. The objective of the scheme is to identify tourist circuits in the country on an annual basis, and develop them to international standards. The aim is to provide all infrastructure facilities required by the tourists within these circuits. The Ministry of Tourism aim at convergence of resources and expertise through coordinated action with States/UTs and private sector.

Scheme of Assistance for Large Revenue Generating Projects

It is recognized that the development of tourism infrastructure projects requires very large investment that may not be possible out of the budgetary resources of the Government of India alone. In order to remove these shortcomings and to bring in private sector, corporate and institutional resources as well as techno-managerial efficiencies, it is proposed to promote large revenue generating projects for development of tourism infrastructure in public private partnerships and in partnerships with other Government / Semi-Government agencies.

Large revenue generating project, which can be admissible for assistance under this scheme, should be a project, which is also a tourist attraction, or used by tourists and generates revenue through a levy of fee or user charges on the visitors. Projects like Tourist trains, Cruise vessels, Cruise Terminals, Convention Centres, Golf Courses etc. would qualify for assistance. However, this is only an illustrative list.

Hotel & Restaurant component will not be eligible for assistance under the scheme either on a stand-alone basis or as an integral part of some other project. Besides hotel & restaurants, procurement of vehicles and sports facilities like stadiums will also not be eligible for assistance under the scheme.

Scheme for Support to Public Private Partnerships in Infrastructure (Viability Gap Funding)

Development of infrastructure require large investments that cannot be undertaken out of public financing alone. Thus, in order to attract private capital as well as techno-managerial efficiencies associated with it, the government is committed to promoting Public-Private Partnerships (PPPs) in infrastructure development. This scheme has been put into effect for providing financial support to bridge the viability gap of infrastructure projects undertaken through Public Private Partnerships.

Scheme for Market Development Assistance (MDA)

The Marketing Development Assistance Scheme (MDA), administered by the Ministry of Tourism, Government of India, provides financial support to approved tourism service providers (i.e. hoteliers, travel agents, tour operators, tourist transport operators etc., whose turnover include foreign exchange earnings also) for undertaking the following tourism promotional activities abroad:

- Sales-cum-study tour
- Participation in fairs/exhibitions
- Publicity through printed material.

Recent Initiatives

During 11th Five Year Plan (2007-2012) Ministry of Tourism propose to continue supporting creation of world class infrastructure in the country so that existing tourism products can be further improved and expanded to meet new market requirements and enhance the competitiveness of India as a tourist destination. In consultation with the State Governments and UTs the Ministry of Tourism have identified several tourist circuits and destinations for integrated development. During the current financial year the Ministry has sanctioned so far Rs.323.00 crore for various projects throughout the country. This is an all time record and will facilitate timely execution of projects during the working season.

Some of the important infrastructure projects which have been sanctioned in the current financial year are:

Beach and Sea Tourism

- MOT has sanctioned a project of Rs.5.00 crore for development and beautification of Beach Promenade in Puducherry.
- Another project for development of walkway along the bank of river Arasalar and Vanjiiar in Karaikal, Puducherry (Rs.4.78 crore)
- The project of Development of Marina bach in Tamilnadu has been sanctioned (Rs.4.92 crore).

Eco Tourism

- A project of Eco tourism for development of Horsely Hill in Chittoor Distt. of Andhra Pradesh has been sanctioned.
- The project of development of Satkosi in Orissa (Rs. 4.25 crore) has been sanctioned in which Interpretation Centre, Landscaping, Elephant camps, Trekking park, Watch Towers and parking facilities, etc. are proposed to be developed.

- MOT has sanctioned a project for development of Eco tourism in Morni-Pinjore Hills and Sultanpur National Park in Haryana for which Rs. 2.63 crore have been sanctioned.
- The project of Integrated Development of Tribal Circuit with special focus on Eco tourism in Spiti in Himachal Pradesh has been approved for Rs. 6.98 crore.
- Development of Wayanad in Kerala for an amount of Rs.2.01 crore.
- Development of Tourist Circuit (Western Assam Circuit) Dhubari-Mahamaya-Barpeta-Hajo has been sanctioned for an amount of Rs.4.97 crore.
- Development of Mechuka Destination (Rs.4.41 crore in Arunachal Pradesh).
- Development of Tourist Destination at Khensa at a cost of Rs.4.58 crore in Nagaland.
- Circuit-Udhyamandalam-Madumalai-Anaimalai, Tamil Nadu Rs.4.39 crore.

Projects for NE Region

- The INA Memorial Complex at Moirang in Manipur is being renovated and tourist facilities are being developed (Rs.82 lakhs).
- Tourism infrastructure is being developed near Pakhai Wildlife Sanctuary in Arunachal Pradesh (Rs. 5.00 crore)
- Gayaker Sinyi Lake at Itanagar is being developed at a cost of Rs.5.00 crore.
- Tourist infrastructure is being developed in Nathula-Memmencho-Kuppu tourist circuit in Sikkim (Rs.4.54 crore)
- MOT has sanctioned a project for development of Tizu Kukha as Adventure Destination in Nagaland (Rs.4.99 crore)
- Projects for Jammu & Kashmir.

MOT has sanctioned a project for development of tourism infrastructure in Leh (Rs.4.95 crore), Bungus Valley (Rs.2.31 crore),

Kargil (Rs.4.84 crore), Poonch (Rs.4.50 crore), various villages around Sonmarg (Rs.1.08 crore), development of Gurez and Telail Valley (Rs.3.66 crore), Patnitop (Rs.2.83 crore), Dandi Pora (3.45 crore), Anantnag (Rs.2.1 crore), Shri Amarnath Yatra Marg (Rs.7.00 crore), Bhaderwah (Rs. 4.12 crore), Kishtwar (Rs. 2.81 crore), Wullar Lake (Rs.2.06 crore) and Rajouri (Rs.4.34 crore).

Tourist Information Centre, Public amenities, approach roads, shelters, signages, etc. will be developed in these projects so that tourists who are visiting Jammu & Kashmir should have trouble free experience the beauty and bounty of the region.

4

Activities in Shopping Tourism

From the beginning of the sixties on, Yugoslavia differed a great deal from other Eastern European countries. The difference did not only show in the political system but also in the personal standard of living, tourism, travelling, shopping abroad and imitating the western life style. In a addition to that Slovenia had a specific position within Yugoslavia: bordering to Italy and Austria, and with strong national minorities in those countries, it was Yugoslavia's most developed and pro-west oriented region. This allowed Slovenia-with the exception of the first post-war years-to be constantly in touch with the two countries and to make realistic comparisons of the standard of living.

Since the mid-fifties the authorities in Slovenia had been striving to approach the level of personal and social standard of living of the neighbouring capitalist countries. However, the system remained a socialist one, despite some capitalist elements it contained.

It was based on egalitarianism, full employment, a high degree of social protection, as well as on the specific socialist ideology and morale. Community (collective), not the individual were given privileged position, although Slovenians are great individuals by nature. A blend of socialist system and capitalist influence from the west created an unusual atmosphere. People did believe in Tito, in self-management, in non-alignment but also in washing machines, refrigerators, TV sets and other postulates of consumer society. Since the laws of market economy and competitiveness were not being fully implemented, the production was unable to comply with the demands of the customers and fashion trends. As a result of that, the only real contact Slovene people had with western type consumerism in the sixties and also in the seventies was through shopping abroad, in which they frequently and readily indulged.

Italy was the first window to the western world for the Slovene (and Yugoslav) people. Incising painfully in the life of people who had until then lived together, first within Austria-Hungary and later, between the two World Wars, under Italy, a new border-to the advantage of Yugoslavia-was set between the two countries in 1957. In some cases the border ran between the houses, crossed gardens, or even-as in the case of village Miren-divided the graveyard into two parts. (At funerals armed border guards are reported to have been present along the provisional demarcation in the graveyard and the coffin was literally pushed from one state to the other by the mourners in order to allow the relatives and friends from both states to take leave from the deceased). In order to preserve a small piece of land for their country, people used to move the provisional demarcation pales until the boundary stones were placed.

The relations with Italy remained tense as long as until 1954 when the so called Trieste question was resolved by the London memorandum (the division of the Free Territory between Yugoslavia and Italy). Border crossings were therefore scarce; only people who lived within the 200 m frontier zone and the so called double owners (i.e. people who possessed land in both states) were entitled to them.

The latter were allowed to take the shortest route to their land in the other state but forbidden to visit bigger villages or towns. In spite of the strict control on both sides of the border they did visit them (on Italian side they were frequently recognised by their "socialist" shoes or by the license plates on their bicycles). As the first buyers of western products people living along the frontier used to smuggle them to Slovenia. The goods were mostly hidden on bicycles or under the garments. One man even built a secret telpher line (lift) across the border to help himself at the smuggling (border guard catched him and he was sent into prison for two years). The most attractive smuggling articles being sugar, coffee, rise, lemons, medications, soap, cameras and other goods lacking in Slovenia (like blue copperas used in wine-growing and even scrubbing brushes and brooms).

The shopping was predominantly based on exchange of goods; in return, meat, brandy, eggs and butter were smuggled to Italy (even today the story about a woman smuggling butter can be heard; hiding it under her blouse it melt and started to trickle exactly when she was at the border crossing). Some smugglers even had an agreement with the police whom they helped to purchase office materials, type writers and similar. In the first half of the fifties foreign fashion articles became an attractive smuggling business; this was especially the case with a sort of raincoats made from synthetic material. The risky smuggling business paid well, and quite some people living along the border made enough money with it to be able to build themselves houses of their own.

In summer 1950 rumours spread along the Yugoslav-Italian border that the residents of the frontier zone from both states were to meet at all major border crossings. Three years after this region was divided by the frontier, the residents from both states were to meet their relatives, renew connections with friends and demonstrate their wish for coexistence. On 6 August, 1950 there was such a meeting at the border crossing Rozna dolina in Gorica and it should be repeated on 13 August, 1950.

On that day thousands of people gathered-predominantly on the Yugoslav side-at the border crossing; they literally pulled it down and scattered subsequently along the streets and shops of Gorica. The unexpected "shopping spree" was described as the "march of the hungry" by the Italian press (although people were mainly buying scrubbing brushes /brooms/, which were lacking in Slovenia), but there was no report about the incident in the Yugoslav press. The press of the Slovene minority in Italy published the following: "On Sunday morning our people pulled down the unjust border at the check-point near Rdeca hisa (red house) and for half a day Gorica regained its position as the centre of Slovene people from the Soca (Isonzo) and Vipava region." The author concluded that sooner or later the artificial frontier would have to be removed; but not just for a few hours.

In his opinion the frontier should be moved to where it belongs, namely to the boundaries of the territory with Slovenian population on the other bank of the river Soea. There were other commentaries, i.e. in the Trieste workers' newspaper Il lavoratore (which supported Kominform-at that time the conflict between Yugoslavia and The Soviet Union was at its height), which wrote: "The Tito government organised jointly with the Italian one a 'legal' crossing of the border to feed its people."

After this unusual incident the border remained tightly closed for the next five years, until the Videm (Udine) agreement was signed. In 1955 Yugoslavia and Italy signed an agreement on the local border (border land) traffic the so called Videm (Udine) agreement. It was the first agreement of its kind to be signed by a capitalist and a socialist state respectively during the period of the cold war. The right to crossing the border was expanded to all the population living along the frontier which resulted in vast increase of border crossings.

People of these regions were particularly keen to visit diverse fairs (i.e. the fair of St. Andrew in Gorica), where they were buying cheap goods. One of the most popular articles was the so called "bambola"-a big baby doll clad in coloured dress; as decoration such dolls were placed on matrimonial beds. Further, people used to buy confetti (for marriages), chewing gum and typical Italian sweets. The goods purchased on Italian stands had a major influence on forming the taste of Slovenian and Yugoslav customers in the fifties, but also later on. Double land owners were not allowed to enter Austria before 1953 when the agreements on frontier traffic and real assets of Austrian double owners on Yugoslav territory were signed. Apart from double land owners, in exceptional cases other residents of the frontier region were granted three-day permits for crossing the border, whereas there were no limitations for doctors, veterinarians and midwives. (In 1958 6000 and 5000 permits for crossing the border were issued on Yugoslav and Austrian side respectively). In 1960 an additional agreement on frontier traffic was signed, according to which residents of the 10 km frontier zone were allowed to enter Austria. These people received permanent permits for crossing the border; they were allowed to go abroad four times a month and stay there up to 60 hours. The same border crossing had to be used upon their return (the regular border crossings between Austria and Yugoslavia totalled 19). A Yugoslav citizen was allowed to take 3500.- dinars (about 12$) abroad every month. However, due to its moderate range of goods available and higher price level, Austria was not as attractive as Italy for Yugoslav shoppers.

People who were not living within the 10 km frontier zone were able to acquire a passport (either a personal, a family or a group passport). Passports were issued by the district departments for internal affairs; application for a passport could be refused without further explanation; further, passports were not issued to men who had not yet served the army.

A visa was necessary for almost all the states; in addition to that, a Yugoslav citizen had to provide a letter of guarantee from the destination state. Until the beginning of the sixties administrative hindrances and also low standard of living prevented Yugoslav citizens from more frequent visits abroad; their travelling was restricted to business trips and visiting relatives. Quite a number of people crossed the border illegally and emigrated afterwards to overseas countries. In the second half of the fifties, however, tourism began to develop which resulted in more frequent visits of foreigners in Yugoslavia.

A lot of them were attracted by diverse trade fairs. A gradual opening towards western culture in the late fifties and in the sixties was also demonstrated by organising fashion shows, song festivals (after San Remo festival in Italy) and miss competitions. In 1958 regular TV broadcast was introduced in Slovenia; in the sixties TV became a mass phenomenon. Its programme (western TV serials, films, music programmes and also commercials) additionally promoted the consumer mentality and affinity for western values; this everything enhanced the wish for travelling abroad. Most Slovenians were able to receive either some Austrian or Italian TV programme; their shopping decisions abroad were therefore frequently based on information gained from commercials. Some Italian and Austrian shop owners (especially those of Slovene origin) gradually started to advertise their products in Slovene newspapers and radio. In the mid-sixties Yugoslavia opened up towards the world and the standard of living increased a great deal.

Passport became available (with hardly any administrative hindrances) to the majority of the citizens; visas for the neighbouring countries were gradually abolished. In 1962 Yugoslav citizens were allowed for the first time to purchase legally foreign currency in the amount of 15 000 dinars (50 US$; a larger sum was only available for the purpose of medical treatment abroad and attending international meeting/conferences).

It was possible to open a bank account for foreign currency. Masses of people went to Austria and Germany to work there; only through employment agencies 62347 Slovenian citizens found work in the west between 1964 and 1969 but there were even more people who moved to the west on their own. For major holidays they were coming back home and bringing products from the west. The western shopping trend gradually moved from jeans (being one of the first citizens of Ljubljana wearing jeans in the fifties, the famous Slovenian actor Janez Hocevar still bears the nickname Rifle), tennis shoes (in Slovenia they are still called "superge", after the popular Italian trademark), cosmetics and washing powder towards washing machines, vacuum cleaners and other domestic appliances and even cars. I can remember purchasing a washing machine Candy (the most popular Italian make for domestic appliances of that time) in Trbiz (Tarvisio) with our neighbours who had already possessed a car.

My mother possessed only a half of the necessary money, but the Slovenian dealer was willing to grant her a credit, so she could pay it on instalments (six months). During that time the Slovenian production and trade were gradually adapting to the needs of their customers: Gorenje started to produce domestic appliances which became popular in Eastern European countries in the following years; self-service stores and department stores started to emerge. However, the supply of goods in these shops was not as good as in the west and the prices were higher.

Like elsewhere in the world, towards the end of the sixties the teenage generation gradually became a very strong consumer group. The socialist supply of goods was not able to cover their demands for all sorts of notebooks with portraits of film stars, felt-tip pens, school bags, fashionable clothes, records and similar articles. Even if this was not so (like in the case of high-quality skis Elan), they were often considered to be inferior and the parents were forced to buy-with their modest socialist salaries-fashionable foreign makes of skis abroad.

As regards the standard of living, the seventies turned out to be the best post-war years for Yugoslavia (Slovenia). The non-aligned Arab friends had prevented Yugoslavia to suffer from the oil-shock; foreign loans were cheap-due to its specific position, they were literally forced upon Yugoslavia. The official policy had defeated the liberal orientation of the sixties; it wanted to prove that the self-managed socialism was the best system in the world. With the help of cheap loans, a large number of Slovenians were building houses of their own in the seventies. Shopping abroad proved this tendency: building material which was either better in quality, cheaper, or not at all available in Yugoslavia was transported in car boots from abroad. The most popular articles purchased abroad were bathroom tiles, wash-basins, water-taps, furniture, diverse (garden) and other tools (even concrete-mixers). There was a great demand for domestic appliances, clothing articles, shoes (Italian shoes have remained to be a byword for quality, despite the good quality of Slovenian products), foodstuffs, spirits and items which were-due to ideological reasons-not available in Slovenia (communion and confirmation clothes, garlands, white shoes and handbags, etc.). Another phenomenon of the seventies was the so called "Ponterosso", where cheap goods and gimcrack were sold. It attracted thousands of Yugoslav buyers who were coming as organised groups by regular trains, buses and cars even from the most distant parts of the country. They were buying everything, even most worthless goods. "Ponterosso" grew into a symbol of consumer mentality, adapted to socialist buyers with little money. Hiding purchases from the customs officers (duty free imports were limited to the value of 100 dinars only) was one of the favourite Yugoslav sports of the seventies, regardless the age or sex of the people involved.

Mass shopping in Italy was also a result of the so called Osimo agreements, which Italy in Yugoslavia-influenced by the spirit of Helsinki-signed in 1975. Yugoslav-Italian border became by far the most open border between a socialist and a capitalist country. In 1978 over 40 million people crossed the border in the Triest region (Trzaska pokrajina); 21 million with passports and 19 million with regular border permits. New border crossing points were opened but there were traffic hold-ups in spite of that, particularly during weekends; a phenomenon which had first started in the sixties.

The frontier zone was increased to 30 km (the residents of Jesenice, a community bordering on Austria and Italy were so entitled to Austrian and Italian regular border permits). The authorities were not enthusiastic about shopping abroad because so much money was spent on it; but on the other hand, foreigners were shopping in Yugoslavia too, particularly petrol, meat and other food which was cheaper in Yugoslavia. Even more important was the ideological reason: how is it possible that people living "under the best system in the world" go shopping to Italy? From time to time therefore articles criticising shopping abroad appeared in newspapers, often with the comment that Yugoslav shoppers were being exploited by the capitalist traders. Particularly communists and public officials/civil servants were advised not to succumb to that shopping fever, but there were no sanctions and no other efforts to reduce shopping abroad (except for customs measures). The third phenomenon of the seventies was the expansion of agency tourism/organised tourism. From the beginning of the seventies on, Yugoslav travel agencies had been organising holidays abroad, particularly in Spain, Italy and Tunisia; further, they organised shopping trips to the main European capitals and even USA (especially New York). Organised shopping tours focused on consumer electronics / audio systems (Munich was considered to be the best place to buy these products), or clothes and leather products (Istambul).

In the eighties Yugoslavia glided into a crisis. The standard of living fell to the level of the mid-sixties. A number of products were rationed or not available at all (petrol, oil, washing powder, citrus fruits). Shopping abroad concentrated therefore on buying foodstuffs; and anyway, due to the growing inflation rate which in the mid-eighties grew to hyperinflation Yugoslav citizens were hardly able to afford to buy anything else. The geographic position of Slovenia allowed its citizens to compensate the shortage by weekly shopping trips abroad (and besides, the supply in Slovenia was better than elsewhere in Yugoslavia). The buying power improved in 1990 when the Yugoslav Prime Minister Ante Markoviæ froze the exchange rate of the national currency dinar in relation 1: 7 to German mark. For a period of a few months Slovenian salaries have reached the level of Italian and Austrian ones, which had an immediate effect on shopping across the border. After the crisis, which led to disintegration of Yugoslavia and consequently to independence of Slovenia, shopping abroad gradually normalised. Goods are abundantly available in shops at home, therefore shopping abroad is not a consequence of insufficient supply anymore; it is rather a matter of lower prices and (or) of prestige.

Border crossings, shopping abroad and travelling have importantly influenced the life style of Slovene people in the post-war decades. They sharpened their sense of quality and influenced domestic production and trade which made effort to reach the western standards. Shopping abroad further exerted indirect pressure on politics, which was-at least to some extend-forced to take account of the demands of consumers and act accordingly. It has to be mentioned however, that shopping was limited-particularly in the fifties and in the first half of the sixties-by the low standard of living. In the course of time a specific consumer ritual was established, a sort of shopping fever to which the majority of Slovenians (and even more Yugoslavs) succumbed. A typical feature of that attitude was that people did not only buy products they really needed. When abroad they had to "take the opportunity" to make the journey "worth the money and time" it took and therefore used to buy everything that came to their hands. This philosophy was in perfect agreement with the belief that saving and rational spending of money made no sense, since in socialism the state was believed to be responsible for providing housing, regular income and solving other problems of the citizens (however, not everything could be implemented and especially Slovenians tended to be more economical; a lot of them bought flats or built houses on their own).

Shopping tourism was only one of the influences that formed the post-war socialist consumer mentality in Slovenia. Its impact has to be seen within a broader context, together with films, music, television, mass motorization, expanding of foreign tourism in Slovenia and economic emigration. Everything this led to the fact, that Slovenians accepted western standards and behaviour patterns as regards the style of home decor, clothing and spending leisure time as early as in the "liberal" sixties (in the second half of the seventies, for example, the more affluent citizens already had access to international credit cards, including American Express).

People took from socialism what was of use to them (free schooling, good health services, full employment), whereas ideology that filled political speeches, newspaper articles and TV news was perceived as the necessary evil. During the last two decades, the self-managed socialism was hardly taken seriously by anyone. This was probably also due to the fact, that both, regime critics and party officials met on their shopping tours across the border.

Draft: National Tourism Policy of India

Tourism emerged as the largest global industry of the 20th century and is projected to grow even faster in the 21st century. India has immense possibilities of growth in the tourism sector with vast cultural and religious heritage, varied natural attractions, but a comparatively small role in the world tourism scene. A New Tourism Policy, which builds on the strength of the national Tourism Policy of 1982, but which envisages new initiatives towards making tourism the catalyst in employment generation, environmental re-generation, development of remote areas and development of women and other disadvantaged groups in the country, besides promoting social integration is, therefore, vital to our economy. It would lead to larger foreign exchange earnings and create conditions for more Foreign Direct Investment.

The Mission

Our mission is to promote sustainable tourism as a means of economic growth and social integration and to promote the image of India abroad as a country with a glorious past, a vibrant present and a bright future. Policies to achieve this will be evolved around six broad areas such as Welcome (Swagat), Information (Suchana), Facilitation (Suvidha), Safety (Suraksha), Cooperation (Sahyog) and Infrastructure Development (Samrachana). Conservation of heritage, natural environments, etc. and development and promotion of tourist products would also be given importance.

Objectives

The objectives of tourism development are to foster understanding between people, to create employment opportunities and bring about socio-economic benefits to the community, particularly in the interior and remote areas and to strive towards balanced and sustainable development and preserve, enrich and promote India's cultural heritage. One of the major objectives is the preservation and protection of natural resources and environment to achieve sustainable development. Given the low cost of employment creation in the tourism sector and the low level of exploitation of India's tourism potential, the new tourism policy seeks to expand foreign tourist arrivals and facilitate domestic tourism in a manner that is sustainable by ensuring that possible adverse effects such as cultural pollution and degradation of environment are minimised.

The New Tourism Policy also aims at making the stay of foreign tourists in India, a memorable and pleasant one with reliable services at predictable costs, so that they are encouraged to undertake repeated visits to India, as friends. This would be in tune with India's traditional philosophy of giving the highest honour to a guest (Atithi debo bhava).

Tourism a Multi-Dimensional Activity

(a) The Government will aim to achieve necessary linkages and synergies in the policies and programs of all concerned Departments/agencies by establishing effective coordination mechanisms at Central, State and District levels. The focus of national policy, therefore, will also be to develop tourism as a common endeavour of all the agencies vitally concerned with it at the Central and State levels, public sector undertakings and the private sector.

(b) It will be the policy of government to encourage people's participation in tourism development including Panchayati Raj institutions, local bodies, Co-operatives, non-governmental organisations and enterprising local youth to create public awareness and to achieve a wider spread of tourist facilities. However, focused attention will be given for the integrated development of identified centres with well directed public participation.

(c) Public and Private Sector Partnership: A constructive and mutually beneficial partnership between the public and the private sectors through all feasible means is an absolute necessity for the sustained growth of tourism. It is, therefore, the policy of the Government to encourage emergence of such a partnership. This will be achieved by creating a Tourism Development Authority consisting of senior officials of the Government and tourism experts and professionals from the private sector.

(d) Role of the Government: Tourism is a multi-sectoral activity and the industry is affected by many other sectors of the national economy. The State has to, therefore, ensure intergovernmental linkages and coordination. It also has to play a pivotal role in tourism management and promotion. The specific role of the Government will be to:

i. Provide basic infrastructural facilities including local planning and zoning arrangements.
ii. Plan tourism development as a part of the over all area development strategy.
iii. Create nucleus infrastructure in the initial stages of development to demonstrate the potential of the area.
iv. Provide the required support facilities and incentives to both domestic and foreign investors to encourage private investment in the tourism sector.
v. Rationalise taxation and land policies in the tourism sector in all the States and Union Territories and in respect of land owned by Government agencies like Railways.
vi. Introduce regulatory measures to ensure social, cultural and environmental sustainability as well as safety and security of tourists.
vii. Ensure that the type and scale of tourism development

is compatible with the environment and socio-cultural milieu of the area.

viii. Ensure that the local community is fully involved and the benefits of tourism accrue to them.

ix. Facilitate availability of trained manpower particularly from amongst the local population jointly with the industry.

x. Undertake research, prepare master plans, and facilitate formulation of marketing strategies.

xi. Organise overseas promotion and marketing jointly with the industry.

xii. Initiate specific measures to ensure safety and security of tourists and efficient facilitation services.

xiii. Facilitate the growth of a dynamic tourism sector.

(e) Role of Private Sector: Tourism has emerged as the largest export industry globally and all over the globe private sector has played the lead role in this growth. The private sector has to consider investment in tourism from a long term perspective and create the required facilities including accommodation, time share, restaurants, entertainment facilities, shopping complexes, etc. in areas identified for tourism development. Non-core activities in all airports, major stations and interstate bus terminus such as cleanliness and maintenance, luggage transportation, vehicles parking facilities, etc. should be opened up to private operators to increase efficiency and profitability.

The specific role of the Private Sector will be to:

i. Build and manage the required tourist facilities in all places of tourist interest.

ii. Assume collective responsibility for laying down industry standards, ethics and fair practices.

iii. Ensure preservation and protection of tourist attractions and give lead in green practices.

iv. Sponsor maintenance of monuments, museums and parks and provision of public conveniences and facilities.

v. Involve the local community in tourism projects and ensure that the benefits of tourism accrue to them in right measure.

vi. Undertake industry training and man-power development to achieve excellence in quality of services.

vii. Participate in the preparation of investment guidelines and marketing strategies and assist in database creation and research.

viii. Facilitate safety and security of tourists

ix. Endeavour to promote tourism on a sustained and long term perspective.

x. Collaborate with Govt. in the promotion and marketing of destinations.

(f) Role of voluntary efforts: Voluntary agencies and volunteers have to contribute their expertise and understanding of local ethos to supplement the efforts of other sectors to provide the human touch to tourism and foster local initiatives. All such efforts shall be encouraged.

Tourism Development Fund and Resources for Development

It would be the policy of the Government to facilitate larger flow of funds to tourism infrastructure and to create a Tourism Development Fund to bridge critical infrastructural gaps.

Priority would be given for development of tourist infrastructure in selected areas of tourist importance and for those products which are considered to be in demand in the existing and future markets so that limited resources are put to the best use.

Foreign Investments and Incentives and Rationalization of Taxes

i. In view of large investment requirements in the tourism sector and the need for maintaining high quality standards in services, hotels and tourism related industries will continue to be in the priority list of industries for foreign investment. Export-house status has been accorded to Hotels, Travel Agents, Tour Operators and Tourist

Transport Operators vide Notification No.33(RE-98)1997-2002 dated 26.11.98 of the Ministry of Commerce. The status needs to be extended to all tourism units irrespective of the annual turnover.

ii. In order to offset the specific constraints of tourism industry and to put in place the required infrastructure as quickly as possible, particularly in less developed areas, appropriate incentive schemes would be considered. It would also be the endeavour of the Government to persuade the State/UT Governments to rationalise taxes, to put a cap of 20% on all taxes taken together on the accommodation and hospitality units, to allocate suitable land for tourism purposes at reasonable prices, harmonize movement of tourist transport across State borders, etc.

Adoption of New Technologies

a. Efforts will be made to adopt the technological advances in the tourism sector to provide better facilities to tourists and to market the tourism product, to the benefit of all concerned.

b. Information technology shall be given the pride of place in the efforts to promote Indian tourism. Every endeavour in this regard would increasingly rely on optimising the use of e-commerce/m-commerce, use of internet for disemination of tourism related information, increasing use of portals as gateway to accessibility to tourism information, development of Handy Audio Reach Kit (HARK) Tourist Guidance System at important monuments and heritage sites, networking of States, setting of tourist information Kiosks, encouoragement to information technology and eco-friendly practices by the private industries and above all keeping abreast with the global technologies for promoting and facilitating tourism. It shall be ensured that Information Technology(IT) and Indian Tourism(IT) become synonymous.

c. The Central Government will set up a Paryatan Bhawan in New Delhi as a modern Tourist Interpretation Centre to cater to various needs of travellers, foreign as well as domestic and to offer facilities for air and train reservation, money changing counters and information about all tourist centres in the country. The Centre will be equipped with e-connectivity and networking facility to all state tourist offices. Efforts will be made to have similar state level Paryatan Bhawans in state Capitals.

The economic and social benefits of tourism and its importance as an instrument of economic growth have to be fully recognised by all sections of the society. It would, therefore, be the endeavour of the Government to bridge the information gap through proper statistical documentation of the impact of tourism and its wide publicity to create awareness so that the economic and social significance of tourism is well recognised and tourism is given due attention and national priority

Tourism Economic Zone, Tourist Circuits, Special Tourism Area and Areas of Special Interests

1. Tourism Economic Zones will be created with private participation based on the intrinsic attractions, potential for development and availability of resources in these zones. Air, road and rail connectivity to these areas will be established to facilitate direct and easy access to these zones from international and domestic destinations. Adequate backward and forward linkages will also be established to ensure flow of benefits to the local community. The development of such zones will be guided by well conceived Master Plans and executed by specific Tourism Development Authorities which will be created by the Government involving senior officers from the Department of Tourism, and other relevant Ministries/ Departments of the Govt. of India, professionals from tourism industry and representatives of Industry & Trade Associations.

2. India with vast cultural and religious heritage and varied natural attractions has immensed potential of growth in the tourism sector. 25 travel circuits and destinations have already been identified for development through joint efforts of the Central Govt., the State Governments and

the private sector. State Governments of Kerala, Tamil Nadu, Orissa and Maharashtra and Union Territory Administration of Daman & Diu have also declared Bekal Beach, Puri-Konark, Sindhudurg, Muttakadu-Mamallapuram and Diu as Special Tourism Area for integrated development. Steps will be taken to work towards the integrated development of all the tourist circuits of the country with the involvement of all the infrastructural departments, State Governments and the private sector.

3. Areas of Special Interest: Government would initiate and support special programmes and schemes for the development of tourism in North Eastern States, Himalayan region and island States/U.Ts with a view to achieve overall economic development of the regions, and as part of the strategy for removing regional imbalances.

Sustainable Development and Perspective Plans

The principle of sustainable development stipulates that the level of development does not exceed the carrying capacity of the area. It will be governments' policy to ensure adherence to such limits through appropriate planning instruments, guidelines and enabling regulations and their enforcement.

Efforts will be made to diversify the tourism products in such a way that it supplements the main stream of cultural tourism. Comprehensive perspective plans for developing sustainable tourism by assessing the existing tourism scenario in each State/ Union Territory with respect to availability of natural resources, heritage and other socio-cultural assets, quantitative/demographic factors like population, employment, occupation, income levels etc., services and infrastructure will be developed by initiating immediate action in this direction.

Conservation and Development : Tourism development needs to be properly guided and regulated to avoid adverse impact on the natural environment and cultural heritage which constitute the tourist attraction. A judicious balance needs to be maintained between conservation and development. Government will continue its policy of trying to maintain balance through planning restrictions and by educating the people in appreciating their rich heritage and by eliciting their cooperation in preserving and protecting it.

Promotion and Marketing : Promotion and marketing is an important component of tourism development and needs to be undertaken along with product development in conformity with consumer profiles and product characteristics. The policy of the Government therefore will be to develop and implement cost effective marketing strategies based on market research and segmentation analysis in each of the tourist generating countries.

International Cooperation: Tourism is a global industry requiring inputs from various international agencies and collaborations with other countries. The policy of the Government therefore will be to foster positive win – win partnership with all the international agencies and other countries.

Professional Excellence : Tourism being a service industry it is necessary to enhance its service efficiency. The new policy will strive towards excellence by introducing professionalism through training and re-training of human resources and providing memorable visitor experience to both domestic and international tourists.

5

Activities in Sports Tourism

Attempting to accurately identify sport tourism motivators seems to be plagued with a number of difficulties. The complexity and copious number of motives for participating in sport and tourism are well documented. Additionally the fact that these motives change over time and cover broad and disparate areas of study further exacerbates the problem.

In sport tourism context the multiple nature of motivators can easily be described. For example the sport tourist travelling to the Euro 2004 soccer championship may want to see their team competing, enjoy the pleasant summer weather, participate in associated cultural festivities or take advantage of the local hospitality.

These combined collective motives illustrates that at this point in time it is unrealistic to identify and link up the almost countless motivational variables found in both sport and tourism. It may be wiser to take a broader view of the sport-tourism nexus by first suggesting that there exists a motivational duality which is both synergetic and reciprocal. Standeven and De Knop highlight this relationship by observing that, '...the nature of sport tourism is about an experience of physical activity tied to an experience of place.' However, Standeven and De Knop's (1999) explanation of the sport-tourism relationship errs on the side of geographical theory rather than a psychological one that addresses the method by which this synergy takes place.

The idea originally proposed was that the sport tourist could be categorized depending upon their primary and secondary reasons for travel. Furthermore, referring to the wider literature concerning intrinsic and extrinsic motivation, it was suggested that secondary motives had an enriching affect upon the primary ones:

Secondary reinforcement refers to a process by which an originally neutral stimulus acquires reinforcing properties through its association with a primary reinforcer. In these terms, an intrinsically motivated activity is simply one in which the reinforcement value of the goal has associatively rubbed off on the behaviour itself".

Therefore secondary motives should not be perceived as inferior or second rate, but rather as sources of enrichment to the primary ones. For example, whilst the primary motive maybe to play golf, the experience of playing will be reinforced by a number of contextual indicators that the environment engenders.

These could include climate, scenery, social elements, the quality of the course or indeed a host of other indicators which add to the overall experience of playing golf (an experience which collectively differs from the experience back home). This example illustrates that for some individuals (in this case active sport tourists) sport tourism offers them the opportunity to experience the best of both worlds. As Ryan (2003:31) succinctly observes, 'Finding something you love to do, of course, creates both meaning and pleasure.'

What could be better than to participate in your favourite activity in your favourite place – or in a place that you had always wanted to go to? Whilst it is suggested that sport and tourism motives combine additively it is less clear to what extent they interact during the experience(s).

For example, it is not known in what ways (if any) negative touristic experiences affect sport related ones and vice versa. Such questions of course focus upon the experience rather than the motive but nevertheless generates some important considerations for both the sport tourism manager and researcher.

A Sport Tourism Framework

Drawing upon the observations of Swarbrooke and Horner (1999); that tourism motives are generally made up of primary and secondary reasons for travel. And that secondary motive positively affect (in terms of reinforcing properties) the primary reasons for travel a sport tourism consumer framework can be outlined.

The main aim of the framework is to, firstly, illustrate the bisectional nature of the subject area, i.e. either from a sport or tourism base (a supposition supported in the sport tourism literature whilst, secondly, highlighting the segment list structure of sport tourism in order to delineate further areas of focus. Although categorizing sport tourism is not new the sub-division to soft and hard categories attempts to demonstrate four distinctive sport tourist types, each with quite different organizational, financial and methodological implications.

For example, the organizational and marketing processes within the Sport Tourism hard definition differs greatly from those utilized in the Tourism Sport hard definition. The following section introduces in a little more detail the four proposed categories.

Sport Tourism

The left-hand side of the framework focuses upon Sport Tourism. This section is devoted to the analysis of individuals and/or groups of people who actively or passively participate in competitive or recreational sport, whilst travelling to and/or staying in places outside their usual environment. The qualifying criteria are that sport is the prime motivation to travel, though the touristic element may act to reinforce the overall experience.

Hard Definition

A hard definition of the sport tourist includes those individuals who actively or passively participate at a competitive sporting event. We can therefore classify a hard sport tourist as someone who specifically travels to and/or stays in places outside their usual environment for either active or passive involvement in competitive sport.

In this case sport is their prime motivation for travel and would encompass participation at sporting events e.g. the Olympic Games, Football World Cup. The competitive nature of these events is the distinguishing factor.

Soft Definition

A soft definition of the sport tourist would be someone who specifically travels to and/or stays in places outside their usual environment for primarily active recreational participation in a chosen sport; for example skiing and cycling holidays. The active recreational elements are the distinguishing factors here.

Tourism Sport

Tourism sport comprises persons travelling to and/or staying in places outside their usual environment and participating in, actively or passively, a competitive or recreational sport as a secondary activity. The holiday or visit being their prime motivational reason for travel. Similarly this can be broken down into two distinct categories:

Hard Definition

Here one can identify holidaymakers who use sport as a secondary enrichment to their holiday (passive or active). Competitive or non-competitive sport may be applied, examples of which are Centre Parcs, Eurocamp and beach holidays. So for these tourists whilst the holiday is their primary motivation to travel, they will also expect to participate in some sport. Therefore sport will act as a secondary reinforcement to their vacation.

Soft Definition

A soft definition of tourism sport involves visitors who as a minor part of their trip engage in some form of sport on a purely incidental basis. For example whilst visiting a seaside resort for the day they play or watch bowls (jeu de boule) or play tennis in a local park; or visitors to Cambridge (UK) may wish to punt on the river. This is deemed "soft" because their participation is purely incidental.The framework was designed in order to first identify four distinct categories of the sport tourist (based upon primary and secondary motives) and secondly, to propose that there are a number of varying facilities and resources that each category of sport tourist would be mostly likely be drawn to.

This is not to suggest that competitive sports events are only going to attract those individuals and groups whose primary motive for travel is sport, for certainly major events will attract a diverse cross section of visitor, but rather to argue that it is these sport tourists that such events are more likely to attract. Since publishing the first article, it became clear that the original framework did not account for either sport tourism attractions or the ever popular sports fantasy camps. Halls of fame, sport museums and stadia tours have been treated as "secondary visitor attractions" and have consequently been included in the hard "Tourism Sport" category.

Of course, similar to the other categories, this is a somewhat uncomfortable generalization, as undoubtedly some of these attractions (e.g. Noucamp in Barcelona, Baseball Hall of Fame in Cooperstown) have become primary draws for domestic and international tourism alike. In contrast, sports fantasy camps can be classed, as soft Sport Tourism activities as the primary aim of these products are active recreational participation.

Application of the Framework

Implicit in the design of the framework is its applicability to a number of motivational, planning and marketing related contexts. Sport today represents a serious consideration to national, regional and urban re-imaging and marketing strategies unsurprisingly, such strategies involve a number of diverse stakeholders from both public and private sector organizations each wishing to establish and enhance their sport and tourism profiles. Indeed, since 1997 and the publication of the original article, we have been approached by local governments, major international entertainment organizations and political policy makers all interested in the applicability of the framework.

It soon became apparent that further clarification and adaptation was necessary. The framework has been revisited since 1997 to provide a more international flavour of activities around the world and of course to illustrate ways of how the framework could be applied to specific sports and places.

The framework can indicate the sport tourism components of a country through including major sporting, leisure and tourism activities that take place there. This could be based on a number of criteria. For example attendance figures, frequency, bookings, number of sports clubs, participation rates, tourism statistics or a combination of these. Similarly this principle can also be applied at a regional level (province, county or district).

In addition cities and towns can also show their sport tourism and tourism sport components by the inclusion of what it has to offer through the definitions described.

In this way specific sport, leisure and tourism components could be identified as potential areas to develop, or indicate areas as inadequate or weak. It may useful to refer back to Rooney's (1974) approach which helped identify a large number of hotbeds of sports activity in North America which compared regional variations with the national per capita level – as well as region to region comparisons.

Cities could potentially analyse their own sport tourist numbers, local sports events or sport attractions and compare them with either the national average (suggesting a need for a sport tourism index) or a host of other domestic and/or international urban competitors.

The inclusion of distinct categories and definitions forms a basis for exploring the motives of the sport tourist, providing a blueprint for further analysis and investigation. National sport and tourism agencies, local government and private leisure companies could use this approach as a starting point for developing their portfolio of sporting products.

Equally tour operators can monitor and evaluate their primary and secondary sporting products. Alternatively one sport could be analyzed through the motivational framework. The sport could then be applied at any of the levels described above. This could benefit particular sport organizations, national governing bodies, tour operators and of course private companies.

The national framework example, incorporating the Netherlands was chosen because the majority of the sport tourism literature features sporting destinations that have developed a relatively sophisticated sport tourism portfolio e.g. Britain, France, Portugal, Australia, USA etc.

Little attention has been paid to those destinations that are not in the media limelight as either a consequence of hosting major international events or as being recognized as major tourism destinations. Similarly, sporting cities such as Barcelona, Sheffield and Sydney have been cited numerous times in the sport tourism literature at the expense of smaller, or lesser known towns.

Although, not immediately associated with sport, for a country its size the Netherlands has achieved considerable sporting success. The fervour with which the Dutch also support and follow their sports (in many ways in a carnival / party atmosphere) is second to none. However this example also serves as a reminder of the ease with which the framework can be applied to any country.

According to the Dutch Central Bureau for Statistics about 25% of the 16 million people are registered to one of the 35,000 sports clubs in the country. About two thirds of the population older than 15 years participates in sport weekly. Additionally, many Dutch enjoy watching sports events. The most popular sports, both for active participation and audience are football, cycling, speed skating and tennis.

In addition in 2003 recreational activity (being away from home for at least two hours) accounted for 1 billion day trips with walking (75% of the population) and cycling (66%) being the most popular and on the increase. The Dutch spend about 16% of their holiday budgets in their own country. Revenues from incoming tourists account for 1.7% of the Dutch gross domestic product (GDP). This is significantly less than the European average of 2.3%. The potential therefore to increase sport tourism revenue is high.

Cruises, walking holidays and cycling opportunities are popular and are well catered for. A range of water sports are also available. These range from swimming, windsurfing, sailing, water-skiing and fishing. There are many canal and river tours. With 300km of coastline, walking is very popular. Walking routes are available for long and short distances and a unique experience is mud walking over the Wadden Sea to the islands offshore.

There are 17000 km of special cycling lanes and paths with a number of long distance routes. Bikes can be hired everywhere and railways allow bikes on trains.. In 2003 More than 40% of day trips undertaken by children were connected with sports activities.

Choosing a city to apply the framework did not pose too much of a problem as there are a number of well-known sporting cities whose particulars are well documented but the usefulness of the framework is not just in identifying the array of existing sport tourism offerings in major urban areas but also to indicate possible future developments in 2nd tier cities. Groningen is not a big sport tourism city, yet exemplifies effectively the dilemma many small cities face when examining their sport tourism and tourism sport profiles. They show possible gaps, over dependence and a different emphasis and perspective on the sport tourist. Groningen is the major city of the Northern Netherlands with a population of 179,000, and is the seventh largest city in the country. From an inspection of figure 3 it soon becomes apparent that there is further potential for Groningen to develop a sport tourism base. This is particularly emphasized by the fact that Groningen is the 'youngest' city in the Netherlands with over half the population being under thirty-five!

"Golf" was selected as the sport to apply to the framework because it not only illustrates well the different categories in the framework but also exhibits a range of different forms and activities. Profiling a particular sport provides an overview for possible market penetration for many organizations interested in developing a sport tourism product.

The application of the framework provides countless opportunities to examine aspects of sport tourism at many levels. These include local, regional, national and international dimensions. However in addition different sports organizations, private companies, tour operators and local government can all utilize the flexibility of the framework to increase their understanding of the sport tourism phenomenon.

Implications of the Framework

Many of the implications discussed in 1997 are unsurprisingly still relevant today. Undoubtedly the primary implication of the Sport Tourism Framework is that it attempts to delineate the sport tourist into four clearly identifiable categories based upon the combination of primary and secondary motives for travel. Consequently the framework may help to better understand the consumer through further research into the individual segments of the sport tourism categories. It also provides a starting point for profiling tourism destinations, plàces, cities, sports, and potentially private companies for sport tourism and tourism sport opportunities. For example, by undertaking a stock-take of what a destination currently offers in the way of sport tourism and comparing it to what is offered elsewhere, managers can either focus their efforts in maintaining and building upon what they already have or to develop particular products and services they may be weak in.

The framework continues to provide a discussion point for the future development of the subject both academically and industrially. From an academic perspective it us hoped that it will help stimulate the sport-tourism nexus debate by illustrating the breadth and diversity of the subject area. Similarly, the framework will aid sport tourism planners and managers in the innumerable opportunities open to them, as well as offering a window into both the motives and possibly the complex expectations of their customers.

Conclusions

The multitude of explanations detailing why people choose to actively or passively participate in sport, together with the many touristic motives for travel illustrates the multi-facetedness of the sport tourist. In sport tourism no single motive can account for the variety of multiple and shared motives prevalent at any one time. It may be over ambitious and indeed obfuscatory to detail the almost innumerable combinations that these primary and secondary motives generate. However, it may be safer to argue that there exists a motivational and indeed experiential synergy which denotes, at a basic level, the beginning of a sport tourist typology. The Sport Tourism Framework aims to illustrate this relationship by categorizing the sport tourist consumer based upon primary and secondary motives, linked to competitiveness, recreation, activity and passivity. Furthermore it also acts as an indicator to those organizations offering sport tourist experiences; outlining what they currently offer against what they might want to develop for the future.

Of course this is only a starting point to building a better understanding of the motives and experiences of the sport tourist. It is still relatively unknown in what ways sport and tourism motives combine and interact and how this might affect consumers' expectations and satisfactions. Nevertheless, the proposed framework aids in our understanding and knowledge of the sport-tourism relationship by outlining four clearly defined and applicable motivational categories. Research now needs to focus more on these categories to examine further the motives of the sport tourist and to assess in more general terms the utility of the framework Sports tourism refers to international trips specifically taken to watch sporting events.

Common examples include international events such as world cups, the Olympics and Formula 1 Grand Prix, regional events (such as the soccer European Champions League), and individual (non-team) participant sports such as tennis, golf and horse racing.

Estimate of Global Market Size

The most popular global sporting events are the soccer FIFA World Cup and the Olympics, followed by the European Football Championships. However other popular sporting events also attract a large number of international visitors. These include the Rugby Union World Cup and Formula 1 Grand Prix.

- The FIFA Football World Cup held in France in 1998 attracted 900,000 international football fans and generated $12.3 billion.
  - It is estimated that the 2000 Olympics in Sydney generated 111,000 additional international arrivals to Australia specifically travelling for sports tourism.
  - Euro 2004 (the European Football Championships) attracted 500,000 sports tourists to Portugal, generating $320 million for the Portuguese economy.
- The Monaco Grand Prix (which alongside the Indy 500 and Le Mans is one of the most famous motor racing fixtures of the year) attracts 200,000 visitors over its four-day duration.
- The 2007 Cricket World Cup staged in the Caribbean was thought to have generated an additional 100,000 visitors who travelled specifically for the tournament.

Whilst the number of sports tourists fluctuates on an annual basis depending on the events taking place (it is greatest during FIFA World Cup and Olympics years), on average an estimated 12 million international trips are made for the main purpose of watching a sporting event.

Potential for Growth

Increased media exposure of sporting events over the last decade has raised the profile of many sports, and although TV coverage is better than at any time in the past, an increasing number of sports fans want to experience live events. The media also has the ability to make national and international icons of sporting stars, thereby generating greater demand, as fans want to see their sporting idols "in the flesh". Sporting events themselves are being made increasingly appealing to attend, with greater levels of comfort, and other events – such as festivals-being created around them (such as horse racing weekends, boating regattas, etc.). Low-cost regional airlines (and more affordable long haul flights), are also driving demand for sporting events as flights become more convenient, more regular, and of course more affordable. Overall, the sports tourism niche market is expected to grow annually at around 6% for the next five years.

Brief Profile of Consumers

Sports tourists are more easily profiled according to the sports they follow. However, in general terms the bulk of the market tends to be young-between 18 and 34 years, and in the C1 and C2 (middle) socio-economic groups. This would also be the typical profile of a sports tourist following soccer matches.

Rugby and cricket followers tend to be slightly older and with greater disposable income. Horse racing has a broad range of followers with no clear demographic structure. Followers of athletics tend to be young, low spenders, whilst those following the Formula 1 Grand Prix circuit tend to be skewed towards males in their 90s with above average disposable income.

Main Source Markets

The main source markets for sports tourism are those that are most interested in the main international sports. These include:

- United Kingdom
- United States
- Germany
- Italy
- Spain
- Scandinavia
- Australia
- South Africa

Main Competing Destinations

The main competing destinations tend to vary depending on where the large events, such as the FIFA World Cup and Olympics are held. However, those holding key annual tournaments of global sporting interest include:

- United States
- United Kingdom
- France
- Australia
- Spain

For specific sports, such as golf, motor racing, or yachting, this list of competing destinations would vary considerably.

Key Tour Operators

There are a large number of sports tour operators. However most of them operate at a very local level, principally serving a specific soccer club for example. However, there are a few that operate as international sports tour operators offering a wide range of sporting events in different countries. It is not uncommon, in particular for the much sought-after events, to find tour operators offering flights and accommodation but without tickets.

An overview of sport tourism: Building towards a dimensional framework

The notion of people travelling to participate and watch sport dates back to the ancient Olympic Games and the practice of stimulating tourism through sport has existed for over a century.

Just recently, however, sport and tourism professionals alike are realizing the significant potential of sport tourism and are aggressively pursuing this market niche. Although the definition of sport tourism may vary based on different people's interpretation of sport and travel, for the purpose of this article sport tourism refers to travel away from home to play sport, watch sport, or to visit a sport attraction including both competitive and non-competitive activities. Sport tourism can be broken down into five main categories: attractions, resorts, cruises, tours, and events. Each of these categories draws from other tourism sectors such as adventure tourism, health tourism, nature tourism, educational tourism, and leisure tourism. This article outlines the benefits and reasons for growth of sport tourism; provides examples of the scope and opportunities within the sport tourism field; and suggests ways to maximize potential by understanding all elements integral to sport tourism.

Sports Tourism Strategy in Australia

Tourism has in recent decades become firmly established as a major Australian industry, providing significant economic and employment benefits. It accounts for 8% of employment, 5.8% of Gross Domestic Product and nearly 15% of export earnings. Forecast growth, especially for inbound tourism, is very strong.

Similarly, the sports sector has a major economic impact, contributing billions of dollars to the economy and employing tens of thousands of Australians. Furthermore, sport occupies a central place within Australian culture and identity, based on a long history of achievement across a wide range of sports.

It is not surprising then that travel for the purpose of participating in some manner of sporting activity is both significant and growing – in Australia and worldwide.

The Key Elements of the Strategy

The aim of the Strategy is to facilitate a viable and internationally competitive sports tourism industry which can maximize its contribution to Australia's economic and social wellbeing, especially in regional Australia.

The draft strategy identifies a number of issues that impact on the development of the sports tourism industry, and discusses developments in these areas and possible actions. The issues include:

- industry coordination
- education and training
- government regulation
- sport and tourism
- infrastructure
- evaluation of the economic benefits of sports tourism
- research and data and
- Strategy implementation.

What is Sports Tourism?

Estimates of the size of the sports tourism sector vary, mainly because there is no single, agreed definition of what constitutes "sports tourism". While definitions of tourism are well accepted and fairly consistent throughout the world, definitions of sports tourism range from narrow ones involving travel solely for participation in competitive sporting activity to broader definitions where the "sporting" activity might be more leisure or adventure activity incidental to the main purpose of travel.

For the purposes of developing a National Sports Tourism Strategy, a relatively narrow definition has been adopted. It is:

- Domestic sports tourism: any sports-related trip of over 40 kms and involving a stay of at least one night away from home; and
- International sports tourism: any trip to Australia a prime purpose of which is to participate in a sporting activity, either as a spectator, participant or official.

The sport or sporting activity under this definition are organised activities – unstructured activities undertaken by individuals have been excluded, as governments' ability to influence such activities is relatively limited. Under such a definition, it appears that sports tourism in Australia might represent about 5% of the overall tourism market, equating to tourism expenditure of about $3 billion per annum.

Tourism and Sport – The World and Australian Markets

Tourism and travel have grown to become not only one of Australia's, but also one of the world's most significant industries. The World Tourism Organization predicts that global international tourism, which in 1999 generated, directly and indirectly, 11% of global GDP, will expand by 4.1 per cent per year over the next two decades. Australian international visitor arrivals are predicted to grow more quickly at around 7 per cent per year through to 2008. Based on these predictions, tourism is destined to continue playing a vital role in Australia's economic and social development.

Accompanying the growth in tourism has been a significant expansion in the worldwide sport and recreation industry. These industries come together in the sports tourism sector, and with the emergence of "niche" markets as a major factor in tourism development, the potential for growth in the sector is considerable.

Apart from economic factors, notably increases in disposable income, there is a range of other factors influencing the future growth. These include: continuing increases in the number of sporting events and accompanying media exposure; increased professionalism in sport and consequent demand for training camps; the growth of mass participation events such as Masters Games; and the growth in "manufactured" events – both made for television and made specifically to help promote tourism to a region.

Opportunities for Australia at the International, National and Regional Levels

The hosting of the Sydney 2000 Olympics also provides Australia with a unique opportunity. Apart from showcasing Australia to the world, both as a tourism destination and as a country with the ability to successfully stage major sporting events, the Olympics will leave a legacy of expertise in a range of sports-tourism related fields as well as a legacy of world-class sporting venues. The challenge for sports tourism development is to take advantage of all the opportunities this presents.

Industry Coordination

Sports tourism opportunities, and especially the tourism

benefits, are sometimes lost or not maximized because the linkages between the sports and tourism sectors are not well established.

Sporting activities, especially events, have historically been organised by sporting organizations for purely sporting purposes. Maximizing the tourism potential of the events has often not been a major consideration for the organizer, representing a potential failure of the market. Further, many sporting organizations rely on volunteers, and may not have well developed business or organizational skills or experience. Both of these factors can lead to lost tourism opportunities.

To overcome this, better linkages need to be established between the sporting and tourism groups at all levels – regional, state/territory and national. Regional "sports tourism clusters" provide a model for building these linkages at the local level. Similar groupings at state and national levels would also be beneficial. While the State and Territory events units are working to improve linkages, there may be a role for the Commonwealth to disseminate information and take on a coordination and facilitation role at the national level.

Education and Training

Education and training is critical to the success of both the sports and tourism sectors. For sports tourism, the issue of education and training is especially important in ensuring that sporting bodies in particular have the requisite business skills both to run successful events and to recognize and take advantage of the tourism opportunities which accompany the hosting of those events.
While training in this area is certainly available, there may be an issue with ensuring such training is appropriate to the needs of the sector and is affordable and accessible.

Regulatory Issues

Government regulation can and does impact on the sports tourism sector– at the local, State/Territory and Commonwealth levels. This can range from the need to obtain permits for road closures etc. at the local level, to visa requirements for international athletes or international visitors generally, involved in a sporting activity. It is important to try to minimize any adverse impacts of such regulation. A basic problem for many organisers is simply trying to deal with what can seem like a maze of different agencies with differing requirements. While some States/Territories have developed information kits to help address this issue, the Commonwealth could also play a major role in assisting organisers to navigate through this maze.

Infrastructure

Most if not all sporting activities and events rely on there being appropriate infrastructure in place. The most obvious form of infrastructure is the sporting facilities themselves, however other infrastructure is often more important if sports tourism opportunities are to be maximized.

Adequate accommodation and transport are often critical to the success of events where large numbers of people may need to be moved and accommodated. This can provide difficulties in regional areas, where accommodation may be in short supply and where transport links, both to and within a region, may be expensive and/or suffer from inadequate capacity.

A starting point in addressing these issues, and one which the Commonwealth and a number of States and Territories have already embarked on, would be to conduct facilities audits to identify just what sporting facilities and at what standard, are available. A further logical step down this track would be to conduct a broader "asset audit" of all relevant infrastructure, to assist organisers in assessing the ability of a region to support a particular sporting activity or event.

Research and Data Collection

Like many niche tourism sectors, the sports tourism sector suffers from a lack of reliable data on which to base strategic decision-making. Even data which might help measure the size of the sector is not readily available. Indeed, there is no agreed definition of just what constitutes "sports tourism", hence any discussion of research and data needs must start with the need to come to some consensus as to just what "sports tourism" comprises. Limited data is available from the major tourism surveys-the International Visitor Survey and the National Visitor Survey. At best, however, the picture they draw is very partial but does indicate that sports tourism is significant in the overall tourism market.

A further issue is that most of the available research tends to focus on individual events and not on improving our overall understanding of the sports tourism market and how it operates at a national or regional level.

Evaluation of Events

There are numerous "models" employed to evaluate events which can lead to different outcomes and a consequent inability to compare results. A more consistent methodology, and in the case of smaller regional events, a simplified methodology, would be of considerable benefit.

The Cooperative Research Centre for Sustainable Tourism, through its events sub-program and its recently established sports tourism "node", may be able to better coordinate activity in this area, and help provide a more "macro level" focus.

Australia can learn from international experience in the sports tourism field. The United Kingdom, through the British Tourist Authority, has developed a sports tourism marketing strategy and has recently appointed a sports tourism coordinator in their Sydney office.

Canada has been pursuing a program of developing sports tourism "clusters" or networks in regional areas, to bring together relevant players, raise awareness and maximize tourism benefits. South Africa also has identified sports tourism as a growth sector.

Implementation

Successful implementation of a national strategy will require a concerted and coordinated effort from a range of organizations, including governments at all levels (Commonwealth, State/ Territory and local), the tourism industry, the sports sector including national and state/territory sporting organizations and researchers.

At the State/Territory level, State departments and events corporations take on much of the responsibility for building these links. At the local level, there may be a greater need for development of networks or clusters focusing on sports tourism development. At the national level, there may also be a need for better coordination. Clearly, sports tourism in Australia has enormous potential. A number of factors, including strong inbound tourism growth, a sporting culture, good sporting and tourism infrastructure, and the catalytic effect of the Sydney 2000 Olympic Games, are combining to make this a key growth area. The challenge is to maximize that growth in a manner that can provide genuine economic and social benefits for Australia and Australians.

This draft Strategy poses a number of questions, with the aim of identifying key measures which would need to be implemented to facilitate growth of the sports tourism industry.

The development of the National Sports Tourism Strategy has its genesis in the National Action Plan for Tourism. The Plan, released in 1998, provides a policy framework for the future growth of the tourism industry in Australia. It identifies the development of a range of niche tourism products as one of the avenues which will promote strong future growth and diversification of the industry, and identifies sports tourism as one of the sectors showing enormous potential for further development.

In November 1999 the Federal Minister for Sport and Tourism, the Hon Jackie Kelly MP, announced the Government's intention to develop a National Sports Tourism Strategy in recognition of the need for a planned and consistent approach to building a larger sustainable base for the sports tourism sector. The development of the Strategy to date has involved extensive consultation with a wide range of stakeholders; desk research; the production of a preliminary discussion paper; and the organization of a series of focus group workshops around Australia.

Why Develop a National Sports Tourism Strategy?

In the past decade tourism has been firmly established as a major industry in Australia, economically, socially and as a job provider for Australians. In 1996-97, tourism directly accounted for 5.8% of expenditure on Gross Domestic Product (GDP). Growth in the tourism industry is forecast to continue well into the next decade, especially for international tourism, with the Tourism Forecasting Council predicting that international visitor arrivals will grow at an average annual rate of 7.3 per cent to 2008 when we will welcome 8.4 million visitors.

In 1999, international tourism to Australia generated export earnings of $17 billion and accounted for 14.9% of Australia's total export earnings. Expenditure derived from domestic tourism was $44.8 billion in 1998-99.

Sport has always been an integral part of Australian life and it is increasingly being recognized that sporting events and activities have the potential to be a major tourism drawcard. Australia has something of a natural advantage in this niche market given our strong international image as a sporting nation. This reputation is largely based on the achievements of our sports men and women and images from international events held here. It also forms part of the Australian "lifestyle", an experience which is consistently rated as a major motivating factor in bringing international visitors to Australia.

The popularity of sports events, which constitute a significant proportion of all events held in Australia, guarantees that they are a major component of tourism agencies' strategies for destination development. For the Australian Tourist Commission (ATC), the promotion of Australia as a destination for a holiday featuring sports activity is a logical development of Australia's strong sporting image and the ATC has incorporated a "sports" theme in its overseas marketing.

Sports tourism, or tourism which is associated with sporting activity, therefore has the potential to develop into a highly significant niche sector which provides Australia with economic and social benefits. The hosting of the Olympic Games in Sydney in 2000 was undeniably a definitive moment for sports tourism in Australia and it brought significant benefits to the Australian tourism sector. While mega-events of this ilk are definitely not the "bread and butter" of sports tourism, the Olympics provided many lessons in organizing, running and capitalizing on the tourism benefits of sporting events.

Strategy to Promote Sport Tourism

The aim of the strategy is to facilitate viable and internationally competitive sports tourism industry and to ensure that the benefits of this niche market are maximized and spread widely throughout Australia. This objective has been identified because of the perception that the tourism benefits which sporting activities and events can provide are not currently being maximized. The strategy identifies opportunities for the development of the sports tourism sector as well as identifying and addressing impediments to the growth of the industry. The key elements of the strategy are a range of possible actions which can help to:

- Improve the coordination and competitiveness of the sports tourism industry ....
- Identify and address education and training issues for the industry ....
- Minimize the impact of regulatory issues (e.g. visas, customs) on the industry ....
- Identify and address the infrastructure requirements of the industry ....
- Identify and address the research and data collection requirements of the industry ....
- Improve the means of evaluation of the economic benefits of sports tourism........
- Coordinate the implementation of the strategy ......

What is Sports Tourism?

Sports tourism is a niche market which can be broadly described as a tourism activity generated by participation in sporting activity. That activity can be a sporting event or competition, a tour of a sporting facility, or a training camp. Participation might involve being a competitor/participant, official, or spectator. The Australian definitions of international and domestic tourism are well understood and accepted and are used as the basis for the definitions of sports tourism adopted for the development of this Strategy. These are:

- Domestic sports tourism: any sports-related trip of over 40 kms and involving a stay of at least one night away from home; and
- International sports tourism: any trip to Australia a prime purpose of which is to participate in a sporting activity, either as a spectator, participant or official.

As to what constitutes a sporting activity in this context some decisions need to be made in relation to activities that could be seen more as recreational (eg fishing, golf, skiing, horseracing) and also to adventure activities (eg sky surfing, para-sailing, rock-climbing, etc.). All of these activities require skill and also offer potential for competition, however they are also frequently pursued by individuals in an unstructured way and maybe entirely incidental to their main reason for travelling. While this may not matter in some respects, structured, organised sports events, tours, camps and so on arguably offer more potential for industry and governments to target with a view to increasing the tourism potential, than do leisure and adventure activities – important though they are in their own right. It is therefore those activities which can be targeted for further development which are included within the ambit of this strategy.

Tourism and Sport-The World Market

Tourism and travel make up one of the world's largest industries. In 1999 the World Travel and Tourism Council (WTTC) also reports that across the global economy, travel and tourism generates, directly and indirectly:

- 11% of GDP;
- 200 million jobs;
- 8% of total employment; and
- 5.5 million new jobs per year until 2010.

World Tourism Organization (WTO) data for 1999 show that 663 million people spent at least one night in a foreign country, up 4.1 per cent over the previous year. Spending on international tourism reached US$453 billion — a growth rate of nearly 3 per cent over 1998. These results are in line with WTO's long-term growth forecast Tourism: 2020 Vision which predicts that the tourism sector will expand by an average of 4.1 per cent a year over the next two decades.

Annual international arrivals are expected to surpass one billion by the year 2010 and reach 1.6 billion by the year 2020. Reasons for this sustained growth include greater disposable income in tourism generating countries, and, especially in some of the emerging economies of Asia, more leisure time, earlier retirement, improvements in infrastructure and transport (particularly air transport), and changes in consumer spending preferences.

Sport and active recreation have become very large and successful industries worldwide. A 1994 European Commission Report on the European Community and Sport estimated that the sports industry is responsible for 2.5 per cent of world trade. The factors influencing the growth of sport and recreation are similar to those influencing tourism growth-notably increased disposable income, greater availability of leisure time and changing consumer preferences. An increased awareness of the benefits for all ages of greater physical activity has also been important.

In addition, the role of the media in promoting sports has been critical. A number of factors have contributed to this greater international media attention on sport and recreation, especially in western economies:

- increased demand for sports programming from television broadcasters to meet consumer demand, the advent of dedicated sports channels (eg. Fox Sports, ESPN, C7 Sports), and the availability of satellite technology allowing live coverage;
- increased prominence of professional sportspersons across a range of sports, e.g. golf, tennis, basketball, baseball, surfing, rugby and soccer;
- large amounts of money being spent by corporations directly and indirectly sponsoring events, teams and individuals for commercial advantage;
- sports associations becoming more like large-scale business enterprises;
- growth of merchandise associated with particular sports, sporting activities and sporting teams;
- significant advertising, promotion, and activity associated with high-profile international sporting events, e.g. the Olympic Games, soccer World Cups, Grand Slam tennis, Formula One Grand Prix, and national sporting competitions;

- increasing opportunities for participation, especially in western economies, through changing leisure patterns, ageing of the population, increased disposable income, and increased awareness of the benefits of physical activity.

Sports Tourism

Having regard to the trends emerging in both the tourism and sports sectors, it is not surprising that significant growth is also occurring in travel for sports related purposes. In fact, this growth is also linked to another trend – that of travelling for specific "niche" purposes, of which sporting activity is one.

The British Tourist Authority and English Tourism Board claim as many as 20 per cent of tourists trips are for the prime purpose of sports participation, whilst up to 50 per cent of holidays include incidental sports participation. This level of activity is broadly consistent with Canadian data, with the 1998 Canadian Travel Survey finding that 37% of domestic trips that year were for sports-related purposes.

In the case of the United States, the Travel Industry Association of America found that in the past five years, 38 per cent of US adults attended an organised sports event, competition or tournament as either a spectator or participant, while on a trip of 50 miles or more. These figures are based on rather broad definitions of the "sport" in sports tourism.

Significantly, perhaps, the sports market, and hence the sports tourism market, is becoming increasingly internationalised. As previously mentioned, the availability of sports-only TV channels which display sports from numerous countries around the world, as well as increasing coverage of an ever-expanding range of sporting events through more mainstream media outlets, means there is an increasing awareness of the range of sporting activities being pursued around the world, including in countries such as Australia.

Tourism and Sport-The Australian Market

Tourism

Tourism has grown to be one of Australia's most significant industries. While a small player in terms of world arrivals, Australia is a major tourism destination in terms of tourism receipts, ranking 12th in the world for 1999. In 1996-97, tourism accounted directly for 5.8% of expenditure on Gross Domestic Product (GDP), and was directly responsible for the employment of over 670 000 persons and indirectly for a further 290 000. This accounts for 11.5% of total Australian employment. In 1998/99, expenditure derived from domestic tourism was $44.8 billion. In 1999, international tourism to Australia generated exports of $17 billion and accounted for 14.9% of Australia's total export earnings.

Tourism is destined to continue playing a vital role in Australia's economic and social development. The Tourism Forecasting Council (TFC) predicts that international visitor arrivals will grow at an annual average rate of 7.3 per cent to 2008 and generate nearly $32 billion in export earnings in 2008. This means international visitor number in excess of 8.4 million in 2008-almost double the current level of tourist visitation to Australia. Much higher levels of growth are predicted from emerging Asian markets including China (21.1 per cent), South Korea (23.7 per cent) and Thailand (18.3 per cent). On the domestic front growth is anticipated to be steady with an average annual growth rate of 1.6 per cent for the period 1998-99 to 2008-09.

Sport

Australia has long been regarded as a sporting nation. Significant interest by the Australian public in sports of one type or another across wide demographic boundaries ensures that the sport industry in Australia assumes a significant economic, social and even political profile.

Involvement in sport and sporting activity not only benefits both the health and general wellbeing of our nation, it also makes a sizeable contribution to the Australian economy. Precise figures are extremely difficult to find – a problem for sports tourism also, and one which is discussed later in this strategy. What is clear is that the sports sector generates many billions of dollars within the economy and provides employment for tens of thousands of people.

Despite its size and significance, many sectors of the industry are not highly commercialized, although some, such as the businesses supplying goods and services which support sporting activities, are very commercially focused. There is a large "not-for-profit" segment of the sports sector, exemplified by the number of volunteers working within it. In 1994/95 there were 112,877 volunteers working in the sports industries which was almost double the formal employment in sports industries at that time. The majority of these volunteers (89 per cent) worked within the sports or in the provision of services to sports, sectors.

Structurally, the sports sector is very decentralised. An important part of the sector is the local sporting club-bodies dedicated to the development of single sports run by and for its members. These clubs often affiliate with regional and state associations which, in turn, unite to form National Sporting Organizations (NSOs). Volunteers administer sport at all levels-particularly the club level. At state and national levels professional administrators begin to play a role, although even here volunteers may still make a significant contribution.

Professional clubs also exist in parallel with this system in the major sports like the football codes, basketball, cricket and baseball. They belong to state or national leagues and are managed predominantly by full-time professional administrators and coaches. Special purpose associations exist to promote particular interests such as sports medicine, coaching, school and university competition, physical education, legal issues and professional development for sports workers. These usually affiliate with an umbrella body which operates at the national level.

Government involvement in sport occurs at each of the three levels of government-local, state and national, through the various departments dealing with sport and recreation, the Australian Sports Commission, the Australian Institute of Sport, and the State Institutes of Sports and Academies. There are also a range of non-government organizations which administer, coordinate and promote particular interests at both state and national levels. Within the government sector, there are a number of vehicles for seeking to discuss and coordinate issues relating to sport industry development. The Sport and Recreation Ministers Council (SRMC) is the peak body for discussion between the Commonwealth and State and Territory Governments for issues concerning sport and recreation needs across Australia. It is supported by the Standing

Committee on Recreation and Sport (SCORS), whose members are senior officials in the sports departments of each State and Territory.

The Commonwealth Government has also given recognition to the many commercial businesses which service Australian participation in sport, through the development of a strategic plan to facilitate the growth of the commercial sports and leisure services sector.

Sports Tourism

Both the tourism industry and the sports industry in Australia come together in the sports tourism sector. Those involved include:

- sport and tourism departments
- major events corporations
- sporting bodies
- facilities managers
- event organisers
- promoters
- tour operators
- accommodation providers
- transport operators
- retailers
- the full range of organizations providing goods and services to both sporting and tourism operators.

However, not all of these groups necessarily perceive themselves as being part of a broader sports tourism industry, resulting in potential lost opportunities associated with the staging of Australia's many and various sporting events.

While it is difficult to establish the size of the industry, some efforts have been made to quantify its value to the Australian economy.

For example, during the focus group process forming part of the development of this draft strategy, a number of participants suggested that the sector accounts for about 5% of the total tourism market, based on the relatively narrow definition proposed in the Strategy. If this is the case across both international and domestic tourism, sports tourism in Australia would account for annual expenditure of about $3 billion per annum.

This estimate is consistent with analysis undertaken by the Bureau of Tourism Research and published in the recent paper Sports Tourism: An Australian Perspective, which found that 6 percent of day trips and 5 per cent of overnight trips taken by Australians in Australia, were taken with sport as the primary motivation. This corresponds to expenditure of $1847 million by domestic sports tourists, of which $461 million was on day trips and the remaining $1386 million was spent on overnight trips.

Australian domestic sports tourists appear to generate a higher dollar yield than other domestic travellers, with 31% staying in hotel, resort, motel or motor inn accommodation on their sports trip compared with 23% for all domestic travellers. Consequently, their estimated average daily expenditure of $130 is higher than the $112 estimated for other domestic travellers.

Opportunities for Australia at The International, National and Regional Levels

Australia has many competitive advantages in the sports tourism marketplace, including a climate conducive to outdoor activities, a diverse range of sporting activities, access to quality sports facilities, well developed tourism infrastructure and an internationally renowned image as a sporting nation and tourism destination.

Even the fact that our seasons are the reverse of those in the major tourism source markets of the Northern Hemisphere provides a range of opportunities in areas such as pre-season training camps. Similarly, our expertise in areas such as sports science and sports medicine, as well as leading edge facilities such as the Australian Institute of Sport, help to encourage international sporting teams and individuals to travel to Australia. These assets form the basis for an internationally competitive tourism product. However they have to be managed in a way that delivers the maximum benefits for the country as a whole. While there are numerous opportunities within the broader sports tourism fields, some sectors and some markets appear to have particular potential for Australia to exploit.

International Opportunities

The Olympics

The sport mega-event is the most widely recognized example of sports tourism. And, with mega-events such as the Olympic Games and the World Cup Football it is not surprising that they involve the largest volumes of spectators and the largest revenues of all special events and festivals. The value of hosting an Olympic Games has been the subject of much research with wide ranging views on the benefits and costs of such an event. A significant increase in tourism is not a guaranteed certainty with many impacts dependent upon the organization and marketing of the Olympic Games. Regardless, the staging of an Olympic Games is recognized as being a unique opportunity for the host city and country to engage in high-profile promotion their tourism products at a worldwide level.

Development of international standard sporting facilities and the upgrading of facilities required for pre-Games training, is both an obvious and tangible legacy. High quality facilities combined with a successful hosting of the Olympics have given Australia a head start in bidding for major sporting events in the years immediately following the Games. It is also in these years that the Tourism Forecasting Council predict Australia will receive a major tourism benefit from the Olympic Games with additional international visitor numbers of 342 000 in 2000, 335 000 in 2001 and 350 000 in 2002. If these numbers are realized, and they may well be, Australia will have received an immediate and major dividend from the hosting of the Games. Many of those additional visitors will no doubt participate in sporting activities while in Australia.

Just as importantly perhaps, the lessons that have been learned by governments, sporting bodies and business will play a major role in the further development of the sports tourism sector. The Olympics will also expose Australia's sporting and tourism assets to vast new audiences and markets, providing significant opportunities in the sports tourism field.

Australia's traditional international "sports tourism" markets have been North America, Europe and New Zealand. Rugby tests in particular, but also rugby league, cricket and to a lesser extent netball, generate significant trans-Tasman traffic flows. More recently, however there appears to be considerable emerging growth potential from upper middle and high income Asian economies, including Japan, Korea and Taiwan. Other emerging markets (e.g. India, Latin America and South Africa) offer similar promise where the distribution of wealth is changing and there is an expanding middle class with an increasing level of disposable income.

National Opportunities

Masters Games

Masters Games provide sports tourism opportunities at the international, national and regional level. They may well prove to be the greatest potential growth area in sports tourism over the next decade. A relatively recent phenomenon, these games have already grown to occupy a central place among sports tourism activities and are keenly fought over and bid for by potential hosts, because of the sheer numbers of participants involved and their demographic profile – i.e. Masters– which generally equates to high levels of disposable income.

At the top of the Masters Games tree – which comprises local, inter-state, national and international events – is the World Masters Games. Recognized as the world's biggest multisport festival, the World Masters Games are considered the premier international event for Masters competitors, allowing them to compete regardless of ability, gender, race or religion. In terms of competition, they are twice as big as the Olympic Games. Held every four years, the World Masters Games are participant focused, with competitors only being required to meet each sports age qualification.

In Australia, the first sanctioned Masters Games were held in 1986 in Alice Springs. The first Australian (i.e. national) Masters Games were held in Tasmania in 1987. Since then the Australian Masters Games have been held in Adelaide (1989), Brisbane (1991), Perth (1993), Melbourne (1995), Canberra (1997) and Adelaide (1999). The eighth Australian Masters Games will be held in Newcastle and the Hunter region in 2001. The overall philosophy of the Australian Masters Games is to provide an incentive for mature age persons to begin, or continue active participation in sport. It aims to provide a focus for individual sports to develop their own mature age sport events and to maintain mature sports as a continuing aspect of their programs and focus. There is a definite aim of the Games to promote community interest and participation in mature age sport and to thereby contribute to the health of its citizens and the nation. The organisers of the 2001 Australian Masters Games in Newcastle have also identified the potential for the Games to have a significant impact on tourism, sport and culture in the Newcastle and Hunter region and to increase both tourism and brand awareness of the area at a domestic and business level.

"Manufactured" Events

Over the past twenty years or so the interest in sport, especially elite sporting events, has grown at a phenomenal rate. Sport is no longer just about playing the game, it is now perceived to have an obligation to provide public entertainment. This growth has been in parallel with advances in technology and the evolution of the digital age. People now expect to be entertained by worldwide sporting events telecast live direct to their television sets-or perhaps on their home computer. According to a survey conducted by the Australian Bureau of Statistics in November 1997, sporting programs were the most commonly watched on television after news and current affairs, and were viewed regularly by over half of all Australians aged over 18 (55%). A relatively recent concept is the "manufacture" of sporting events for television – events such as the "One Summer" sporting festival of beach related sporting events is a case in point of what is almost exclusively a television event. There can be a number of tourism-related benefits, including marketing benefits, from events such as these.

Another variation on the "manufactured" event theme is an event which is designed from the outset to promote tourism, rather than being designed as a purely sporting event with the tourism aspect an added extra. The main emphasis in events of this nature, of which there are still relatively few, is on the promotion of tourism to the region where the event is being held, rather than just on the event itself. An excellent example is the Jacobs Creek Tour Down Under in South Australia, which sees cyclists racing through regional South Australia, receiving national and international media coverage and by careful planning and route selection, promoting the region to potential tourists. One of the major benefits of this type of event is that they can be designed using existing locations, and to suit the capabilities of the region. Examples include cycle races, triathlons, road races, "challenges" such as the Omeo challenge, etc.

Critically, these events can be introduced to even out peaks and troughs in tourism activity, and can be tailored to fit into a regional tourism package of events, attractions and activities.

They can also spread the accommodation load across a region if necessary. Given that the region which created the event then "owns" the event, they can be conducted on an annual basis which in the longer term reduces the costs associated with their staging.

Regional and Local Opportunities

Masters Games and "manufactured" events can have significant impact at the regional and local level, as well as nationally. Indeed, there are numerous market sectors within sports tourism which lend themselves to regional areas and the lower level of facilities and infrastructure which these areas generally possess. A key issue for regional areas is to identify the range and level of resources and infrastructure which they do possess, and to use this information as the basis for identifying and pursuing suitable sports tourism opportunities. Some examples of events which might well lend themselves to hosting by regional or local areas include:

- Schools and underage championships, which can vary in size from quite small to very large (eg Albury has been very active in pursuing this part of the market);
- National or indeed international events in "lesser" sports (eg Corowa has hosted a world parachuting championship recently while Manilla is a world-renowned paragliding centre);
- Regional championships in a variety of sports; and
- Sports which can be held at a number of locations throughout a region.

Marketing Opportunities

Sports tourism events at the international, national and regional levels have a double-barrelled effect – the direct effect of the attendance of the competitors and/or spectators and accompanying persons, and the indirect effect of the marketing of the destination which will lead to subsequent tourism flows. This indirect effect can be very large – most of the tourism benefits of the Olympics are expected to be of this nature. Even for non-mega events, for example events like the Gold Coast Indy Car Race, the Australian Formula 1 and 500cc Motor Cycle Grand Prix and even events such as the Australian Surf Life Saving Championships, this impact can be very significant. There is a marketing effect through the word-of-mouth recommendation of attendees at the event, (such as with Masters competitions) but potentially a much greater effect if the event attracts widespread media interest – especially live television coverage. The marketing spin-offs from sports tourism events can vary enormously depending on a range of factors, including whether the tourism aspects were considered as an integral part of the event and were "built-in" to the development process. For example, the Gold Coast Indy Car race is deliberately designed to showcase Australia's premier beach destination – the Gold Coast – with parts of the track running right beside Surfers Paradise beach. Given Australia's status as a relatively little known tourism destination in world terms, the marketing benefits from events, particularly from mega-events such as the Olympics, may be greater than for countries which are already well known tourist destinations. This presents a genuine opportunity for better showcasing Australia's tourism assets through sporting events.

Industry Coordination

It is clear that major sports events can play a significant role in generating tourism activity on a national and international scale. Such events can have positive economic and social benefits, and have in recent years been increasingly recognized by both national and State governments as a legitimate focus for tourism and general economic development strategies. One manifestation of governments' support of events-based strategies is the provision of funding for events and infrastructure by Commonwealth, State and Territory sport departments, and the creation in most states of dedicated events corporations. As this investment in events increases, Governments are being increasingly required to justify their expenditure in these areas, with the attendant challenge being how to enhance sporting events as tourism products so as to maximize returns on investment.

Developing a Strategic Approach

The Commonwealth government developed Strategic National Plan for the Sport and Leisure Services Industry. The plan articulated a vision for the industry and ways for the industry to become world class in the provision of sport and leisure goods and services. Success in realising this vision required advanced business networks and better relationships between business, governments, sporting organizations and consumers of leisure activities. A similar challenge faces the sports tourism sector. The sports tourism focus group discussions identified the need for the sports tourism sector to identify itself as a discrete industry group and to establish the linkages necessary to capture commercial opportunities.

The current lack of an identity and cohesiveness was identified as one of the major impediments to the growth of the sports tourism sector. In addition, the lack of recognition by both government and the private sector of the economic potential of sports tourism has led to many opportunities being overlooked. Some of the key issues which need to be addressed to encourage and enable the growth of sports tourism include:

> *establishing linkages to enable the raising of awareness of the mutual benefits and advantages of establishing alliances; coordinating planning and the sharing of resources and information; and identifying opportunities and mechanisms for maximizing the tourism benefits of sporting activities.*

Establishing Linkages

The fact that most events are organised by sporting bodies as sporting events first and foremost with tourism almost an optional extra, represents a failure of the market. Sporting bodies arguably have little incentive to pursue the tourism benefits which can flow from sporting activities, especially sporting events, because they themselves cannot directly capture many of those benefits. The great majority of those benefits accrue to other parties – tour operators, accommodation providers, transport operators, retail outlets, restaurants and so on. And yet many of these people may not even perceive that they stand to benefit significantly from tourism activity associated with sporting events.

To some extent, States and Territories have moved to address this by establishing major events corporations, to bring together the sports and tourism players and to bid for events. This works very well for some events – most notably the larger, higher profile events on which the events corporations generally focus.

However, the needs of second-tier or regional events are not necessarily adequately met through this process. At a regional level, governments could play a role in facilitating the establishment of "cluster" groups comprising the full range of stakeholders in the sports tourism process. A useful model could be the cluster formed in Cairns following the focus group conducted there – "Sports Tropical North Queensland". Significantly, the Cairns group is being coordinated by the economic development corporation, reflecting the broad benefit which sports tourism events can provide throughout the regional economy.

Sharing of Resources and Information

At the regional level, clusters or networks can play a number of roles to help coordinate activities, assist in the sharing of physical resources and encourage information sharing. For smaller sporting bodies, the level of resources required (eg. signage, barriers, marquees) may be a deterrent to running events, as can be the lack of knowledge for first time organisers. Simply sharing these resources can assist in the planning and running of successful events, with regionwide benefits for both sporting and tourism groups. At a national level, the Commonwealth could play a role which would largely be one of the provision of nformation, including providing links and referrals to the enormous range of information already available, much of which has been produced by States and Territories, but which is currently not being accessed by event organisers or tourism groups.

Maximising the Tourism Benefits

There are a number of ways to maximize the returns from investment in events. These include:

- improving the yield from existing events;
- staging more events;
- targeting and supporting events that offer the biggest potential returns in terms of tourism;
- spreading the benefits of new and existing events to more regions, rather than just the major metropolitan centres; and
- better coordination of sporting events with other tourism related activities to maximize visitor stay and yield.

Success in each of these areas relies on the establishment of alliances between sport and tourism bodies at all levels-national, state/territory and regional-and greater emphasis on cooperative planning and coordination. This emerged as the top priority in almost every focus group discussion held around Australia. Recent international experience such as that in the UK has illustrated that simply bringing the sport and tourism sectors together is not sufficient to encourage the development of working alliances. It will therefore be important to demonstrate clearly to both the sport and tourism sectors the practical advantages of creating and encouraging alliances. While sporting events continue to be organised purely as sporting events with tourism a secondary consideration, progress towards fully capturing the business opportunities associated with sports tourism will remain difficult. What is required is for events or activities to be seen as sports tourism opportunities and for organisers to give equal weight to the requirement to run a technically and administratively successful sporting event and the opportunity to maximize the visitation and yield by producing an appropriate tourism package.

Possible Commonwealth Facilitation Role

One of the key suggestions arising from the focus group discussions is for the Commonwealth government to play a facilitation role for the development of sports tourism in Australia. In doing so, the Commonwealth government could help address a perceived general lack of coordination between private sector, government, and sport and tourism bodies, and rectify the absence of an effective and appropriate mechanism for the dissemination of information throughout the sports tourism sector. This facilitation role could focus primarily on the provision and dissemination of information, referral to appropriate agencies, and the encouragement of better communication between key sports and tourism players.

Project Facilitation

The Commonwealth government could also play a role in the facilitation of major projects – the so-called mega events – which impact on national interests as well as individual State/Territory interests. A possible model could be the approach adopted for the Olympics, where a coordination unit brought together the many Commonwealth agencies necessary to make the event a success. This role would be undertaken on an "as needs" basis, when events of this magnitude are being considered or planned.

Network Facilitation

More generally, as already mentioned, there is a need to help facilitate the establishment of sports tourism networks or clusters, especially at a regional level, to ensure opportunities are not lost and are indeed maximized. There are existing models in other industries. By way of example, as part of the Furnishing Industry Action Agenda, which aims to improve the competitiveness of the furnishing industry, the Commonwealth Government has recently announced the establishment of a Furnishing Industry Unit within the Department of Industry, Science and Resources. This unit will act as a focal point within the Commonwealth for issues of concern to the sector, and will aim to improve networking and statistical data collection. A similar mechanism could be established for sports tourism and might play a similar role, although broader, to that being undertaken by Soar International in Canada. Soar International is a sports information and event management company contracted by the Canadian Tourism Commission to facilitate the development of sports tourism networks in regional areas.

6

Planning and Activities of Conventional Tourism

Sustainable tourism is an overhearing concept. All forms of tourism can be sustainable – even mass tourism- when it's managed properly! But certain types of tourism tend to be viewed as being more inherently sustainable as others, namely ecotourism, pro-poor tourism, community-based tourism, fair-trade tourism, cultural tourism and rural tourism. The relationship between forms of tourism considered sustainable and those considered unsustainable can be seen in the diagram below.

Non-sustainable Growth of Tourism

Sustainable Tourism Development

Unplanned activities e.g. building a guest house ad hoc, without knowing if it is beneficial; building a slope for downhill skiing – could not be successful, but ecological damage remains; duplicate activities in a region, useless competition and resource squandering.

Development concepts and plans responsible business plans; of tourism development in a region Makes possible a responsible and coordinated use (therefore in decreased amounts) of accessible resources. Central planning and decision-making decisions about regional projects are made in Bratislava; when making plans, regions are not considered, and the like. Decisions made at local level, involving local people and businessmen subsidiary; true public participation in zoning plan preparation; (entrepreneurs and citizens decide what they want and what they don't want in tourism, of course assisted by experts) Unlimited development when planning and implementing tourism-related activities, the tourism interests are considered only, nothing else; Regulated development in time and space restrictions are respected, e.g. acceptable number of visitors in village, nesting time of birds, carrying capacity of a territory, etc.

Intensive use of landscape and resources things get concentrated on a few places; effort is made to get the most out of a client; negative impacts of intensive development are ignored.

Extensive use of landscape and resources effort is made to disperse visitors in the territory; to get out of the client only what is necessary; efforts to regulate impacts are respected.

Understanding tourism as a universal remedy for social and economic problems in a region unprofessional approach that ignores the basic economic and logical aspects of development; cannot depend on one sector – high risk, low capability to withstand threats; low rate of using the potential of landscape and community. Understanding tourism as one of the tools for solving social and economic problems in a region it is necessary to have a wider portfolio of branches, so if one fails or faces problems, the others can keep the economy going; better use of the potential of the landscape and community Focus on economic goals only orientation on financial profit. Harmonisation of economic, social and environmental goals benefits include not only financial profit, but also e.g. good feelings, education, cultural exchange, pleasant atmosphere, clear conscience, pretty and diverse landscape, and the like. Universal support of tourism activities without differentiation no priorities are determined, resources are just scattered with no true result required; difficult-to-measure results, though usually there is no interest to measure them.

Differentiated and targeted support of tourism activities defining priorities–what is important for the region, what has to go first and what can wait; well measurable results, effort to transfer experience in to next phases.

Implementation of individual projects in the region individual interests are promoted, interests and needs of others are not respected; however, this could be "only" a consequence of bad coordination. Coordination of projects in the region effort is made to increase synergy in the region. Construction and development for the purpose of satisfying unlimited demands-"the more visitors the better" method absence of professional analysis (or they are not respected) – they define what is best for the region and where is the focus meaningful. If having a lot of visitors, low income is sufficient and so the quality can be worse; effort to get quick money, not reflecting consequences.

Determining the limits of a territory-"the most proper visitor" method analysis and surveys are prepared and respected; rather to have fewer but better paying visitors – this, however, requires higher standards and quality (long-term process).

New constructions (lodging, recreation centres, various parks, etc.) easier way, but causes more damage to the environment (occupying new areas, influencing biodiversity, etc.); quicker money, easier preparation.

Use of existing objects usually complicated and more expensive; however, the strengths of the region are promoted and used. Copying not local and not typical models and construction technologies in architecture uniformity; global materials, technologies and companies it is an easier way but decreases the quality of experience.

Implementing architectural elements and construction technologies typical for the region difficult way, but increases the quality of experience however, biases exist and results are expectable in midterm horizon. Use of cars intricate problem, difficult to solve; the entire society is based on cars; have a strong negative impact on the environment – exhausts, spatially demanding, safety problems, degradation of tourism, etc. Promoting public and non-engine ways of transportation difficult goal because public transport (PT) is usually less comfortable and low quality; PT – significantly less pollution, considering the number of transported people; non-engine transportation – positive impacts on health, no pollution, more intensive experiences. Seasonal character of demand and/or offer being satisfied with the peak time periods when enough money is made for the year but it is accompanied by a number of social (seasonal employment, crowded centres) and environmental impacts. Permanent demand and/or offer easier on the social and economic environment.

Stereotypic and universal products for everyone degrading the visitor to a „piece"; decreasing the quality of experience, stronger feelings of dissatisfaction, and the like; the visitor is then less sensitive to the landscape and community.

Tailor-made products for small groups atmosphere of friendship and pleasant experiences; good feeling from visiting the region; visitor supports the community and landscape protection.

The visitor's passive acceptance of the environment lying on the beach, going up and down on skis, etc. the visitor is then less sensitive to the landscape and community.

Interactive relation between the visitor and the environment visitor learns more and then understands the need to protect the community and landscape and is supportive of this protection. Favouring cheap but unqualified labour force attempts to have increased profit, even for the price of long-term losses; frequently, this is also a consequence of a bad external situation.

Efforts to employ highly qualified people thinking in long-terms; investing in local people, who live in the place and presumably will stay there for longer.

Use of labour force from outside of the region exploitation of employees and violation of human rights; low quality of work; Use of local labour force this is a responsible approach to the region where profit is acquired; this way, usually, the visitor's experience is better, out flow of financial profit from the region too.

Ecotourism and Sustainable Tourism

There tends to be a lot of confusion in definition between the two terms. In some countries the term ecotourism is used instead of sustainable tourism. Ecotourism, however, should be considered as a concept separate to sustainable tourism. It is, as mentioned above, a type of tourism or tourism sector, which is considered to be inherently more sustainable than other forms.

Definition of ecotourism: "responsible travel to natural areas that conserves the environment and improves the well-being of local people."

Sustainable Tourism in Protected Areas

Protected areas (PAs) are important destinations for a growing tourism segment (nature or ecotourism) which uses intact and diverse nature, landscapes and biodiversity as major attractions. This represents both a potential threat to, and an opportunity for conservation goals. On the one hand, negative environmental and other impacts have to be minimised; on the other hand, nature tourism can provide significant benefits, both for conservation agencies and for local people living in and around PAs. One of the most important challenges that many PA agencies and conservation NGOs face today is satisfying these requirements in a sustainable way.

Tourism in protected areas should be based on the special character of the protected area and includes:

Tourism based on appreciating nature, such as studying, photographing or painting nature or landscapes and activities such as mountain walking, climbing, caving, diving, cross-country skiing, cycling or canoeing, where they are enjoyed primarily to discover nature, rather than as a sport. Cultural and educational tourism aimed at increasing people's understanding of the protected area and its surroundings, for example, school visits, nature camps, visiting natural and cultural sites, learning local crafts. Quiet, small-scale or small group activities which maintain the area's peace and quiet and wild qualities.

Strategic Planning for Regional Tourism Development

Why Strategic Planning?

There are four main reasons why strategic planning is useful for tourism development. These are mentioned in this section.

A region could have great potential for tourism development. It is, however, necessary to consider this potential carefully in order to ascertain how this potential can be used in a way, which will make tourism development good for the region. A good strategy can help to do just that! It helps the people managing such development to create sound conditions for tourism development in the region, it also enables individual stakeholders to recognise their position in the development process and it sets out guidelines for the implementation of tourism activities in a profitable way. Tourism development in a destination is a long-term, systematic process. In contrast the projects of individual stakeholders are almost always of a short-term, rarely midterm, character. It is, therefore, necessary to create a framework, into which the individual projects will fit, thus supporting the long-term character of tourism development. Strategic planning provides this framework. The tourism products of a region are influenced by a number of different factors and consist of a variety of major or minor products and services, which are provided by various stakeholders. If a region intends to create conditions for tourism development there and to sell tourism product harmonising and coordinating these products is necessary. Strategic planning can assist and organise this process.

Having a good strategy is also helpful when applying for financial support from banks, funds, etc.

Basic Requirements

If a tourism development strategy (or any local/regional strategy) is to be successful and effective, it must be created through a process of cooperation between all stakeholders and adopted by them in a form which is convenient. The final document should be an outcome of intensive discussions and negotiations amongst stakeholders. General agreement must be achieved in visions and goals, as well as in actual measures towards meeting them.

When creating a tourism development strategy it must be clear in advance that the stakeholders actually want it and that they will respect it and therefore stay true to it's contents. It can only be viable as a document when it is supported and required or at least confirmed by the people, who will use it, i.e. by the stakeholders. In addition, it should not be initiated when the main aim behind it is to make money from various sources.

Even if a strategy is officially adopted, e.g. by local parliament or a tourism association, it remains an informal and voluntary tool. A strategy should achieve its goals through the voluntary commitment of all the stakeholders. A strategy is flexible and open. Neither the process of preparing a strategy nor the final document should be fully defined in advance. Only the basic framework is predetermined. The strategy and action plans which are derived from it, should be realistic and achievable and should not focus on activities and goals which maybe tremendous but which are unrealistic. A well designed sequence of small, realistic steps can lead to the completion of larger goals, which may have previously seemed improbable.

Tourism development strategies should determine and coordinate the steps to be taken for each industry sector in a region, not just one (e.g. public administration or hotel service).

Essential Parts of a Strategy

A strategy usually consists of five basic parts:

1. Diagnosis of the present state and a problem analysis
2. Defining the vision and goals of tourism development
3. Identification of strategies
4. Programmes and projects put into action
5. Monitoring and feedback

Diagnosis of the Present State and Problem Analysis

The diagnosis of the present state of an area, is a description of the existing situation in the field of tourism. It clearly defines a common basis for determining goals, programmes and for joint decision-making and can include:

Analysis of the present situation in the region: natural features (landscape, interesting fauna and flora, rich biodiversity, geological formations, water, protected areas, etc.); cultural features (historical monuments, typical architecture, traditions, customs, music, gastronomy, events, etc.); tourism infrastructure (lodging, eating, attractions, services, etc.); other basic data (distances from cities, airports, bus/train stations; means of transportation to and within the region, density of shopping network, health care, banks, police, various services, etc.,); marketing data (existing market segments; visitors' interests, needs and motivations; modes of marketing; modes and channels of promotion, etc.); legislative environment (national and regional tourism concepts and plans, small business legislation, zoning plans, nature conservation and historical monuments protection, etc.).

Analysis of the external environment: identifies relevant threats and opportunities that need to be faced or used in the tourism development (e.g. trends, political situation, expected legislation, demographic development, etc.). The present situation can be defined and the problems analysed through a number of steps, which include: an inventory of the above mentioned elements; SWOT analysis; benchmarking – the comparison of selected regional parameters with those from another region, which is considered to be at a further point of development; creating scenarios – estimation of possible scenarios for various versions of development. Usually the best and worst scenario are thought out and then compared. The result of this process is the initial identification of aspects which are especially important for tourism development.

Defining the Vision and Goals of Tourism Development

A vision is developed with the aim to answer the following questions: "Where are we going?" and "What do we want to achieve?". The vision justifies the tourism development and defines the development goals, from the perspective of regional and social development. The vision and goals need to be defined through a creative process, where bold, even utopian ideas should explored.

Identification of Strategies

After defining the vision and goals, the basic and strategically important areas of long- term tourism development should be defined. The main direction of the goal-achieving process also needs to be determined. Factors which need to be specified are: what needs to be developed, what given features of the region will be used, what procedures will be pursued, and who will be the main actors.

Depending on the perspective, a number of strategies can be identified. These can be divided into two basic groups:

a) Sectoral strategies, e.g.: *diversification strategy* – if it is apparent that the existing products/market segments are not sufficient this strategy looks at what new products will be introduced into the market and what market segments addressed; *human resources development strategy*

– identification of professions that need to be developed and determining the focus and extent of this development; *marketing strategy* – detailed identification of market segments (target groups) and the selection of a way of marketing, which will attract these segments to the region;

b) Cross-sectional strategies (all sectors are regarded), e.g.: *win-win strategy* – conflicts that have hindered tourism development need to be solved. This helps to satisfy any doubts that stakeholders or the local population may have about the development and also means that the conflicts no longer block further development; *sustainable development strategy* – defines the principles of a sustainable tourism development.

Operation Programmes and Projects

The strategies identified above should then, in so called *operation programmes* or *action plans*, be converted into the steps that are required for achieving the development goals. *Operation programmes* define, among others, (a) the measures which lead to the goals being met, (b) the organisation and finances required, (c) the time schedule, etc.

The operation programmes are usually sectoral, i.e. deal with measures and actions to be taken within one sector. In the case of tourism development in a region, they can include: creation/ improvement of conditions for business in tourism; protection of nature, landscape and the environment; development of human resources in tourism; building infrastructure for tourism; transportation; ensuring clean and safe public areas; marketing and promotion, etc.

Operation programmes, or the measures defined within them, form the basis for decisions about individual projects. Projects are comprehensive groups of short-term activities with real goals. A project should deal with real problems and it's activities and outcomes should be described thoroughly in the operation programme. A number of projects can be included in one operation programme; they can be implemented parallel to or after one another. All projects have a manager and follow a clear project cycle (preparation – implementation – evaluation– feedback).

It is appropriate to create projects and ideas that are related not only to project activities but also to the manner of project management, financing, communication, etc. The following components need to be clearly defined when carrying out projects (in the operation programme or project supply): project justification (i.e. what measures of the operation programme are implemented and what goals of the strategy are intended to be achieved by the given project); project description (localisation, goals and description of activities); description of project outcomes; principles of project financing (indicative budget, financial management, follow-up costs and the way of handling them etc.); people/ institutions responsible for project implementation; description of the project management; plan of activities and project milestones.

Operation programmes should be consistent, mutually interlinked and the following aspects should apply to them: they should consist of short-term but complex measures focused on tourism development in the region; these measures should be prioritised, i.e. it should be determined what is more important and what less; programmes focused on operation and maintenance should be perceived as being supportive of development and innovation but not as an individual goal of the strategy; operation programmes should follow an integrated approach, i.e. effort should be made to link those measures from various sectoral operation programmes, which are (a) common/shared, (b) have the same manager, or (c) are possible to finance from the same resource; similarly, individual projects, will be integrated into a "central project". If the individual projects share some of the project activities; these can be interlinked and will also influence one another; projects should have a multiplicative effect, i.e. several new activities should arise from one project. They should, however, not be dependent on the original project; programmes and projects should be innovative, i.e. they should look for and encourage new views and solutions. An innovative element is usually tested on one project and if it is successful, it is included in other projects as well.

Innovations can be implemented in products, methods and approaches. Creativity is an essential part of innovations; particular measures and projects should be as concrete as possible. They should provide deadlines and define the people/institutions responsible for carrying out the measures etc.

Adaptive Management and Monitoring

Tourism development strategies, like any other strategy or development plan, are accompanied by a certain amount of risk and uncertainty. This can be increased when innovations and creative thinking are implemented into the strategy and also in the strategy's preparation process. This is, however, perfectly natural. Nothing can be planned perfectly in advance. When implementing a strategy, unexpected development should be taken into account and if necessary, changes to the strategy and its operation programmes should be made. Quick reactions to inappropriate or unexpected development is the basis of adaptive management. To achieve this, it is important to take into account the fact that the feedback mechanism is an important part of the process, e.g. feedback from the strategy and its stages, operation programmes and their stages, and the fact that all projects should be evaluated. In addition, the acquired knowledge has to be included in the updated version of the strategy/operation plan, used in the next stage or project. When monitoring the implementation of a strategy, it is necessary to determine what should be monitored, how aspects of the projects should be measured, what the results of the measurement will be used for, who is responsible for what, etc.

Regarding feedback: in the process of a strategy preparation, it is important to remember that updates will be elaborated (e.g. in regular intervals or after achieving a goal). It is; therefore, important to develop a mechanism of evaluation and to incorporate the results of this evaluation in the actualised version of a strategy.

Basic Principles of Developing and Implementing a Strategy

The process of strategy preparation is as equally as important as the strategy itself. During the strategy's preparation, it is already decided whether the given strategy will be a formal, unused document or whether it is will be an actual framework for tourism development in the region. The following two areas need to be considered:

Ownership of Strategy

A tourism development strategy can be only be successful if it is widely accepted by the public in a given region. It should be understood and accepted not only by the authors but also by stakeholders (e.g. entrepreneurs, local parliaments, state institutions in the region, etc.) and primarily by the local population. The reason or group of people behind the strategy preparation process is important in determining the future use of the strategy. This reason or group of people can be one of the following:

a) Bottom-up – the demand for the strategy development, its principles and content (to some extent) comes from the local population or from a group of public professionals, who do not have the right to make decisions (usually businessmen in tourism). This approach is ideal because it creates "ownership feelings" towards the strategy among quite a large number of people. These people then not only accept and implement the measures defined in the strategy more willingly, but also demand that the local authorities do the same. At the same time, this approach is the most difficult, because it requires extensive communication with the public interesting.

b) Top-down – the demand for a strategy comes from local authorities (self- administration or state). The local people are then convinced (or forced) to accept the strategy and the measures derived from it. Although this is the approach, which is used most frequently, it is actually the one, which is the most ineffective because people tend not to trust the authorities and their decisions. When deciding on, whether or not they should accept a strategy, people often look at who is behind the strategy (Popular or unpopular politician? Did I vote for him or not?

What political party is he/she a member of?, etc.) before making their decision, rather than at its content. In addition, the wishes and interests of the public are not incorporated into the process or they are taken into consideration but in a formal and ineffective way, which does not have any significant influence on the final strategy.

c) Middle-out – the demand for a strategy comes from local experts, research institutions or organisations on the middle management level (ones that do not have the rights to make decision but which have the executive capacity and expert knowledge to carry out the strategy). This approach depends strongly on the capability of local experts to take the public interest into consideration and their ability to assert themselves among the local people and on decision-making levels. This approach can be either successful or unsuccessful, depending on the way it is executed.

d) A combination of the above mentioned approaches – this is the least system- atic approach but the one which still occurs quite often. It should, however, be avoided because it creates an intricate set of unclear relations. It is unclear who is responsible for what, who is the author and "owner" of which part of the strategy etc. In addition, those who are to accept and implement the strategy may not know what their tasks are.

Participants in the Strategy Development Process

A successful strategy incorporates the entire community, e.g. the local people, relevant social groups, decision making structures, professional and executive institutions it its preparation and should not be the result of the work of just a small group of people (or even by just a few authors). Generally at least one representative for each interest group should be involved in the process. To suget the best possible results from this approach the following issues should be dealt with:

Who will be responsible for the preparation, implementation and evaluation of the strategy? This is something which needs to be clear to everybody involved and accepted by a large (as large as possible) number of stakeholders.

Who will participate (what people and what institutions) in the strategy preparation? Here, two viewpoints need to be distinguished: the involvement of various types of "action-takers", e.g. leaders, innovators and creative people, "hard-workers", pedants, "decision-makers", etc. so that the result is as harmonic as possible; involvement of representatives for all stakeholders groups and groups of local people (parliament members, entrepreneurs, officers, etc.) in the preparation process as well as the final stages of the strategy implementation. The adoption of the strategy by the public will be less problematic with this approach. At what stages, to what extent and in what activities should the particular stakeholders, or local people, participate?

How (in what form) should the individual stakeholders be involved in the strategy preparation and adoption?

How can a consensus, compromise and generally accepted decisions be achieved? How will the suggestions, ideas, interests and needs of stakeholder be collected?

Though the participation of the local population and the stakeholders is an inevitable prerequisite of a good strategy, equally important is the effective participation of experts – both local experts and those from outside of the region. Tourism, like other industry branches, has its rules, verified procedures and methods. It is essential that the strategy is a methodically correct document – otherwise it will not meet the expected goals. This is why experts should be invited to take part in the procedure and assigned responsibilities. Strategic planning cannot be done without them.

Creating a Vision

What is a Vision?

A vision describes a state in the future, towards which development should be directed. A vision does not provide detailed goals, it is not a state that is truly intended to be achieved but is more the direction that people intend to follow, a description of an ideal state that people dream of. Creating a vision means asking "Where do we want to go?".Developing a vision is a creative process, which allows daring and utopian ideas. Visions can sometimes be quiet easy to achieve and sometimes it might be impossible. Whether the vision is achievable must be clear to the managers, stakeholders and the local inhabitants of the planning process.

What is Visioning?

Visioning (vision building) is a managed process used by a

group of people (community, group of businessmen, local government, company, etc.) to create and build a the vision itself. It is used for participative approaches in a long-term policy agenda setting, using the imagination of the stakeholders as a source of ideas. It allows the participation of a wide public in the development of long-ranged regional plans. It is a democratic way to obtain disparate opinions from every stakeholder and to look for common ground among participants for exploring and advocating strategies for the future.

Visioning determines the direction people want to go in with development activities. It also defines goals, whilst respecting the opinions, needs and wishes of all the participants of the visioning process. This is a strong prerequisite if the goals of the development are to be defined properly and also for designing a good strategy to achieve those goals. Visioning brings the different tourism scenarios, issues, problems, different points of view and competing demands to the forefront. The collected scenarios serve as a basis for generating the end vision. The end vision is based on the opinions, ideas and the diverse perspectives of many people and can therefore be considered a democratically-derived consensus.

Vision building connects stakeholders, refines the environment where the development will take place, creates necessary networks and makes discussions possible. In addition, a vision leads towards the adoption of common goals, programmes and projects.

How to Create a Vision?

Creating a vision with a range of stakeholders or the general public is done through surveys, meetings and voting. There are, however, many different approaches to the process of visioning and towards the adoption of a common vision. Some of these are mentioned below: The creation of a vision in a single or in several stakeholder meetings, informing the public about it afterwards and then discussing the results with stakeholders and the general public which should finally lead to the adoption of one of the visions.

The conduction of a public survey to find out the publics issues with, concerns about and ideas for tourism development and biodiversity conservation. From the results different options for the vision should be developed and discussed. The stakeholders and general public should then vote for one of the options. The conduction of a public survey to find out the issues with, concerns about and ideas for tourism development and biodiversity conservation. Discuss the results in stakeholder meeting(s) and create a vision based on the discussions.

Surveys and discussion not only lead to the adoption of a common vision, but should also identify priorities and major concerns, which need to be integrated into the tourism management plan. They can also provide ideas for goals, which will be derived from the vision and for their implementation. These ideas can then be used in the next steps of the planning process.

It is important to recognize that visioning will require time, staff and will need to be well prepared (for further information on methods of visioning see the literature list at the end of the guide).

Methods

There is a number of methods that can be used to create a generally acceptable vision, most of them being based on, what is called, guided imagination. When implementing this approach, the participants should firstly imagine the ideal state of the place where the tourism is to be develop, secondly, they should try to describe it and write some notes on their ideas and finally they should create a vision. The method of guided imagination for visioning is described in detail in the interactive part for this topic.

Tourism Associations

Tourism Associations as Leader of Marketing

In the tourism sector, the effort of only one producer or hotel manager is usually not sufficient to promote the sustainable tourism products of a region. Cooperation, coordination and joint action are, therefore, important issues for tourism promotion and marketing in a region. Mutual organization, e.g. a tourism association, is generally considered appropriate for the marketing of one or several tourism products or of a tourism region as a whole. A tourism association can be established by local or regional administration or by a cooperation of tourism providers, e.g. hotels, restaurants, guides, tour operators, agencies etc. The association can focus on the promotion of the whole region as a tourism destination, thus fostering the long term success of many providers instead of concentrating on the individual short term revenues of only one. In countries where the tourism service is highly developed, e.g. in Austria or Switzerland, tourism associations have been effectively functioning for more than 100 years. They were established by local stakeholders and their aim is to develop tourism in their region. Membership in these associations is frequently obligatory for tourism businesses. In Tirol, Austria for example it is a legal requirement.

The goal of this seminar is to examine various forms of tourism organisations and to explain particularly the role and advantages of tourism associations.

Functioning of an Association

Essential features of tourism associations an open structure with content and responsibilities, which are clearly defined; efficiency and expertise; acceptability by decision-making bodies and sufficient competence; enough personal, financial and methodical resources; management and coordination skills.

Membership

Possible members of an tourism association are:

> *Individual tourism providers and providers of additional services. Communal government: Its membership has a specific character but it is very important if an association wants to be successful because it improves the coordination of activities and contributes to the image building of the destination. Communal governments often support associations financially but their votes, however, do not have extra weighting in decision-making processes. Non-governmental organizations, citizens' initiatives, local museums, galleries, civic associations and cultural institutions*

Financing

There are different ways to finance the association: Each member of the association pays a membership fee that is either a lump sum or is calculated according to selected criteria. Enrolment fees are single payments paid when a member registers. The generation of individual income for the association, e.g. income from TIC (tourist information centre) operation, from providing information about accommodation, selling souvenirs, organising events, etc. External sources such as visitors' taxes and fees are also a source of income for associations. This is typical for Austria, Germany and Switzerland. State and EU funds can provide support for non-profit organizations, structural funds, etc. Gifts from large businesses and corporations, from dedicated individuals, etc. Sponsorship from other businesses.

Internal Structure

The associations usually have a different legal structure. Most of them are civic associations or associations of legal entities. Their structure usually includes the following:

General assembly of members – elects members of the association's bodies, votes on principal decisions and plans; Board of trustees – is in charge of supervision and control of the association's financial management; Executive body – takes care of the day to day functioning of the association and organises its programme; Board of directors – makes decisions on and manages the work of the executive body.

Preparation committee – has a specific task, which is to specify the image of the association-to-be, prepare data and a proposal of initial documents and open a public discussion about the association, its function and goals. In addition, it should define the associations tasks (issues that the association will focus on) and place them in a realistic time frame and also prepare the founding meeting of the association.

Goals and Tasks of an Association

Tourism product development and coordination of regional tourism development

Tourism associations help to develop the region's tourism products through a continual process that involves as many stakeholders as possible. As a result the services are continually being improved and extended and the ability of the region to compete with other tourist destinations is maintained. In principle, the development of tourism products is the task of a tour operator. If, however, the association helps the individual tourism providers with this work, individual tourism providers can then focus on other things. To foster tourism development, tourism associations can organise events that are attractive for visitors, i.e. cultural, social or sport events, which are part of a region's tourism product.

Tourism associations also have an important role in marketing tourism destinations as well as activities that are focused on improving the product and services provided, such as training those working in the tourism sector.

Visions and Concepts of Regional Development

All stakeholders should get engaged in influencing or even creating a tourism development policy (as well as regional development in general). This is not the exclusive task of local governments or local state administration authorities. Members of tourism associations should be actively involved in defining the development objectives of a town or region, while the association itself can be used as a platform for communication. In addition, the association can manage this communication and take part in the preparation and implementation of particular strategic steps of regional development – it links people and interests of tourism stakeholders. An association, which functions well and which is representative also has the power to influence communication with the state administration authorities as well as with the local government. It is therefore able to bring its own particular interests (e.g. adjusting the open-hours in museums or in the process of developing a zoning plan) to the forefront and to promote them. The association puts effort into promoting tourism in the town/ region and works towards helping stakeholders make their voices heard at decision-making levels.

Acquiring Public Support

Successful tourism development is only possible if the local public has a positive attitude towards tourism. The association should therefore communicate its work, objectives and plans to local citizens (top-down). At the same time, it creates a platform for a bottom-up communication approach at regional or national levels where the interests of the association's members are promoted. Communication between the association and citizens can be carried out in a number of forms. These can include media activities, various events, publications, training courses (study trips, seminars), round table, discussions, exhibitions, etc.

Operational Function

The association carries out practical activities that benefit a great variety of tourism stakeholders. These are often non-profit activities.

Business Advisory Service

Tourism associations provide or help to search for experts and consultants in various fields.

Marketing

Tourism associations carry out surveys and analyse the level of visitor satisfaction, produce and distribute promotional materials, prepare workshops and presentations for potential partners, invite journalists to the region, who can write about the given destination and its attractions. Tourism associations coordinate the cooperation of tourism stakeholders and public administration, e.g. the public administration makes sure that the infrastructure for the development of the region is sufficient, while the association is responsible for promoting the destination and its product among the competing tourist sites.

Moderation of conflicts

The association can also serve as an independent non-biased institution, which deals with visitor complaints or problems or handles conflicts between two stakeholders.

Typical Problems for Tourism Associations in Central and Eastern Europe

Even today there are not many tourism associations in central and eastern Europe that function well. The main reasons for this include:

Psychological barriers: in the past, especially in states in Eastern Europe, the organization of public life was enforced by state authorities and because of this people usually distrust collective institutions. Lack of appropriate legislation: There are no rules and regulations that would (a) guarantee financial resources to associations and (b) assign them certain rights in tourism development in the region.

Lack of Financial Resources

Absence of a clear and concrete programme: Many tourism destinations have not prepared good regional development plans. These plans would indicate the need of tourism development plans and „justify" the foundation and existence of a tourism association.

Lack of professional staff: The activity of an association must be managed by experienced professionals. Associations, however, usually do not have the money to pay such professionals for their work.

Unreasonable expectations: Inadequate expectations of the way associations' work are induced and cultivated among its members. This often occurs when the association is founded. Lack of motivation: Individual tourism providers have no motivation to be- come members of a tourism association, they are not able to see the potential of such an association.

Certification in Tourism

What is Certification?

Certification is the implementation and fulfilment of certain criteria or requirements given by the particular certification scheme within a facility, service, product or other entity. The facility etc. receives a certificate or a logo when the schemes requirements or criteria have been fulfilled. The logo may then be displayed by the facility and serves as confirmation to clients that the facility etc. meets the requirements and respects the goals of the certification scheme whose logo it displays. This logo is generally used for marketing reasons. It shows that the facility or product has fulfilled certain criteria and this can be used to attract more customers.

It is a voluntary procedure that, through assessment, monitoring as well as written assurance, shows that a business, product, service, facility etc. meets specific criteria and therefore a particular standard.

Certification programmes in sustainable tourism are also often known as eco-labels. Certification is important because it introduces standards into tourism. This is useful for facilities etc. and for customers. Labels are clear benchmarks for products etc. that are of acceptable standards or that are particularly sustainable. Unfortunately not many people are aware of certification schemes and what they entail or mean.

Reasons for Certification in Sustainable Tourism

Certification can be a good tool for the individual/ company implementing the scheme because it can be used to reach the goals that they are trying to realize. If a tour operator is trying to become more sustainable then a certification scheme can give them the incentive and direction to become more sustainable. It provides smaller steps, which they can apply so that they eventually get to their larger goal.

As mentioned above certification is a good marketing tool for a facility/product or business. Certificates tend to be focused on and therefore attract specific target groups e.g. environmentally friendly/ sustainable tourists, people who by organic produce etc. If a facility is certified for something, e.g. a hotel wants to be certified as being environmentally friendly, the certificate/logo not only informs the target group automatically that the hotel has certain environmental standards but it also increases the attractiveness of the hotel for the target group.

Certification is also useful for customers who use the labels for product/facility orientation. A facility or other entity, which is certified generally shows some kind of good quality and gains the facility credibility in the eyes of the customer.

A certification scheme also shows that the individual, company or facility which is certified, obviously believes in/respects/supports the topic/issue of certification and that their interest is not just in better marketing.

The Basic Characteristics of Certification Schemes

* They are voluntary.
* They exceed the standards which are required by law.
* They usually cost money.

* They allow the facility etc. to use a logo, which makes the facility stand out from its competition.
* They award a logo/ brand to the entity.

This logo is however only allowed to be displayed when the entity obtains the certification, in other words, if they fulfil the criteria set by the scheme. These criteria reflect the goals of and issues behind the scheme.

The rules of the certification scheme are generally clearly stated. They define the criteria, mode of application of the certificate, the way it will be evaluated and how the certificate will be presented, how monitoring and control of the scheme takes place as well as the time limit for its application and regional specificities.

Certification schemes include a formalised evaluation process. This process includes self evaluation, external verification, spot checks, evaluation through customers and checks at regular intervals.

The certification scheme should be well marketed. This is necessary if the scheme is to be successful. Without good marketing the certification scheme itself and the benefits it should bring to the facilities implementing the scheme will most likely fail.

Orientation of Certification Schemes

Process-orientated

Goal: continuous improvement, without fixed figures. Certification schemes which focus on process are especially created for facilities or products which are interested for example in becoming more sustainable but want to achieve this by continuously striving to reduce the impacts they have on the environment without actually trying to reach a certain target. For example a hotel may get a certificate of this type may meet the goals defined by the certification scheme (these are usually more general than the criteria) but not individual criteria. An example of a goal might be for example under the heading rubbish: attempting to increase the amount of recycling and reuse of resources in a firm. Whereas criteria for rubbish could be: to use recycled toilet paper.

Almost any facility can achieve this type of certification, which reduces the marketing value of the certification.

Performance-orientated

Goal: Achievement of clearly defined criteria.

These types of certification scheme certify facilities etc. which do want to reach a certain target through the fulfilment of criteria. In sustainable tourism certification schemes based on fulfilment this means that just meeting the goals of the scheme is not enough. The individual criteria must be met if certification is to be obtained. This means that the facility has to make a lot more effort where its levels of sustainability are concerned. It has to take all the criteria into account and change its approach accordingly.

This certification is more difficult to obtain but has therefore a stronger marketing effect. On the other hand the fact that it is so difficult to obtain means that fewer facilities want to make the effort to become certified.

Types of Certification

Affiliation with a trademark (franchising) the facility fulfils the criteria/goals of a certification scheme, which means that they can benefit from a given affiliation. These benefits may include being able to use the companies logo, marketing strategy, products etc.

Increase in comfort specific target groups criteria that need to be met involve improving the quality and comfort of a facility for particular target groups so that it is more attractive for them.

Quality the facility attempts to increase the quality of their service for clients or to fulfil set international standards. This is generally involves improvements in the area of management but also other areas.

EMAS, ISO-Standardization Systems

Sustainability the facility attempts to reduce their impacts on the natural and cultural environment.

Regional identity the facility attempts to fulfil criteria which state to what point the facility fits into a certain region. The facility should generally sell regional products, cook regional specialities, promote regional tradition and culture etc. These certificates can also be applied to and are often orientated towards a number of different entities. These may include improving the (environmental) management of a facility, improving the sustainability and quality of (tourism) products e.g. beaches, bathing areas (blue flag), accommodation, tour operators etc., certifying food which has been produced organically etc. Certification schemes may actually strive to improve more than just one of the above mentioned areas and also more than one of the above mentioned entities.

The Development Process

Initial steps:

* Declarations, codes of conduct, contest/awards

Implementation:

- Public seed funds
- consultations and networking
- advising and training measures
- "soft" criteria and self evaluation
- marketing
- stricter criteria and control measures
- financial sustainability

Introduction to Marketing in Tourism

Why Marketing in Sustainable Tourism?

The lack of marketing expertise and knowledge of the tourism's industry distribution channels is the main reason why entrepreneurs in sustainable tourism fail. They often assume that because they have an authentic and exciting tourism product, tourists will be interested, failing to understand the nature of the tourism industry as a marketplace. Many donors and policy makers also underestimate the challenge and the costs of distributing the tourism product and do not recognize marketing as a key to economic success, which, in the case of sustainable tourism development, is a part of the sustainability of tourism development. The aim of this seminar is therefore to clarify and emphasise the fact that marketing is an essential part of sustainable tourism development and that its basic principles should be understood if economic failure, disappointment and discouragement of the ones engaged in sustainable development is to be avoided.

What is Marketing?

Once sustainable tourism development begins, stakeholders of the region design tourism products, create management plans to monitor and prevent unwanted negative impacts and take measures to make the best use of tourism benefits. At this point, just "waiting for the visitor" won't do. Tourists will only purchase the product if they find out information about the product, the product meets their needs and interests, they are able to buy it.

Marketing involves these issues: To have a product which is of interest for a potential visitor, to find out about the customer who might buy it, to make sure that the potential customer is informed about the product, to bring the product to the market, so that the customer is able to buy it, and to keep in contact with the customer and the public to ensure further purchase of the product. Market analysis, product development, distribution and advertising, or more general, promotion are all parts of marketing.

The Key Stages of Marketing

There are many different ways to structure marketing. The stages of marketing management may be different according to the product, the markets and goals of a business. The stages of marketing presented here simply give an overview of the different issues and strategies which should be considered in tourism marketing. For this purpose, marketing here is divided into four stages: analysis, goals and strategies, marketing mix and implementation and control.

Analysis

The first step of marketing is to gain profound knowledge about the potential or given tourism products which one has to sell, about the environment in which the business is developed and about the market, that is, potential customers and existing or future competitors.

According to product development there are two approaches: either to develop the tourism product first and then determine the appropriate market segments where the product may be purchased, or to have a look at the potential customers first: to find out what their interest and needs are, what their budget for a holiday is, what their expectations about quality are, etc., and then develop a product which meets these interests and needs.

Sustainable tourism product development tends to follow the first approach, because it is based on the use of the given environment (natural and cultural resources) and aims not to change the region's lifestyle, characteristics and original features but to provide tourism which the tourist will enjoy. But ignoring the point of view of the visitor may lead to unsatisfying outcomes. The key to a successful tourism product development is a combination of the two approaches, balancing what it is possible to offer with the wishes and needs of the tourists.

Goals and Strategies

This stage is about the creation and operationalisation of an overall marketing strategy. The segmenting strategy aims to select market segments: to which type of tourist should the products be offered? make decisions about targeting: will the product be offered to one or more market segments, to local, regional, national or international markets? Will there be new products introduced or will a diversification of products take place? Is the aim to penetrate the existing market or to develop a new market?

The competition strategy decides whether the differences between the own product and other products (here: other providers or other regions) should be pointed out, or whether a 'Me-too-Strategy' should be followed, which means taking advantage of an already existing strong market leader, or whether a Cooperation Strategy should be established with other competitors. This option of particular interest for tourism associations and non-commercial stakeholders in the tourism sector. The customer strategy concentrates on the identification of the right target groups for the product and involves finding out about new, additional target groups, e.g. special interest groups.

The outcomes of this strategy may lead to a change in the developed tourism product or to a diversification of products to meet the needs and wishes of the identified potential customers.

The positioning strategy decides on the main focus of the marketing: quality or price. Combination of strategies Normally, the strategies presented don't exclude one another. A mix of the different strategies will generally take place. There may be different strategies for different business segments.

Marketing Mix or Tactical Marketing: Promotion and Distribution

To implement the marketing strategies, the optimal combination of marketing methods must be selected according to the developed goals and considering the given environment. There are different instruments, often summarized as the four P's: product (or services), price, place (distribution policy) and promotion (communication policy).

Product policy: The product policy concentrates on the adequate product design for the selected market segment. It may consist of combining various product elements (tourism product chain) to achieve the right tourism package or of the design of a single product. The distinction between competing products is part of the product policy. It decides whether to continue with what is already on offer or to change the products on offer (elimination, variation or innovation). In the tourism sector, product policy often concentrates on the improvement of services (e.g. for hotels), or, in the case of tour operators, the selection of agencies and staff, the quality of consultation and the creation of additional services (guide books, information meetings, etc.).

Price policy: The price policy can be market oriented, that means that the price of a product is not determined by considering the costs, but by evaluating the current market situation and competition. Different price policy strategies include price differentiation, high pricing (quality, exclusiveness), low pricing (discount offers) and price balancing (financing the discount on one product through another product which has a high price).

In the tourism sector, price policies are often based on price differentiation of the following factors: time: peak season-off-peak season, weekend-working day, stand-by- offers customer: families, kids, students, seniors volume: rebates for groups, prices for contingents distribution chain: discounts for tour operators point of time of payment: discount for early booking/payment spatial criteria: different prices for different departure points/ geographically separated markets commercialisation of "free goods": climate, air, water, location, view, orientation ("ocean view")

Distribution policy: The main decision here is whether the product is purchased directly by the customer or via tour operators. On this decision depends the selection of agencies, booking systems and strategies of motivation and as well as guaranteeing the loyalty of tour operators or agencies (through information meetings and trips, commissions).

Communication policy: The communication policy consists of making the potential customers, tour operators and a wider public aware of the product and guarantee the continuing interest of customers.

The corporate identity (CI) is "the message", philosophy or of the tourism product, the provider or the region. It is a useful starting point for the other parts of communication and helps to position the product in the market.

Public relations (PR) describes the communication of a company with the wider public. It is usually unspecific, giving general information about the product and the provider and it focuses on contact with the media to ensure ongoing and positive media coverage. Advertising transmits specific information to specific target groups. Forms of advertising are TV spots, ads in the press, the internet and elsewhere. Advertising and PR are areas which overlap.

Promotion: The ongoing activities in advertising, sales and public relations are often considered aspects of promotion. The aim of promotion is to keep the product in the customer's and tour operator's mind and to stimulate the demand for the product. Various methods can foster incentives to buy the product. Tour operators which resell the tourism products and journalists can be invited to FAM (familiarization) or press trips. Decoration services, presentations at fairs and direct merchandising like little presents and customer's cards can motivate tourists to buy a product.

Implementation and Control

The implementation takes place after developing the product and other decisions about the presented strategies and it consists of the concrete organization of the marketing measures, considering resources, costs and time. Controlling the outcomes of marketing by comparing the goals with the results is not only required at the end of the process, but also throughout the process through constant monitoring, tests and surveys ensuring appropriateness of the selected strategies.

Tourism Product Development

What is a Tourism Product?

A tourism product is a combination of services, commodities and other material or immaterial items that enable the clients to have a „complex experience", which starts at them leaving their home and ends out their return. The experience consists of what the tourist does and learns during his stay and the individual impressions he gets from visiting the destination.

The so-called original tourism product consists of the natural and cultural attractions of a region. Derived tourism products are developed at a later stage at the destination either to increase tourism or because of an increase in tourism, e.g. transport facilities, hotels, restaurants, information and communication services. The socio-cultural environment and the infrastructure of a destination for example politics, education, communication, transport, supply and disposal, can be considered separate or can partially come under both of the above categories. There are a large number of stakeholders (businesses, institutions, people and associations etc.) responsible for the maintenance of the above mentioned tourism attractions categories. Some of them can be seen in the list below:

Accommodation: Hotel managers, private accommodation landlords. Gastronomy: Restaurants, cafes, Kiosks, retailer (tradesmen), farmers. Service: Local authorities, tourism departments & associations, travel agencies.

Infrastructure: the town or regions building authority, the trade promotion office, culture and sport administration etc. The character of the destination: Regional Planning Authorities, Towns building authority, citizen initiatives.

The surroundings: Nature and conservation authorities, planning authorities, farmers, the village citizens, nature conservation initiatives. Transport: road construction administration, communal transport businesses, civil engineering office, national railways, police.

Specific Features of Tourism Products

When compared with other products, a tourism product has a number of specific features: It cannot be produced on stock, it cannot be stored, and it is always prepared for a particular customer and for a certain time. It always consists of items that the product's initiator cannot influence, but that must be considered (e.g. weather, character of landscape, history, etc.). Part of the tourism products are immaterial items such as hospitality, customs and traditions. Tourism products are bound to a particular territory – it is not possible to transport them elsewhere. A tourist buys a product even though he hasn't seen/experienced it. Finally, the product user-the tourist-has an impact on its quality. He/she can decide about the content and form of the product, even when it is being used.

The Structure of the Tourism Products

It consists of a number of basic elements: preparation, travel to, stay at, travel back from the destination and activities to be completed after returning home. The topic of this lecture deals mainly with one of these elements – the stay in the region, therefore, the term regional product will be used. From a practical point of view, the product consists of four basic parts: the itinerary, lodging, eating and additional services (e.g. travel, money exchange, purchase of maps and camera films etc.). These items are not products themselves but when they are combined they become a part of a regional product.

Who can Produce a Regional Product?

In principle, three basic „producers" can be identified: Individual service providers (e.g. hotels, restaurants, tour guiding) coordinate their products and each of them tries to sell their own service, which is supplemented by the service of other partners. They generate profit mainly by selling the primary service that they provide.

Travel agencies and tour-operators sell a tourism product

which is a combination of services from other providers, mainly providers and organizers of itineraries, lodging and catering. The tour operator then sells this product under its own name (or in cooperation with vendors). The income of the travel agency/tour operator is generated from percentages received from providers of individual primary services or by increasing the total price of individual products, or by the combination of both methods. Destination management organizations (DMOs) (e.g. tourism association, tourist information centres, tourism department of the local administration), similarly to a tour operator, create products from services of other providers.

They do not, however, sell this product but provide it for vendors. The profit is generated from the percentages received from the vendor (who generates his income based on percentages received from primary service providers) and/or from percentage gained from the income of primary service providers.

Packages

A tourism package is a form or even a synonym of a tourism product, for the package is what is sold to the customer by the vendor. Producing a package involves a number of steps:

Offer Inventory

A detailed summary of everything that the region can offer the client. It is important that existing attractions and activities are included in the list, not the potential ones. The inventory should not, for example, include "folk customs", if there is nobody to present them to the client; "good traditional cuisine", if no restaurant offers local dishes or "gothic churches" if it is not possible to visit them. For the purpose of a creating a tourism package, each of its elements should be an independent service with a clear provider, price and conditions.

Combining Offers to a Package and its Organisation

When the list of existing offers of the region is completed, its individual elements need to be combined. It is usually necessary to create a balanced composition, where the following features of the individual elements should be included: Focus – the product should have a certain character, a unifying element (e.g. mining history of the region, active relaxation in nature, etc.). From this perspective, the product items should be combined so that they compliment each other – e.g. noisy discos should not be included in a relaxation programme for seniors, highly technical tours of architectural monuments should not be a part of a programme of active relaxation in natural surroundings, etc.

Quality – the individual items should be of similar quality. For example an old bus which hardly works should not be used for rich clients with high purchasing power who are accustomed to high standards. Equally it would not be correct to organize a seminar for them in a noisy restaurant, etc. Length – particular items of a tourism package should have an appropriate and complementary lengths. A client should be given enough time to experience the "full flavour" of everything that is part of the product.

A perfectly prepared programme also leaves a certain amount of time for the client to do activities on his/her own (e.g. going for walks, spending time in cafes, taking naps, etc.). It is important that the itinerary is planned realistically so the clients do not need to be rushed or stressed. This can give them a negative impression of the package they have paid for. Variability – even though each package has its own focus, a certain level of variability also needs to be included, e.g. alternating between active parts and parts for relaxation, indoor and outdoor activities, etc. Morning activities should be differ from the afternoon programme, places to eat should vary and so should the character of activities. Appropriateness of activities – the client's wishes, habits and values need to be respected. Someone who appreciates good food should not be taken to a fast-food restaurant, a nature conservationist should not be offered a colourful plastic aqua park, a Muslim client should not receive pork for lunch, etc.

Marketing of the Package

When the package is ready, it is necessary to find the proper market for it. Identification of the market segments, communication channels, sale methods, etc. is necessary. More attention is given to this topic in TOPIC 8. The above described procedure is obviously subject to change. The points 2 and 3 are often interchanged, i.e. appropriate market segments for a region are identified first, and then the available attractions are used to make a package for the identified market segments.

Frequent Mistakes of Product-making

Services that cannot be guaranteed are included in the package – a typical example is when churches are advertised as a great attraction of a region but entries into them are not always possible.

Tight programme – too many activities are planned for one day. This can result in late arrivals, nervousness and a bad impression of the product. On the other hand, long and boring periods of time whilst waiting for the next point of the programme (e.g. waiting too long to enter a museum), also needs to be avoided. Good knowledge of local services and ability to foresee and solve complications are therefore required.

Too much organization – effort is made to arrange the entire programme for the client and he does not get the chance to experience the magic of wandering in quiet historical streets, sitting in cafes, talking to local people, etc.

Improperly set price – tour-operator is afraid to include an appropriate price for their service (for making the product and organization work) in the total price. As a result, they do not generate sufficient profit for future work.

Unequal offer – in an effort to satisfy the customer as much as possible, things that were not part of the original package are offered to him as a surprise. Such additional and operative products are all right if provided to each client. Problems may occur if this is not possible because a client may find out about the new product and, if he did not receive it and paid the same price as those who did, his satisfaction is at risk. Extra services need to be guaranteed for all clients, or each client has to pay for them additionally.

SWOT Analysis

Meaning and Goal of a SWOT Analysis

* S – Strengths
* W – Weaknesses
* O – Opportunities
* T – Threats

The SWOT Analysis is an effective tool for assessing the current situation. It is necessary for developing a master plan, a strategy or operation programme for a distinct region, town or any other location. It helps to determine existing gaps, potentials and risks as well as to identify the desired direction of future development. It serves as a foundation for further planning and development in any sector. This applies to business and town management as well as tourism development.

When implementing the SWOT method, four basic groups of factors can be identified.

These can be put in two main groups: Internal factors (strengths and weaknesses): Factors that are inherent to a region, society, project or other units; they can be influenced or changed, they are present in a given territory, their owners are identifiable, etc.

External factors (opportunities and threats): Factors that are outside of an analysed region (organization, project or feature), we cannot influence. They can however have an effect on any of the areas examined

General proceeding of a SWOT Analysis:

1. Taking the inventory: determining the current situation by carrying out surveys and investigations; gathering all accessible facts and information
2. Drawing the SWOT Chart: evaluation of the current situation by identifying the strengths, weaknesses, opportunities and threats. Include any of the acquired facts in one of the above described groups of factors.
3. Outlining a further strategy (plan, procedure, programme) with the aim to: Promote strengths and/or use them Eliminate weaknesses Use the opportunities offered Eliminate threats

The procedure of a SWOT Analysis is simple and highly effective, which makes the analysis a convenient tool to be used not only by experts but also by the general public. It can be used in several stages of tourism development, e.g. at the beginning of a process to find out what the properties are, the potentials and needs of a region, and how these should be developed further. The SWOT Analysis can be also be used for the evaluation of the existing situation and methods and thus to find out if it is satisfactory and if the most effective solution was proposed for the given environment and objectives. Carrying out a SWOT Analysis remains the same for every purpose. Only the thematic areas to be evaluated change depending on the field you are working for.

Thematic Areas for Tourism Planning

Frequent Errors when Realising a SWOT

Not distinguishing between the strengths and opportunities, or between weaknesses and threats. This means that the authors do not follow the essential principle. This is that the strengths and weaknesses should refer to the internal features of the analysed object, while the opportunities and threats refer to the external situation, in which the analysed object is situated.

Steps to be Taken Instead of Opportunities: It is wrong to believe that opportunities are in fact possibilities or steps that should be taken to improve the analysed object.

SWOT Without Participation of Residents: The involvement of the local population is important in all steps of tourism planning. They are the most eligible persons for the analysis of the region, be- cause they have an inside view of what activities and services are missing. In addition, they should get involved in the strategy preparation, thus increasing the sense of "public ownership" of the strategy.

Recent Development In Tourism Industry

Tourism is the act of travel for the purpose of recreation, and the provision of services for this act. A tourist is someone who travels at least eighty kilometres from home for the purpose of recreation, as defined by the World Tourism Organization. A more comprehensive definition would be that tourism is a service industry, comprising a number of tangible and intangible components.

The tangible elements include transport systems; Air, Rail, road, Water and now, space; hospitality services, accommodation, foods and beverages, tours, souvenirs; and related services such as banking, insurance and safety and security. The intangible elements include: rest and relaxation, culture, escape, adventure, new and different experiences. Sometimes *Tourism* and *Travel* are used interchangeably. In this context travel has a similar definition to tourism, but implies a more purposeful journey.

Health tourism & leisure travel; It was not until the 19th century that cultural tourism developed into leisure and health tourism. Some English travellers, after visiting the warm lands of the south of Europe, decided to stay there either for the cold season or for the rest of their lives.

Others began to visit places with supposedly health-giving mineral waters, in hopes of relieving a whole variety of diseases. Leisure travel was a British creation due to sociological factors. Britain was the first European country to industrialize, and the industrial society was the first society to offer time for leisure to a growing number of people. Initially, this did not apply to the working masses.

Winter Tourism; Winter sports were largely invented by the British leisured classes. Organized sport was well established in Britain before it reached other countries. The vocabulary of sport bears witness to this: rugby, football, and boxing all originated in Britain, and even Tennis, originally a French sport, was formalized and codified by the British, who hosted the first national championship in the nineteenth century, at Wimbledon. Winter sports were a natural answer for a leisured class looking for amusement during the oldest season.

Mass travel; The father of modern mass tourism was Thomas Cook who, on 5 July 1841, organized the first package tour in history by chartering a train to take a temperance campaigners from Leicester to a rally in Loughborough, some twenty miles away. Cook immediately saw the potential for business development in the sector, and became the world's first tour operator. He was soon followed by others, with the result that the tourist industry developed rapidly in early Victorian Britain. Initially it was supported by the growing middle classes, who had time off from their work, and who could afford the luxury of travel and possibly even staying for periods of time in boarding houses. For a century, domestic tourism was the norm, with foreign travel being reserved for the rich or the culturally curious. *International mass tourism;*

Increasing speed on railways meant that the tourist industry could develop internationally. By 1901, the number of people crossing the English Channel from England to France or Belgium had passed 0.5 million per year..

Attempts to move towards "quality tourism" are difficult given competition from cheaper, unspoilt holiday destinations on the one hand and the legacy of decades of over-exploitation on the other.

Receptive tourism is now growing at a very rapid rate in many developing countries. In recent years, second holidays or vacations have become more popular as people's disposable income increases. Typical combinations are a package to the typical mass tourist resort, with a winter skiing holiday.

Special Forms of Tourism;

* Medical tourism
* Disaster tourism
* Virtual tourism
* Bookstore Tourism
* Vacilando
* Ecotourism
* Educational tourism
* Health tourism
* Space tourism
* Adventure Tourism
* Cultural tourism
* Agritourism
* Heritage tourism.

Future Trend of Tourism Industry; The World Tourism Organization forecasts that international tourism will continue growing at the average annual rate of 4 percent. By 2020 Europe will remain the most popular destination, but its share will drop from 60 percent in 1995 to 46 percent. Space tourism is expected to "take off" in the first quarter of the 21st century, although compared with traditional destinations the number of tourists in orbit will remain low until technologies such as space elevator make space travel cheap. On the ocean tourists will be welcomed by ever larger cruise ships and perhaps floating cities.

World Tourism Day

Since 1980, September 27 is celebrated by the World Trade Organization as World Tourism Day. The purpose of this day is to display awareness that tourism is vital to the international community and to show how it affects the social, cultural, political and economic values worldwide. The adoption of the statutes is considered to be a milestone in global tourism.

Water Recreation and Disease

Background

Recreational use of inland and marine waters is increasing in many countries. It is estimated that foreign and local tourists together spend around two billion days annually at coastal recreational resorts. The World Tourism Organization predicts that by 2026, 346 million tourists will visit Mediterranean destinations annually, representing about 22% of all arrivals worldwide (WTO 2001).

It has been estimated that 129 million people visited the beach or waterside in the United States of America between 2000 and 2001, an increase of 6% from 1995 (NOAA 2004). In the United Kingdom it is estimated that over 20 million people use the British coast each year, in addition to inland waters and their surrounding areas, for a variety of reasons. The National Centre for Social Research (1998) reported there were 241 million day visits to the sea/coast in Great Britain in 1998, with people prepared to travel an average of 43 miles to reach the coast. However, perceived risks involving recreational water use may have important economic repercussions in areas that depend to a large extent on recreational tourism as a source of income. An example is the decline in tourists visiting Lake Malawi in South Africa because of news reports about schistosomiasis cases (WHO 2003a).

Indoor water recreation is also hugely popular. Pools may be private (domestic), semi-public (hotels, schools, health clubs, cruise ships) or public (municipal or governmental). Pools may be supplied with fresh, marine or thermal water. Specialist pools, such as hot tubs are used for both pleasure and medicinal purposes and are generally filled with water at temperatures over 32ºC (WHO 2005). 'Natural spa' is the term used to refer to facilities containing thermal and/or mineral water, some of which may be perceived to have therapeutic value and, because of certain water characteristics, may receive minimal water treatment (WHO 2005). Water-based recreation and tourism can expose individuals to a variety of health hazards, including pathogenic micro-organisms. Sports which involve intimate contact with the water such as surfing, windsurfing and scuba diving are growing in popularity, and technology is changing the behaviour of recreational water users – the use of wet suits for example, now encouraging prolonged immersion in water even in temperate or cool areas. The type, design and use of pools may predispose the user to certain hazards. Indoor pools, for example, may be subject to higher bather-loads relative to the volume of water. Where there are high water temperatures and rapid agitation of water, it may become difficult to maintain microbiological quality, adequate disinfectant residual and a satisfactory pH (WHO 2005).

The vast majority of research to date in the field of recreational water quality and health has focused on microbial hazards, in particular gastroenteric outcomes arising from contamination of water by sewage and excreta. Mild gastroenteric symptoms are widespread and common amongst recreational water users. A cause effect relationship between bather-derived pollution or faecal pollution and acute febrile respiratory illness (AFRI) is biologically plausible, and a significant exposure response relationship (between AFRI and faecal streptococci) has been reported by Fleisher *et al.* (1996). AFRI is a more severe health outcome than self-limiting gastrointestinal symptoms, but probabilities of contracting AFRI are generally lower and the threshold at which the illness is observed is higher (WHO 2003a).

Despite the acknowledged constraints of current bathing water quality monitoring practices, considerable information has become available to recreational water users in recent years concerning the microbial quality of the water they are using for recreation. The relatively minor illnesses associated with poor microbial quality of water and non-microbial hazards have been identified in the WHO *Guidelines for Safe Recreational Water Environments* (WHO 2003a; WHO 2005). Less information is available on the more severe potential health outcomes encountered by recreational water users resulting in symptoms which are not self-limiting and require medical attention.

Waterborne microbial pathogens are capable of causing illness depending on the dose and the physical condition of the individuals exposed. It should be stressed that exposure to waterborne pathogens does not always result in infection, nor does infection always lead to clinical illness.

The total global health impact of human infectious diseases associated with pathogenic micro-organisms from land-based wastewater pollution of coastal areas has been estimated at about three million disability-adjusted life years (DALYs) per year, with an estimated economic loss of around 12 billion dollars per year.

Researchers in the United States have estimated that the health burden of swimming-related illnesses at two popular beaches in California, USA exceeds US $3.3 million per year. The annual costs for each type of swimming-related illness at the two beaches were estimated to be: gastrointestinal illnesses, US $1,345,339; acute respiratory disease, US $951,378; ear complaints, US $767,221; eye complaints, US $304,335.

Although most illnesses contracted through recreational water contact are mild (e.g., self-limiting diarrhoea) diseases with a range of severities may also occur. A number of viruses, bacteria and protozoa associated with more severe health outcomes may plausibly be transmitted through use of contaminated recreational water. Bacteria and protozoa may induce illnesses with a wide range of severity.

Bacteria may cause life-threatening diseases such as typhoid, cholera and leptospirosis. Viruses can cause serious diseases such as aseptic meningitis, encephalitis, poliomyelitis, hepatitis, myocarditis and diabetes. Protozoa may cause primary amoebic meningoencephalitis (PAM) and schistosomiasis is caused by a flatworm (trematode). In addition, gastrointestinal disorders are amongst a number of illnesses that may be attributed to unidentified or unspecified micro-organisms.

These hazards to human health should be weighed against the benefits of using water as a medium for relaxation and aerobic, non-weight bearing exercise. Physical exercise has been shown to positively affect certain cardiovascular risk factors such as insulin resistance, glucose metabolism, blood pressure and body fat composition, which are closely associated with diabetes and heart disease. With increasingly sedentary life styles in many societies, routine daily exercise of moderate intensity is highly recommended to reduce cardiovascular risk.

Swimming is often recommended by the medical profession because of its potentially beneficial effect on the joints and indeed on people's general sense of well-being. For example, non-swimming dynamic exercises in heated water have been shown to have a positive impact on individuals with late effects of polio, with a decreased heart rate at exercise, less pain, and a subjective positive experience. Although it is difficult to quantify the psychological benefits of exercise, Van de Vliet *et al.* (2004) have shown that fitness training embedded in a cognitive-behavioural treatment programme is associated with positive changes in clinically depressed patients. This includes enhanced coping strategies, sustained efforts to continue activities, and improved awareness of physical well-being.

Evidence for Adverse Health Outcomes Associated with Recreational Water Use

The first reviews of the incidence of disease associated with the use of recreational waters were undertaken by the American Public Health Association in the early 1920s. Simons *et al.* (1922) attempted to determine the prevalence of infectious diseases which may be transmitted by recreational water contact. Major epidemiological studies were conducted between 1948 and 1950 by the United States Public Health Service to investigate the link between bathing and illness. The findings concluded that there was an appreciably higher overall illness incidence rate in people who swam in Lake Michigan, Chicago, the United States, in 1948 and on the Ohio River at Dayton, Kentucky, the United States, in 1949 compared with non-swimmers, regardless of the levels of coliform bacteria found in the water quality tests. It was concluded by Stevenson (1953) that, based upon the results of this study, the stricter bacterial quality requirements could be relaxed without a detrimental effect on the health of bathers.

Moore (1959) undertook a similar study in the United Kingdom. His study was based on five years of investigation of 43 beaches in the United Kingdom and concluded that there was only a 'negligible risk to health' of bathing in sewage polluted sea water even when beaches were 'aesthetically very unsatisfactory' and that a serious risk would only exist if the water was so fouled as to be revolting to the senses. Moore insisted that pathogenic bacteria which were isolated from sewage contaminated sea water were more important as indicators of the disease in the population than as evidence of a health risk in the waters. The subject became one of controversy for many years. It was acknowledged in 1972 by the United States Environmental Protection Agency (US EPA) that there was a lack of valid epidemiological data with which to set guideline standards for recreational waters. There followed a number of epidemiological studies throughout the world. In many of the studies identified, the occurrence of certain symptoms or symptom groups was found to be significantly related to the count of faecal indicator bacteria or bacterial pathogens. Credible associations were found between gastrointestinal symptoms (including 'highly credible' or 'objective' symptoms) and indicators such as enterococci, faecal streptococci, thermotolerant coliforms and *E. coli*.

The WHO *Guidelines for Safe Recreational Water Environments* reviewed the scientific evidence concerning the health issues associated with using waters for recreational purposes and concluded that enteric illness, such as self-limiting gastroenteritis, and AFRI are the most frequently investigated and reported adverse health outcomes in the published literature. The *Guidelines* also concluded that there is an association between gastrointestinal symptoms, AFRI and indicator-bacteria concentrations in recreational waters (WHO 2003a; WHO 2005). The *Guidelines* represent a consensus view and assessment among experts of the health hazards encountered during recreational water use. It includes the derivation of guideline values and explains the basis for the decision to derive or not to derive them.

There are relatively few studies which report associations between indicators and other symptoms although there is limited evidence of an association between ear, eye and skin ailments with swimming.

Evidence suggests that bathing, regardless of water quality, compromises the eye's immune defences leading to increased reporting of symptoms after bathing in marine waters. Infection could also be due to person to-person transmission. In addition, the statistical probability of contracting an ear infection has been found to be generally lower than for gastrointestinal illnesses which are associated with higher thermotolerant coliform concentrations (WHO 2003a). Several studies have found that symptom rates were more frequent in lower age groups.

The main focus of effort concerning the health implications of the recreational use of water focuses on the effects of faecal contamination of bathing waters and the incidence of gastrointestinal diseases and other transmissible diseases to participants in water recreation. The data concerning some of the other hazards is weaker. There are very few epidemiological studies which have considered special interest activities. Evans *et al.* (1983) found no evidence of any particular health risk from short-term immersion in Bristol City Docks, UK. However, Philipp *et al.* (1985) studied the health of snorkel swimmers in the same body of water who were immersed for 40 minutes and revealed that statistically significantly more swimmers reported gastrointestinal symptoms compared with the control group, even though the water complied with the European Union (EU) bathing water standards.

Medema *et al.* (1995) investigating the risk of gastroenteritis in triathlete swimmers estimated that the exposure of triathletes during a competition was between 15 and 40 minutes and exposure was relatively intense; 75% of all triathletes in his study were comapred with biathletes and it was reported that although the health risks for triathletes were not significantly higher than for run-bike-runners (biathletes) symptoms were higher in the week after the event in those athletes that had been exposed to water. (6.8%) than those that did not (3.8%). The percentage of triathletes swallowing water was 72%.

Dwight *et al.* (2004) compared rates of reported health symptoms among surfers during two winters. Their findings showed that for every 2.5 hours of weekly water exposure, surfers experienced a 10% increase in probability of illness (a variety of different symptoms were tracked including highly credible gastrointestinal illness, stomach pain, vomiting, diarrhoea, and others). These activities are important to consider since the difference in risk between the various uses of recreational waters lies primarily with the duration of exposure and the quantity of water ingested.

Different behaviours of different populations of swimmers are an important risk factor for infection. For example, swimming in unchlorinated open waters is much more common in warmer climates and this may increase the risk of illnessto swimmers. For several reasons, children are at particular risk of contracting recreational waterborne illness. Children have greater opportunities for exposure; they tend to be more frequent users of recreational waters for longer periods of time compared to older age groups, and their activities, which may involve play, often increase exposure to contaminated water through accidental ingestion.

The documented health risks posed by poor quality bathing waters usually relate to acute infections acquired whilst bathing. Most of the epidemiological studies conducted to establish a link between bathing and illness do not address the more severe health outcomes or possible sequelae. This is probably due to the low occurrence of severe health outcomes in recent decades in the temperate regions where the majority of studies have been conducted, and because investigations of rarer outcomes usually require larger study groups.

Severe Outcomes

For the purposes of this review, consideration of whether an illness is severe or not is based on three factors:

- acute symptoms of the disease which are debilitating;
- the ability and probability that the illness will lead to sequelae; and
- the effect of the disease on certain susceptible subpopulations.

Each factor can be considered in its own right or in combination with one or both of the other factors. WHO microbial guideline values for safe recreational water environments are in fact based on evidence of the transmission of relatively mild gastrointestinal illness and AFRI. However, the guidelines make provision for adjustment where there is more severe disease plausibly associated with recreational water use circulating in the population. The use of DALYs is suggested as a useful approach to do this. Management approaches developed in the WHO *Guidelines* when implemented as suggested will help to mitigate both mild and severe infectious illnesses transmitted through recreational water.

Infections with Potentially Severe Acute Symptoms

Although the majority of illnesses transmitted through recreational water use arerelatively mild and often self-limiting, there are a number of waterborne pathogens that can cause illnesses with severe outcomes even in average populations.

These include: *Campylobacter* spp., *E. coli* O157, *Salmonella typhi*, *Shigella* spp., *Leptospira icterohaemorrhagiae*, HAV, *Cryptosporidium parvum* and a number of others described throughout this review. Some of these have been known for many years; others, such as *Helicobacter pylori*, are emerging as new pathogens or re-emerging after many years (WHO 2003b). Although not always severe, infection by these pathogens can result in hospitalisation, surgery and death. For example, leptospirosis has been found to have a case-fatality rate as high as 22% if left untreated and a hospitalisation rate of 30–50%. The primary disease symptoms caused by infections with these pathogens.

Evidence for Sequelae of Waterborne Diseases

Sequelae are increasingly important to food and drinking-water risk assessment. It has been estimated that around 5% of waterborne diseases result in sequelae. There has been little agreement over a scientific definition for sequelae. The Oxford English Dictionary defines a sequela as 'a morbid affection occurring as a result of previous disease'. Parkin *et al.* (2000) reviewed scientific publications for definitions of chronic sequelae and developed a definition as follows: 'the secondary health outcome that (1) occurs as a result of a previous infection by a microbial pathogen; (2) is clearly distinguishable from the health events that initially result from the causative infection and (3) lasts three months or more after recognition'.

The sequelae symptoms may be completely different from the symptoms of the acute illness and may occur even if the immune system successfully manages to eliminate the primary infection. The action of the immune system may initiate the condition as a result of an autoimmune response. However, it is also possible that the initial infection may not have passed when the secondary symptoms appear. For the purposes of this review, sequelae which may last less than three months are also included and, therefore, according to Parkin's definition are not chronic.

The evidence that micro-organisms or their products are directly or indirectly associated with sequelae ranges from convincing to circumstantial, due to the fact that it is unlikely that such complications are identified or epidemiologically linked to the initial illness because the data are not systematically collected. In addition, host symptoms caused by a specific pathogen or product of a pathogen are often wide-ranging and difficult to link with a specific incident, particularly as the time of onset of sequelae may vary.

Typically, for example, if symptoms of Reiter's syndrome (reactive arthritis) appear then it will be one to three weeks after initial infection with *Salmonella* spp. Symptoms of haemolytic uraemic syndrome (HUS), if they are to appear, are usually seen within 15 days of infection with *E. coli* O157:H7. However, sequelae such as hypertension and renal failure may not manifest themselves until 15 years later.

Leptospires, the bacteria causing leptospirosis, may persist in the brain – in one report, 4 out of 11 patients had persistent headaches for between 6 and 34 years post-infection; ophthalmic involvement with blurred vision has been reported to persist for decades following acute infection. Where there is a long time-period between the initial symptoms and the sequelae, it becomes more difficult to prove an association between the initial disease and the delayed sequelae. A summary of sequelae associated with some micro-organisms which may be found in recreational waters. These will be discussed in more detail throughout this review. It is stressed that the development of a sequela is incidental to exposure to recreational water, i.e. the sequelae described in this section result from infection with certain pathogens.

Lindsay (1997) raises a further issue which is not widely discussed in the literature: the effect of chronic disease on human personality factors as a result of symptoms such as continual pain from arthritis, irritable bowel or other conditions such as chronic diarrhoea. However, these will not be discussed in this review.

Severe Outcomes in Special Populations

Diseases that are normally mild and self-limiting in the general population can have severe manifestations in susceptible sub-populations with certain attributes. A variety of host factors impact susceptibility to severe disease outcomes. Human immune status can be affected by diseases (HIV, cancer), age, medications taken (e.g., chemotherapy treatment of cancer weakens the immune system), pregnancy, nutritional status, genetics and other factors. Host factors can influence both the severity of the acute symptoms and the propensity to develop sequelae.

The population of immunocompromised individuals is growing. This population is more susceptible to water-borne infections and tend to experience more severe outcomes (e.g., debilitating illness, death) following infection. A number of studies have shown that enteric diseases are the most common and serious problems that affect persons with acquired immunodeficiency syndrome (AIDS).

Between 50% and 90% of people with HIV/AIDS suffer from chronic diarrhoeal illness, and the effects can be fatal. People with reduced immune function due to cancer treatment have been shown to have a case-fatality rate for adenovirus infection of 53%. Likewise, in the 1993 *Cryptosporidium* outbreak in Milwaukee, Wisconsin, USA, 85% of the deaths occurred in people with HIV/AIDS. People with liver diseases are at particularly high risk of fatal septicaemia after ingestion of, or percutaneous exposure to, *Vibrio vulnificus*.

The case-fatality observed for enteric pathogens in nursing home patients in the USA who are more susceptible to infection compared with the general population.

Management of Severe Illnesses

The possible adverse health outcomes associated with recreational water result in the need for guidelines that can be converted into locally appropriate standards and associated management of sites to ensure a safe, healthy and aesthetically pleasing environment (WHO 2003a). The management interventions that may be required to ensure a safe recreational water environment are outside the scope of this publication but include compliance and enforcement measures, water quality monitoring, sanitary surveys, animal waste control measures, wastewater treatment, risk communication and information dissemination to increase public awareness. The reader is referred to the WHO *Guidelines for Safe Recreational Water Environments, Volumes1 and 2* (WHO 2003a; 2005) which illustrates how this can be best achieved through an integrated framework for assessment and management of risk for water-related infectious diseases.

Summary

There are many unanswered questions regarding the severity and frequency of illness associated with recreational water use. The difficulties associated with attributing an infection to recreational water use are numerous and the majority of research in this field has focussed on infections associated with the use of recreational waters resulting in minor, self-limiting symptoms. However, it is plausible that more serious illnesses could result from the recreational use of water and this association has not yet been investigated to any great extent. It is also increasingly apparent that a number of micro-organisms or their products are directly or indirectly associated with secondary health outcomes or sequelae and a number of these sequelae may result from water-borne infections. The acute diseases attributable to water-borne pathogens and their epidemiology have been well described, but the sequelae that can result from these diseases have not. Assessing potential sequelae of water-borne infections is a critical part of microbial risk assessment and the formulation of public policy.

Tourism-History

Wealthy people have always travelled to distant parts of the world to see great buildings or other works of art; to learn new languages; or to taste new cuisine. As long ago as the time of the Roman Republic places such as Baiae were popular coastal resorts for the rich. The terms *tourist* and *tourism* were first used as official terms in 1937 by the League of Nations. Tourism was defined as people travelling abroad for periods of over 24 hours.

Tourism-Health Tourism & Leisure Travel

It was not until the 19th century that cultural tourism developed into leisure and health tourism. Some English travellers, after visiting the warm lands of the south of Europe, decided to stay there either for the cold season or for the rest of their lives. Others began to visit places with supposedly health-giving mineral waters, in hopes of relieving a whole variety of diseases from gout to liver disorders and bronchitis.

Leisure travel was a British invention due to sociological factors. Britain was the first European country to industrialize, and the industrial society was the first society to offer time for leisure to a growing number of people. Initially, this did not apply to the working masses, but rather to the owners of the machinery of production, the economic oligarchy, the factory owners, and the traders. These comprised the new middle class. The British origin of this new industry is reflected in many place names. At Nice, one of the first and best-established holiday resorts on the French Riviera, the long esplanade along the seafront is known to this day as the *Promenade des Anglais*; in many other historic resorts in continental Europe, old well-established palace hotels have names like the *Hotel Bristol*, the *Hotel Carlton* or the *Hotel Majestic*-reflecting the dominance of English customers.

Tourism-Winter Tourism

Winter sports were largely invented by the British leisured classes initially at the Swiss village of Zermatt (Valais), and St Moritz in 1864. The first packaged winter sports holidays (vacations) followed in 1903, to Adelboden, also in Switzerland.

Organized sport was well established in Britain before it reached other countries. The vocabulary of sport bears witness to this: rugby, football, and boxing all originated in Britain, and even Tennis, originally a French sport, was formalized and codified by the British, who hosted the first national championship in the nineteenth century, at Wimbledon. Winter sports were a natural answer for a leisured class looking for amusement during the oldest season.

Tourism-Mass Travel

Mass travel could not really begin to develop until two things occurred.

- improvements in technology allowed the transport of large numbers of people in a short space of time to places of leisure interest, and
- greater numbers of people began to enjoy the benefits of leisure time.

A major development was the invention of the railways, which brought many of Britain's seaside towns within easy distance of Britain's urban centres.

The father of modern mass tourism was Thomas Cook who, on 5 July 1841, organized the first package tour in history, by chartering a train to take a group of temperance campaigners from Leicester to a rally in Loughborough, some twenty miles away. Cook immediately saw the potential for business development in the sector, and became the world's first tour operator.

He was soon followed by others, with the result that the tourist industry developed rapidly in early Victorian Britain. Initially it was supported by the growing middle classes, who had time off from their work, and who could afford the luxury of travel and possibly even staying for periods of time in boarding houses.

However, the Bank Holiday Act 1871 introduced a statutory right for workers to take holidays, even if they were not paid at the time.

The combination of short holiday periods, travel facilities and distances meant that the first holiday resorts to develop in Britain were towns on the seaside, situated as close as possible to the growing industrial conurbations.

For those in the industrial north, there were Blackpool in Lancashire, and Scarborough in Yorkshire. For those in the Midlands, there were Weston-super-Mare in Somerset and Skegness in Lincolnshire, for those in London there were Southend-on-Sea,

Broadstairs, Brighton, Eastbourne and many others. In travelling to the coast, the population was following in the steps of Royalty. King George III is widely acknowledged as popularising the seaside holiday, due to his regular visits to Weymouth when in poor health.

For a century, domestic tourism was the norm, with foreign travel being reserved for the rich or the culturally curious. A minority of resorts, such as Bath, Harrogate and Matlock, emerged inland. After World War II holiday villages such as Butlins and Pontins emerged, but their popularity waned with the rise of package tours and the increasing comforts to which visitors became accustomed at home. Towards the end of the 20th century the market was revived by the upmarket inland resorts of Dutch company Centre Parcs.

Other phenomena that helped develop the travel industry were paid holidays:

- 1.5 million manual workers in Britain had paid holidays by 1925
- 11 million by 1939 (30% of the population in families with paid holidays)

Similar processes occurred in other countries, though at a slower rate, given that nineteenth century Britain was far ahead of any other nation in the world in the process of industrialisation.

In the USA, the first great seaside resort, in the European style, was Atlantic City, New Jersey.

In Continental Europe, early resorts included Ostend (for the people of Brussels), and Boulogne-sur-Mer (Pas-de-Calais) and Deauville (Calvados) (for Parisians).

History of Recreational Tourism

The earliest forms of leisure tourism can be traced as far back as the Babylonian and Egyptian empires. A museum of "historic antiquities" was open to the public in the sixth century BC in Babylon, while the Egyptians held many religious festivals attracting not only the devout, but many who came to see the famous buildings and works of art in the cities. The local towns accommodated tourists by providing services such as: vendors of food and drink, guides, hawkers of souvenirs, touts and prostitutes. From around the same date, Greek tourists travelled to visit the sites of healing gods. Because the independent city-states of ancient Greece had no central authority to order the construction of roads, most of these tourists travelled by water, hence seaports prospered.

The lands of the Mediterranean Sea produced a remarkable evolution in travel. People travel for trade, commerce, religious purposes, festivals, medical treatment, or education developed at an early date.

Guidebooks became available as early as the fourth century BC, covering a vast area of destinations, i.e. Athens, Sparta and Troy. Pausanias, a Greek travel writer, produced a noted "description of Greece" between AD 160 and 180, which, in its critical evaluation of facilities and destinations, acted as a model for later writers. Advertisements, in the form of signs directing visitors to wayside inns, are also known from this period. However, under Romans rule is where international travel became first important. With no foreign borders between England and Syria, and with the seas safe from piracy due to the Roman patrols, conditions favouring travel had arrived. Roman coinage was acceptable everywhere, and Latin was the common language. Romans travelled to Sicily, Greece, Rhodes, and Troy, Egypt and from the third century AD, to the Holy Land.

Domestic tourism also flourished within the Roman Empire. Second homes were built by the wealthy within easy travelling distance of Rome, occupied particularly during the springtime social season. Naples attracted the retired and the intellectuals. Before the sixteenth century, those who sought to travel had three modes in which to do so. They could walk, ride a horse or they could be carried, either on a little or on a carrier's wagon. The development of the sprung coach was a huge advance for those who regularly travelled, and by the mid 1600's, coaches were operating regularly in Britain. In the eighteenth century the introduction of turnpike roads, which provided improved surfaces for which tolls would be charged. The later introduction of the metal, leaf spring suspension also added to comfort.

Travel also requires accommodation, and at that time, it was basic. To accommodate the new demand for travel inns was provided. They provided fresh horses, and lodgings were available for rent to visitors when they arrived at their destination. From the early seventeenth century, a new form of tourism developed as a direct outcome of the freedom and quest for learning heralded by the Renaissance. Young men who wanted positions at court were encouraged to travel to the Continent to finish their education. Others soon adopted this practice in the upper echelons of society, and it soon became customary for the education of a gentleman to be completed by a "Grand tour" of major cultural centres of Europe, accompanied by a tutor and often-lasting three years or more. The appeal soon became social, and leisure seeking young men travelled, predominantly to France and Italy, to enjoy the rival cultures and social life of cities such as Paris, Venice, or Florence. By the end of the eighteenth century, the custom had become institutionalised for the gentry.

Passports have their origins in the medieval testimonial. A letter from an ecclesiastical superior given to a pilgrim to avoid the latter's possible arrest on charges of vagrancy. Later, papers of authority to travel were more widely issued by the state, particularly during periods of warfare with neighbouring European countries. Spas were already well established during the time of the Roman Empire, but their popularity, based on the supposed medical benefits of the waters, lapsed in the subsequent centuries. Renewed interest in the therapeutic qualities of mineral waters has been ascribed to the influence of the Renaissance in Britain, and elsewhere in Europe.

Bibliography

Burkart, A and Medlik, S: *Management of Tourism*, The, London, Heinemann, 1975.

Clark, Mona: *Interpersonal Skills for Hospitality Managers*, London, Chapman Hill, 1995.

David L: *International Tourism Policy, New York*, Van Nostrand and Reinhold, 1990.

Donald M.: *Customer Service in the Hospitality and Tourism Industry*, Englewood Cliffs, Prentice Hall, 1994.

Douglas C: *Practical Tourism Forecasting*, Oxford, Butterworth Heinemann, 1996.
Douglas C: *Practical Tourism Forecasting*, Oxford, Butterworth Heinemann, 1996.
Eberts, Marjorie: *Careers in Travel, Tourism, and Hospitality*, Lincolnwood, VGM Career Horizons, 1997.

Elio, C.: *The Hospitality Law Desk Reference*, Miami, Southern Beverage Journal, 1994.

Elliott, James: *Tourism*: *Politics and Public Sector Management*, London, Retailed, 1997.

Foster, Douglas: *Travel and Tourism Management*, London, Macmillan Educational, 1985.

Fowler, Peter: *Heritage and Tourism: In the Global Village*, London, Retailed, 1993.

Ghimire, Krishna: *The Native Tourist*: Mass Tourism within Developing Regions, London, Earthscan, 2001.

Graham M S: *Language of Tourism*, The, Wallingford, CAB International, 1996.

Hoffman, Edward: *Project Management Success Stories: Lessons of Project Leaders*, New York, John Wiley & Son, 2000.

Hubert, B.: *A Host of Opportunities: An Introduction to Hospitality Management,* Chicago, Irwin, 1996.

Ireland, Lewis: *Quality Management for Projects and Programs,* Upper Darby, PMI, 1991.

Judi Radice: *Restaurant & Food Graphics,* Glen Cove, PBC International, 1994.

Judy A: *Tourism: Management of Facilities,* London, Pitman: M & E, 1993.

Karski, A: *Urban Tourism* - A Key to Urban Regeneration?, 1990.

Kotler, Philip: *Marketing for Hospitality and Tourism*: New Jersey, Prentice-Hall, 1998.

Labarge, Margaret Wade: *Medieval Travellers: The Rich and Restless,* London, Hamish Hamilton, 1982.

Larkham, P J: *Building a New Heritage: Tourism, Culture & Identity in the New Europe,* London, Routledge,1994.

Leivadi, S: *Sociology of Tourism, The: Theoretical And Empirical Investigations,* London, Retailed, 1996.

Lewis, Robert C.: *Cases in Hospitality Marketing and Management,* New York, John Wiley, 1997.

Madhukar Manoj : *Hospitality Industries in Next Millennium,* Rajat, Delhi, 2001.

Martin, B.S. : *The Efficacy of Growth Machine Theory in Explaining Resident Perceptions of Community Tourism Development,* Clemson University, 1996.

McNicol, B.J. : *Views of Residents, Developers and Government Planners About Tourists and Tourism Resort Developments in Canmore, Alberta,* The University of Galgary, Alberta, 1996.

Moscardo, G. : *Tourism Community Analysis,* London and New York: Routledge, 1999.

Nijkamp, Peter: *Sustainable Tourism Development,* Aldershot, Avebury, 1995.

Norman G.: *Hotel, Restaurant, and Travel Law: A Preventive Approach,* Albany, Delmar Publishers, 1993.

Peter J.: *College & University Foodservice Management Standards,* Westport, AVI Pub. Company, 1985.

Prentice, R: *Conceptualising The Experiences of Heritage Tourists,* 1997.

Ratti Manish : *Hospitality Management : Theories and Practices*, Rajat Pub, Delhi, 2007.

Richards, G. : *Culture, Crafts and Tourism: A Vital Relationship*, Tilburg: Atlas, 1999.

Robert C.: *Cases in Hospitality Marketing and Management*, New York, John Wiley, 1997.

Rosemary E.: *Managing Employee Relations in the Hotel and Catering Industry*, London, Cassell, 1995.

Rosenzweig, J. E.: *Organisation and Management*, New York, McGraw Hill International, 1963.

Sethna, R.J. : *Social Impact of Tourism in Selected Caribbean Countries*, Washington, DC: George Washington University, 1980.

Sharma Sunil : *Planning and Development of Tourism and Hospitality*, Rajat Pub, Delhi, 2007.

Shrivastava Atul : *Modern Hospitality and Tourism Management*, Centrum Press, Delhi, 2010.

Slinn, Judy A: *Tourism: Management of Facilities*, London, Pitman: M & E, 1993.

Smith, G. : *International Tourism and Hospitality Careers through Education and Training*, CHRIE Annual Conference, Washington DC, 1996.

Smith, V.L. : *Hosts and Guests: The Anthropology of Tourism*, Oxford: Blackwell, 1978.

Stallworthy, E.: *Waste Management Towards a Sustainable Society*, Auburn House, New York, 1990.

Swarbrooke, J.: *Marketing Tourism, Hospitality and Leisure in Europe*, London, International Thomson Business Press, 1996.

Thomas, F.: *Introduction to Management in the Hospitality Industry*, New York, Wiley, 1995.

Timothy R.: *Cases in Hospitality Management: A Critical Incident Approach*, New York, Wiley, 1995.

Tribe, John *Corporate Strategy for Tourism, London*, International Thomson Business Press, 1997.

Var, Turgut: *Tourism Planning*, London, Retailed, 2002.

Wahab, S A: *Tourism Management*, Tourism International Press, 1975.

Index

□□□

HBP / RTK - Anmol - 62938